T0352880

# LIFE AT FULL TILT

# LIFE AT FULL TILT
The Selected Writings of Dervla Murphy

*Edited by Ethel Crowley*

*Foreword by Colin Thubron*

ELAND
London

First published by Eland Publishing Ltd
61 Exmouth Market, London EC1R 4QL in 2023

Introduction copyright © Ethel Crowley, 2023
Extracts copyright © Dervla Murphy
except as specified in the acknowledgements

ISBN 978 1 78060 211 0

A full CIP record for this book is available from the British Library

Cover image: *Dervla Murphy in Canada*, 1991

Printed and bound in Great Britain by Clays Ltd, Elcograf S.p.A.

# Contents

# Acknowledgements

This anthology has been a labour of love and I feel very privileged to have been in the position to create it with Eland Publishing.

My heartfelt thanks go first and foremost to Dervla Murphy herself and Rachel Murphy. The open-hearted trust they placed in me will stay with me forever. It was such a terrible shame that Dervla's health went downhill so fast and she didn't get to see it coming to fruition. She passed away in the early stages of its production. I had so many questions to ask her, in the process of compiling the book. I really hope she would have been happy with the result.

My thanks also to Rose Baring and Barnaby Rogerson for being so open to this idea and being such a pleasure to deal with in the process. They were always communicative, warm and professional. Thanks also to Stephanie Allen for being so friendly and encouraging along the way, and for her capable input on promoting the book. Thanks to Colin Thubron for his gracious foreword. Finally, thanks to Jim MacLaughlin, *mi media naranja*, for doing without me for long stretches of time while working on this and for his constant support.

## Publisher's Acknowledgements

For permission to reprint copyright material, grateful acknowledgement is due to Lilliput Press for material from *Visiting Rwanda* and John Murray for material from *Eight Feet in the Andes*, *Through Siberia by Accident* and *Silverland*.

# Foreword

The intoxication of travel can become an end in itself. 'I travel not to go anywhere, but to go,' wrote Robert Louis Stevenson. 'I travel for travel's sake. The great affair is to move.'

Among modern adventurers this compulsion was famously exemplified by the intrepid Dervla Murphy. Few people, in any age, can have travelled a wider range of countries so arduously. It is possible to ascribe this passion to her mother's immobility – crippled by rheumatoid arthritis and grounding her daughter as caregiver for sixteen frustrated years. More likely Dervla Murphy was born with wanderlust.

In her starkly reflective autobiography, *Wheels within Wheels*, she portrayed herself as a morose and sometimes insolent small girl, whose pleasures were the private ones of the imagination. An only child, she recounted to herself endless fanciful stories, and for years of make-believe the teddy bears inhabiting an elm tree in her parents' garden developed uncontrollable characters of their own. In one of her earliest memories Murphy raged at other children intruding on the private magic she created.

Then, on her tenth birthday, she was given a bicycle and an atlas, and 'a few days later I decided to cycle to India'. The little girl saw nothing odd in this, but she kept silent about it to avoid the condescension of adults. Later she began obsessively reading a haphazard mélange of writers: Shelley, Fielding, George Eliot, Ruskin, Oscar Wilde, Freya Stark.

On her mother's death her repressed ambition burst into action, and she was off on her bike to India. The subsequent book, *Full Tilt*, made her name and became something of a template for the dauntless early travelogues that followed: in Nepal, Ethiopia, India, Kashmir, Peru.

In the galaxy of her travel-writing contemporaries, Dervla Murphy was unique. Not for her the literary manipulations or overwrought description (even fictionalising) of some more writerly writers. She wrote in a down-to-earth style, whose graphic poetry arose as if spontaneously from her subject. Her note-taking was done in diary form during her journeys, often in exacting surroundings, sitting on a sack in the Himalayas by candlelight, or sharing a teahouse floor with Afghan tribesmen.

Hardship came easily to her. She even exulted in it. 'Soon I was discovering for myself that our real material needs are very few,' she wrote, 'and that the extras now presented as "needs" not only endanger true contentment but diminish our human dignity.' Her Spartan travelling placed her beyond the reach of the tourism she hated and drew her closer to the hard lives around her. But solitude was vital. Her preferred transport was by foot, bike or package mule, and she refused guides or escorts. A delight in wilderness – in mountains above all – shines through her writing: 'seeing only hoof prints in the dust, with all around the healing quiet of wild places'.

Over fifty years of travel the injuries she sustained, and the diseases she contracted, were stupendous. In a humorous passage in her *Through Siberia by Accident* she wryly listed them: amoebic dysentery, heatstroke, hepatitis, concussion and a fractured coccyx (in a car accident), a triple tooth abscess, a disabling scorpion bite, malaria, brucellosis, mumps, gout (from Madagascan alcohol), tick-bite fever. She survived at least five attempted robberies (two sadly successful), numerous rape attempts (unsuccessful), with multiple broken ribs, torn tendons and a fractured pelvis. Only after she was brutally robbed and lay sleepless in a vermin-infested Ethiopian hovel did she disclose that she crawled out shivering into the starlight, broken in spirit.

Yet within the paradigm that readers imagined there beat a complicated heart. The product of a remote father and a mother she heroine-worshipped, Dervla imagined that she inherited from her father 'a certain shyness and gaucherie or tendency to self-effacement'. She recoiled from the publicity that attended her books' publication, and was shy of public speaking. 'Unwittingly,' she wrote, 'my mother gave me an inferiority complex I was never to outgrow.' In her native Lismore she lived reclusively, eschewing creature comforts, even a television or washing machine, let alone a car.

But her sympathies and alertness to injustice grew ever more intense, and midway through her career political concerns brimmed into her books, sometimes replacing their raw adventure. An uncompromising and trenchant book on nuclear power was followed by destinations more immediately controversial than before: Northern Ireland, Romania (after Ceausescu's execution), Rwanda (soon after the genocide), post-apartheid South Africa, Laos, Cuba, the tragedy-riven Balkans, and above all the Palestinian West Bank and Gaza.

Some of her readers regretted her move away from pure adventure. Murphy acknowledged this, but was driven by deeper concerns. Her big-hearted outrage at political corruption and blindness overpowered all else. Even in her earlier books there had been embedded a pressing regard for those among whom she travelled, as well as a distaste for urban life. 'I am utterly repelled by the luxury of my immediate surroundings, and by the noise, bustle and smells of twentieth-century life,' she wrote, emerging into Islamabad after months in the Karakoram mountains. 'I miss the snow-peaks, the silence, the contentment.' These, in the end, absolved all the travails of the road. 'It must only be a matter of time before we go back…when we can leave all jeep-tracks behind and follow small paths over high passes.'

*Colin Thubron*
*London 2023*

*Can it be that as a species we're on the way to mass-suicide, driven by a combination of unregulated greed and arrogant technological-scientific ingenuity? Our failure to take adequate measures to slow (or halt) climate change suggests that eventually we may become extinct because we're so stupid. A melodramatic scenario, yet not implausible. For pre-human aeons there was life on Earth and perhaps there will be for post-human aeons. Homo Sapiens is an interesting evolutionary development, as were numerous other creatures no longer with us. Are human beings really necessary? Is there any reason to suppose our planet will sustain for much longer a species that has proved so lethal to most other species?*

Silverland, *2007*

# Introduction: A Maverick's Life

It was 8 a.m. and the phone rang. My immediate thought: who's dead? On tentatively answering the 'withheld' number, I heard, 'Good morning, is that Ethel? This is Dervla Murphy.' To say I was shocked would be an understatement. I had been reading her books since I was a teenager; she was 'one of our own', the premier Irish travel writer who fuelled my own dreams of travel far beyond my local world.

This was 2013. I had written a book called *Your Place or Mine?* in which I had included a section on Dervla. Having sent her a copy, I thought no more of it until that phone call. Thankfully, she didn't mind what I had written and we had a great chat. She then gave me her private phone number and we made a promise to meet before long.

From my first visit to her home in the Old Market in Lismore, we clicked. I was welcomed with warm hospitality, food or drink never far from my elbow. I returned with Jim, my other half, and he was a welcome addition to the party too. She had had friends for forty or fifty years, so we were relative newcomers in her life. It was, however, at a time in her life when the trips and the writing were starting to wind down – as they might when you're in your eighties – so she had more time for visits and phone calls from newer friends like ourselves. We were also delighted to meet her daughter Rachel and family, as well as some of her beloved friends in Lismore.

I have treasured memories of our visits to Dervla's place over the last eight years of her life. We would spend three or four hours traversing the whole world, without leaving the study. Each new subject might start with 'But isn't it terrible what's happening in...?' or 'Have you read...?' or 'I heard an interview on Al Jazeera...' She loved to keep current and it bored her silly to talk about her past trips. Once they were done and written up, that was it – move on. Her time was precious and she didn't want to spend it going over old ground with 'traveller's tales', preferring to keep fresh and informed instead.

Dervla was *all* about books: reading books, writing books, researching books, and reviewing books – dissecting them with a scalpel. This last metaphor is apt because she said that her other chosen profession would have been that of a surgeon, if life's randomness had led that way. If her father had found work in Dublin rather than moving to a rural town like Lismore, would Dervla have followed a more conventional educational path and aimed to become a surgeon, of which she often dreamed? Then maybe she would have been Professor Murphy, eminent vascular surgeon, instead of travel writer extraordinaire.

Regardless, she applied that precision to her observations of the world – that analytical scalpel always kept sharp. She was genuinely the most open-minded person and best conversationalist I've ever known. She never seemed old to me, despite inhabiting the body of a woman in her late eighties with plenty of aches and pains. She was, above all, a survivor.

The idea for this book emerged organically over time. I wrote a newspaper piece to celebrate her 90th birthday in November 2021. It got such a positive response, eliciting such love from readers for her work, that it spurred me to suggest producing an edited collection of her writing. She was initially reluctant due to her modesty – 'But would anyone be interested?' – but then, having discussed it with Rachel and her publishers at Eland, we all agreed to proceed. I had offered that she could keep any royalties, but Rachel and herself decided that they would be happier for them to be donated to a charity of their choice. So it was all systems go.

Unfortunately, very shortly afterwards, her health took its ultimate downturn. Right up until the very end of her life, she was enthusiastically discussing the potential contents and structure of this book, as well as her usual detailed analysis of current affairs.

On the last day that we had a good chat about the book – as she said, an 'editorial meeting' – I had to borrow a few copies of her books that I didn't yet own. I retrieved them from the glass-fronted case where she housed her own books, a copy of each edition preserved for her family. I blew literal dust and cobwebs off them, as she never consulted them once published. I opened them up under the overhead skylight in the kitchen. I joked that these actions were an apt metaphor for the aim of the anthology – blowing off dust and shining new light on these books that spanned over fifty years. We had a little giggle about that, clinked glasses and toasted the book.

Choosing the extracts for this collection was not easy. Rather than just foisting my own favourites upon the reader, I developed a set of criteria for inclusion. I tried to ensure that each set of extracts reflected the spirit and essence of each book and Dervla's own character. These criteria were based on her evocative descriptions of places; examples of her strength, both physical and mental; the numerous illnesses, incidents and accidents that befell her on the road; her long, empathetic conversations with the people she met; her reportage, or objective, detailed reporting of events; her explanations of very different social and cultural practices and her sharp socio-political analysis.

As well as the book extracts, I include a small sample of newspaper articles from the *Irish Times* and *Irish Independent*, spanning six decades. These also deserve new light shone upon them, such is the quality of the writing.

*

Dervla Murphy defied convention throughout her life. Life is about playing the hand you are dealt as best you can; both the cards she was given and the way she chose to play them were unconventional. I aim to contextualise her life in the Ireland that produced her. She was such an individual, though, that her character cannot be attributed to any one factor. She was very complex, a true maverick who existed outside of social and cultural expectations. The origin of the word 'maverick' is an unbranded animal on a cattle farm, the stray one at the edge of the herd who escapes the branding iron: that's Dervla.

When most of us consult a world map, we might be able to point to certain places to which we have flown – the cities where we land and maybe a couple of other spots. Dervla's exploration of her countries of choice was much more thorough. She liked to cycle or walk if possible rather than use any other type of transport. She will have made friends along the way, and she would know the details of the physical terrain, the cultural mores and how much a beer cost in each place. While she has known many, many such *routes* throughout the world, her *roots* are in Lismore, Co. Waterford, in the genteel hills of the south-east of Ireland. Dervla shared the details of her early life in *Wheels within Wheels*, so there is no need to repeat too many biographical details.

However, for the duration of her life, her connection to Lismore's surrounding landscape was closer than to any of its inhabitants. She largely kept to herself – at the edge of social life. When asked to write about her place for the *Irish Times* in 2011, at the age of eighty, she chose to write a beautiful elegy to the River Blackwater and her love of swimming in its depths. This piece is included here. Throughout her life, she was a keen wild swimmer. This early discovery clearly laid the foundation for her lifelong ecological worldview. Lismore was her *springboard*, the spot from which she projected herself out into the wider world. But she always returned home, to settle herself into her writing and reading – until the next trip.

Dervla grew up alongside the emergent Irish state itself. The Irish constitution was ratified in 1937, when she was six years old. But the monolithic, authoritarian Catholic Ireland that its leaders envisaged didn't leave much room for free spirits like her. Most women who had a combination of adventurous spirits and religious faith joined a missionary order of nuns in order to get away; this was a socially legitimate means of escape.

Young people (especially women) often had to try to find ways to flourish despite, rather than with the help of, the adults in their lives. As Dervla reached adulthood in the 1950s, this often meant emigration and getting out of Ireland completely. The poverty, desolation and social oppression drove young people out in their thousands, in search of new and better lives in Britain, the US, Australia and elsewhere. It was on the one hand a social safety valve and on the other, a terrible loss of youthful potential – a 'brain drain'. In 1957 alone, 1.8 per cent of the population left the country. Cattle boats in Dublin doubled as emigration vehicles. As Fintan O'Toole says, 'The export of live people and live animals in the same vessels epitomized the economic backwardness of the country.' Working class and small farming people didn't have much choice but to go abroad in search of 'the start', planting new roots in London, New York and the rest. Two uncles of mine left by ship for Chicago from Cobh (not far from Dervla's home in Lismore) and rebuilt their lives there. Two others moved to London. This multi-generational story is replicated in most Irish families; our collective emotional cartography has been stretched to incorporate distant locations. This was travel as well, but the type of travel taken by the economic migrant, forging themselves anew permanently.

This was the decade that saw Dervla locked into caring for her mother as she got more and more infirm, so emigration in the traditional sense was an impossibility for her, even if she had wanted to try it. Her personal goal was to go on interesting journeys and see what they would bring, especially in terms of writing material. She took several cycling trips to mainland Europe – notably to Germany in 1949, aged only eighteen, and to Spain in 1954 and in 1956. She did write a Spanish travel book, but it eluded her to find a willing publisher at that time. The bigger, ultimate dream of cycling to India had to wait until early 1963.

Dervla lived in a kind of parallel universe to the intensely conservative Ireland in which she happened to have been born. This was a place where everyday life for the majority was scheduled around the Catholic calendar – Christmas, Easter, Mass, holy communions, confirmations – and woe betide anybody who didn't fall into line ideologically. In this context, it was a challenge to exercise individual agency, but Dervla seemed to sidestep it all quietly. She had her bicycle as her trusty partner along the way, taking her places both near and far and enabling as much personal liberty as possible in the circumstances. She seemed to manage by not angrily resisting but by blithely ignoring the power structures around her. I'm sure other people did the same, flying below the radar and getting away with it.

The Catholic Church, culturally dominant throughout the 20th century, was obsessed with controlling sex and inculcating shame and guilt in the populace. The sexual act was for procreation only, to produce the next generation of believers. The idea that it could be a source of pleasure or fun was repressed and condemned. Sex was equated with sin and sin equated with sex. The Church didn't show too much interest in any other kind of sin – morality was located below the belt only. Despite their avowed concern with the purity of their flock, we now know that hypocrisy was the order of the day. The so-called moral guardians of the Irish people were often not so moral behind closed doors. A culture of denial, secrecy and fear ensured that the clergy got away with widespread sexual abuse of children, which only came to light in recent years. Even those who weren't actually doing it themselves certainly knew about others who were; stories are still emerging even now.

This obsession with the evils of sex was especially obvious in the mind of Archbishop John Charles McQuaid, who was Primate of Ireland and Archbishop of Dublin for over three decades, from 1940 to 1972. He operated his fiefdom hand in glove with the very conservative Eamon de Valera, who was either Taoiseach or President for most of the time from the 1930s through to the early 1970s. After Independence, the structures of Church and state were rigid and inflexible, to say the least. Historian Maria Luddy says that women's sexuality and even their bodies were seen as 'suspect and in need of restraint'. This state-sponsored misogynistic ideology was needed in order to ensure that women stayed in the home and out of public life.

Ireland was a misogynistic prison under the cosh of McQuaid and de Valera. In the Magdalene asylums, unmarried girls who got pregnant were hidden away, treated as 'fallen women' and were not deemed fit to live in normal society. There were 945 women incarcerated in these hate-filled institutions in 1956 alone. The repressive state apparatus imprisoned young girls and women for 'moral' misdemeanours and bullied their parents into toeing the Church line.

McQuaid, with his omnipotent power, attempted to render Ireland a blinkered theocracy in all but name. The culture of censorship seems unbelievable to us now. Any media images showing even a glimpse of a female thigh or bellybutton were swiftly censored. Lots of Irish writers' work came under his censorious eye. This had serious repercussions for some. The writer John McGahern had his book *The Dark* banned in 1965 and was subsequently fired from his job as a teacher, thereby losing his livelihood. The audacious McQuaid actually even considered it his business to endeavour to have tampons banned in 1944.

The very characteristics we associate with Dervla were exactly those that the mid-twentieth-century Irish Catholic Church despised in young women: an independent mind, an adventurous spirit and a dismissive attitude to structures of authority. Dervla was about as far from their ideal of womanhood as it was possible to get. They specialised in keeping a tight lid on women's potential for greatness. Not everybody obeyed, of course. There is always a big difference between official discourse and everyday reality. Resistance is almost always possible, especially if you didn't rock the boat too much.

There have been many other pioneering Irish women in the fields of science, medicine, law, business, journalism, sport, the arts and literature. Glass ceilings have been shattered left, right and centre during Dervla's lifetime. However, most of these have depended upon the existence of a university course and access to it. This provided a structure to join, to be as good as the boys or better. As well as those who got educated, there were also the women who were the everyday heroes. These were the wives and mothers who lived hard lives, caring for husbands and children and stretching too little money as far as they could. I'm sure a lot of them would have loved to be able to take off on a bicycle too, given half a chance. They mightn't have reached India, though, as they'd have had to be home by tea-time. They were heroes simply by surviving.

Dervla didn't fit into any of these groups of women. Her achievements were completely individual – self-taught, self-motivated, self-propelled, self-employed. In a way, she existed outside of society and was to a large extent unaffected by social changes. The same summer that her mother died – 1962 – saw the early months of the first Irish television station, Telefís Éireann, and the first episodes of the iconic *Late Late Show* that was a beacon of change at the time. While this was a key defining moment in modern Irish history, Dervla would have been oblivious to it, as she never watched television throughout her life.

When discussing Irish society since the 1950s, the dominant trope is liberalisation – albeit achieved kicking and screaming. The women's movement has played a huge role in fighting for women's rights. However, changes in women's educational achievements, employment patterns, political participation and community engagement are really irrelevant to understanding the 'making' of Dervla Murphy. She had no part in it; she was not a 'joiner'. In fact, she expressed criticism of the women's movement for downgrading and undervaluing the work of mothers and housewives. She was flippant about the struggle for equal pay and issues around the inheritance of property. This is possibly because she was so divorced from conventional society; she was an only child who was never paid to work at anything except her writing, over which she exercised near total autonomy.

Like some other women travellers, she 'shifted uncomfortably when the mantle of feminism was laid upon them', as observed by Mary Russell. Yet while she didn't call herself a feminist *per se*, she was still always tuned into life as seen through local women's eyes. In Afghanistan in the early sixties, she observed, 'two women were travelling on the roof [of the bus] amidst everyone's goods and chattels – very symbolic!' These women were very unwell and to see them treated so badly upset her deeply. Many years later in Rumania, she was also very distressed by the numerous gynaecological horror stories she heard from women there.

*

Dervla existed in a sort of liminal zone between Ireland and England. Dervla's father was an Irish Republican, as was his father before him. They both had joined the old IRA in the struggle for Irish independence. She said he was 'sprung from generations of rebels' and he served time in English prisons for his activities. However, despite this family history, she worked mainly with British publishers. London, rather than Dublin, was the capital of her personal republic. In conversation, London often came up, while Dublin never did except to refer to her early family origins. She saw it as natural to incorporate England into her mental map, simply seeing it as a place of culture and of opportunities to publish her work, as did so many Irish writers, before and since. She thought nothing of hopping on the bus near her home and getting the ferry from Rosslare in the south east of Ireland and the bus across to London. On exploring it as a girl, she mused, 'Half of me seemed to belong in Britain.' I can't help but wonder if she had lived in a more inaccessible part of Ireland, would that have changed her outlook? Knowing her, probably not. Her fate was to travel, in a highly intrepid manner, and to put words on pages, writing great books. Her geographical location would hardly have thwarted her.

She never compromised on her Irishness though; she made it clear wherever she went. But despite her Irish passport, she occasionally sought help from the British Council in times of trouble on the road. She earned two major awards in the UK for her travel writing: the 2021 Stanford's Lifetime Achievement Award and the 2019 Ness Award for the popularisation of geography from the Royal Geographical Society (RGS), of which she was also a

Life Fellow. Historically, the RGS was at the heart of the British establishment. Throughout the nineteenth century, travellers and explorers were published in its *Geographical Journal*, which became a major source of information about far-flung places. It was a highly prestigious publication, whose pages were filled by the likes of Burton and Speke, whose crucial travel reports were then used for military and colonial purposes; it underpinned imperial geography during the Victorian era. The irony of this ethical mismatch would not have been lost on her.

Within this world, those with whom she identified were also on the margins of any kind of convention. Dervla takes her place in the pantheon of brave women travellers like Isabella Bird, Mary Kingsley and Freya Stark. All of these great travellers and writers inspired her as a child and she carried them in her heart throughout her life. There have been many others, of course, including some historical Irish women who have led adventurous and often philanthropic lives, such as Beatrice Grimshaw, Flora Shaw and May Crommelin. However, we only have room to briefly mention three of Dervla's major influences here.

Dervla wrote to Bill Colegrave: 'I think of long dead authors as my friends. Among the dearest is Isabella Bird, a clergyman's daughter, born exactly a century before me in 1831.' Isabella Bird (1831–1904) was an English explorer, naturalist, photographer and writer, who defied all conservative Victorian convention to head off into the unknown. In 1892 she became the first female Fellow of the RGS (followed much later by Dervla herself). She set off on three major world trips in her life. The first was to the New World, through Nova Scotia and down to the Great Lakes. The second was to Australia and New Zealand and on to the Sandwich Islands (Hawaii). On that trip, she sailed into San Francisco, starting the trip that led eventually to her best known work, *A Lady's Life in the Rocky Mountains*. This famous travelogue was based on a four-month-long, 800-mile trek on horseback across America in 1873. In her introduction to the 1988 edition of it, Dervla wrote, 'It is hard to think of any other travel book, of any period, that so spontaneously conveys the author's sheer delight in travelling.' This book was comprised of her letters home to her sister. (Indeed, Dervla's own first book was also based on letters sent home to a friend in Ireland.) Her third expedition was to Japan, China and Malaya. After her husband died (after only five years of marriage), she travelled extensively in Asia, returning to China and Korea where she founded several hospitals. She died after her final trip, trekking across Morocco at the age of seventy-two.

Dervla opined that Mary Kingsley (1862–1900) was 'the best writer and wittiest commentator' of the Victorian women travel writers. There were major parallels between Kingsley and Dervla herself. Firstly, she was also self-taught, using the library of her scholarly father and later becoming his amanuensis. Secondly, Kingsley was a dutiful Victorian daughter who cared for ailing parents until their deaths in 1892. Soon afterwards, she went to West Africa for six months, hitching a ride on a cargo ship. She was the first European to visit several parts of the region. Her classic *Travels in West Africa* resulted from a long trip there. She is well known as a great defender of African cultures against what she termed 'the thin veneer of rubbishy white culture' that British officials and some missionaries were attempting to impose. On her third African trip, she volunteered as a nurse during the Boer War, where she sadly caught typhoid. She died prematurely at the age of thirty-eight and was buried at sea.

Dervla's third role model, Freya Stark (1893-1993), specialised in travel in the Arab world. Fluent in Arabic, she became an expert on Arabic dialects and worked for the British Ministry of Information in Aden and Cairo. She travelled extensively in Persia and Arabia. Her most famous work, written in her lyrically descriptive style, is *The Valley of the Assassins*. For the *Great Lives* series on BBC Radio 4 in 2009, Dervla chose Stark as her subject. She said that she was a considerable influence on her as a child when she was deciding where and how she wanted to travel. Her mother was a big fan of Stark and read her books to her when she was very small. They were excited when they saw that 'there was a new Freya coming out on the John Murray list' and she used to save her pocket money as a teenager so that she could buy her own copies. Stark didn't go to school, but read a great deal on her own – a pattern more or less copied by Dervla herself. Stark's chosen area was the Middle East and Arabia. In that radio interview, Dervla said, 'Even Freya, devoted as I was to her writing, couldn't attract me to the desert. I hate heat. I go for the mountains and cold places.' She met Stark three times, the last time when a newspaper sent her to interview her on her 90th birthday. She said that her memory had gone and she was impossibly vague, but she autographed her first editions for her in Arabic, so she loved that. Like Dervla herself, Stark stayed travelling and writing well into her twilight years.

We can spot parallels between each of these with Dervla's own life, naturally enough. However, each woman's story stands on its own, the product of a unique life trajectory. Spirited individuals like these are destined to carve out interesting lives for themselves, leaving a path for others to follow. They're not called trailblazers for nothing. One big difference, however, is that Dervla was Irish.

*

Dervla had a very learned but idiosyncratic upbringing. Her father's job as county librarian was an esteemed position but not particularly well paid. There certainly wasn't much money floating around and she was reared modestly and frugally, creating the habits of a lifetime. In terms of education, she left school at fourteen to care for her disabled mother at home. Her reading material from the home library was highly elevated, conferring upon her a random kind of cultural capital. She had no programme of study as such, but was more or less an autodidact who made the best of her very unconventional personal situation. Her parents were both solidly upper middle-class and it was the norm to have complex philosophical debates at the dinner table, while listening to Beethoven on the wireless. Indeed, many years later, when she was interviewed for BBC Radio 4's programme *Desert Island Discs*, two out of her eight choices of music were composed by Beethoven, along with Haydn, Monteverdi and some world music from Ethiopia and Madagascar.

Classical literature also featured strongly in the household and her parents always encouraged her love of reading and writing. For Christmas or birthday presents, they'd ask her for a short story or an essay she had written. Eventually, her writing talent grew to fit the space created by that praise. How lovely to have such encouragement, especially considering this was the 1930s and 1940s, not known as an enlightened era in Ireland. Writing became as essential to Dervla's existence as breathing itself.

Dervla's formal schooling fell by the wayside, like so many others of her generation. Her education didn't follow a conventional path and her prodigious reading was not converted into educational credentials to be used in the job marketplace. Sometimes people can also get on in life with symbolic capital, or social connections with a prestigious social milieu – a word in someone's ear at a race meeting or golf game. Dervla had to do without this too; there was nobody pulling any strings for her. She was very much on her own in life – an independent girl who was happy to entertain herself in her local landscape. Her wealth lay in her reading, which opened up the world to her. She told me, 'I wasn't just a bibliophile, I was a bibliomaniac.' However, her personal circumstances prevented her from straying too far from home and experiencing the world in reality – yet. There was an internal dilemma that was waiting to be solved by freedom.

Dervla's imagination, stoked into life by her copious reading, lured her eastwards towards India. During those years, most of her generation dreamed of going to America, where the streets were paved with gold, and all that jazz. One of her oft-quoted rules of travel was to find out where most people were going and then go in the opposite direction. So she obeyed her own rule on the grandest of scales from the outset. She went east – long before the hippy trail was even heard of. The adventurous version of herself had hitherto only been allowed alluringly short European cycle trips. After both her parents had died, she was off – like a rocket, couldn't wait another second – to make up for lost time. She has said that the feeling of liberty she experienced then ran through her body like an electric shock. This time, she didn't have to come back for a long time. How was she to finally explore her potential except to follow that dream, hit the road and see what happened?

Her fate was to become a freelance traveller and writer – not an easy one, but this independent life suited Dervla. The sheer scale of the achievement of that first big trip and the quality of the writing was recognised when it got into Jock Murray's hands. He was exactly the right person to set her on her way towards becoming a world-renowned travel writer. It is well-known that it was Penelope Chetwode, whom she met in Delhi, who encouraged her to approach the prestigious John Murray publishing house but she reiterated with me that she really never would have had the nerve otherwise, as she had tried three or four other publishers to no avail. This was certainly a fortuitous meeting – she was on the right path now. No doubt, she would have found other publishers, but perhaps none who connected deeply with her and appreciated her like Murray in the earlier years, and Eland later on.

\*

Dervla's travel choices defied the gender expectations of mid-twentieth century Ireland. Fortified by the example of the likes of Freya Stark as well as the confidence imbued in her by her parents, she felt there was nothing she couldn't do. The physical stamina she showed defies description – almost superhuman at times. Her books are peppered with stories of being mistaken for a man on her trips, to the extent that it has become one of the standard clichés about her. She regularly unbuttoned her shirt on African trips to establish her feminine credentials. In Uganda, she had to ditch her combat pants because there was a very real danger that she could have been mistaken for a mercenary and shot dead. Historical women travel writers actually disguised themselves as men sometimes to accord themselves more freedom. When women were corseted and skirted, it was seen as scandalous for women to wear trousers, sitting astride a bicycle or horse. Dervla just wore functional, practical clothing – roomy shirts, trousers, jackets – standard practice now.

The threat of violence is always a possibility for travellers of any gender, but for women, it is the ever-present threat of sexual violence that looms large. Dervla was no exception. However, she said there was no point in worrying about things until they actually happened, so she didn't let this put a stop to her gallop. In *Full Tilt* alone, she told of averting one attempted rape with a warning shot from her pistol and another by engaging a strategic knee. She trekked in Bulgaria and Turkey in 1968 while pregnant. She told Mary Russell, 'While hitch-hiking from Ankara to Van, I had to fight off eight would-be rapists in eleven days. This marathon was garnished by two lesbian invitations to bed – providence perhaps felt that I risked being bored by all those over-excited males.'

She took risks with her personal safety that most of us would never dream of, tackling the world with gusto. Reckless? Probably. She had near-death experiences on many occasions – risk was grist to her mill. However, she got annoyed if you called her brave. She told Hilary Bradt, 'It's being afraid when something *actually* happens but not being afraid that something *might* happen. That's the difference.' So the anticipation of disaster didn't stop her. When I raised this issue with her, she said, 'If you're fearless, you don't need courage. It's only if you're fearful that you need courage to overcome your fears.' I persisted, 'Ah, come on, Dervla.' 'Well, over so many decades of travel, there was very little to alarm me. I might have been shaken at times, but not enough to affect future plans.' She developed this fearlessness when very young indeed, under her parents' tutelage. 'At the age of 16, in 1947, it was my mother who suggested that I cycle through the Continent alone – not many mothers did that!'

Dervla was not remotely interested in the arguably more macho reason to travel: breaking records or accomplishing 'feats'. It was for others to 'collect' the highest mountains or the longest rivers, or to be the first in particular spots. She would laugh at the idea of ticking items off on a 'must do' or 'must see' list. However, she can actually be termed an explorer; she accomplished some major feats, quietly and modestly. During the years that Dervla was branching out, Edmund Hillary and Tenzing Norgay were the first to reach the summit of Everest in 1953, for example. Men like these 'conquered' mountains. Just a decade or two later, Dervla hiked and biked over them and enjoyed them (many times), revelled in them, wondered at them, was rendered breathless by them. Not one to join mountaineering expeditions, she climbed many serious mountains on her own and later, with Rachel, in Pakistan and Peru. Rachel has also been a brave traveller since her childhood and was an enormous help to Dervla on the trips they shared, even when very young. Dervla called her 'a compass in human form'. Dervla did things her own way – no strict plan, no team, no bearers, just with a little help from some friends sometimes. She was in competition only with herself. And she survived.

Dervla chose to set off using the simplest possible mode of transport that wasn't simply walking (which of course she also did, later). She loved cycling, which allowed her to be part of her surroundings as she travelled, as well as making it easier to meet people along the way. When she had to travel in a car, bus or train, she often felt wistful because she couldn't get out and walk. Cycling or walking also allowed her to maintain control over her trips, determining her own schedule. Her preferred, low-tech modes of transport kept things simple. Her bicycle, Roz, was her only partner of choice in the early days. On a good day, cycling is the closest thing to flying while still on *terra firma*. For Dervla, work and play were really one and the same.

She freely admitted that she was no technical whizz; she was actually a self-confessed Luddite. Other women travellers have used cars, boats, airplanes or parachutes to get places, but not her. She had no affinity with mechanics, to put it mildly. She usually had to rely on help, of varying levels of competence, to maintain her bicycles on her trips. She was a mass of contradictions. Surprisingly, she also disliked flying and had a phobic fear of spiders. She had little problem with rats (while I shudder to even write the word), mice and other vermin, but spiders... I unsuccessfully stifled a chuckle when she told me this and she said, a little indignantly, 'Well it is a well-documented condition – it's called arachnophobia!'

It goes without saying that many of the places she travelled to were beyond the limits of conventional tourism. But also within each country, the more remote and challenging the destination, the better she liked it. She travelled on the edge of the edge itself.

\*

Towards the latter part of Dervla's life, she constantly pushed the envelope regarding social expectations for older women. She continued travelling into her eighties, and researching, writing and reading up until very shortly before she died. She had written some years earlier, at the age of seventy-six, 'It seems odd that the wanderlust, unlike other lusts, does not diminish with age. As departure date [for Laos] approached my excitement level rose as uncontrollably as though I had never before left Ireland.' The unquenchable spark of her curiosity could be ignited by a conversation with a friend or just a feature on a radio programme.

She had been witness to enormous historical events. She remembered hearing Hitler's broadcasts on the radio as a child; she cycled through Germany after WWII and witnessed it being rebuilt; she cycled through Franco's Spain in the 1950s; she met the Dalai Lama (twice); she attended Nelson Mandela's inauguration as President of the new South Africa. She avoided trouble (mostly) in such hotspots as Northern Ireland, Rwanda, the Balkans and Palestine. In terms of longevity, she is comparable only to her great contemporary travel writer, Jan Morris. However, the comparison ends there. The rough conditions she was willing to endure are absolutely unparalleled – she stayed in a basic concrete structure in a Palestinian refugee camp in her eighties.

She dedicated her last decade and a half to getting under the skin of the Palestinian issue. She made several trips to Gaza, the West Bank and Israel, resulting in two impressive books, published in 2013 and 2015 at the ages of eighty-two and eighty-four, respectively. Her last major trip was to Amman in Jordan in January 2016, after she had turned eighty-five. She had an incident there which caused her to fracture her pelvis, prompting an early return home. She told journalist Isabel Conway that 'it wasn't a fall but a silly way of slipping as I was sitting down'. The manuscript of this trip remained unfinished, as she didn't feel able to continue with her customary copious research and writing at that point.

During her later travels, she could no longer carry her normal rucksack and had to resort to a wheelie suitcase, which as any traveller knows, is not the same at all. However, she felt that the disadvantages of ageing were offset by the major advantage of needing so much less sleep, adding several hours to her day for reading and writing. Books were her constant companion, right up to the end.

*

Travel writing is an amorphous genre that can slip between the cracks and does not always garner the respect or fame it deserves. Dervla is better known for being a tough traveller than a great writer. People only have room for one version of a writer. They remember dramatic incidents with guns and robbers rather than the sometimes sublime writing that she produced, illuminating worlds beyond most of our limits. If she had been a fiction writer, she would have been placed closer to the heart of the Irish literary canon. A comparison can be made here with her exact contemporary, Edna O' Brien, who is very famous and universally lauded.

Travel writing can contain just about anything. Hers is old-school, though, and all the better for it. It contains history, geography, adventure, witty anecdotes and some beautifully lyrical literary tracts that bring us to far-flung places in our heads. As Freya Stark put it in *Riding to the Tigris*, 'One can only really travel if one lets oneself go and takes what every place brings without trying to turn it into a healthy private pattern of one's own and I suppose that is the difference between travel and tourism.'

Dervla certainly did let herself go on her trips; she thrived on producing an honest and entertaining report on each one. She had a very keen eye and ear for minutiae. She told us exactly what happened when she boarded a train in snowy Siberia, entered an African village at dusk or rode her bike onto a South African white farmer's yard. She reported her encounters in a clear-eyed fashion and her empathetic nature sought out the essence of each person, whether a missionary or a mercenary. Maintaining the integrity of the writing was her priority, surpassing any quest for popularity.

The instinctual and individual approach of the intelligent, independent traveller differs greatly from the rule-bound writing of the academic. In academia, one's authority is founded upon using established, respectable research methods, following the line of a school of thought. Validation from peers is essential for success. In travel writing like Dervla's her 'authority' came from having such challenging trips, talking to people in little-known places, and hearing their views and stories first hand. She bore witness. She could say 'I was there. I saw it with my own eyes.' In academia, this is akin to an ethnographic approach within social science, prioritising the details of the everyday life. Dervla wasn't an academic, so she didn't have to worry about the validity of her research methodology as such. However, she could have gone down this road, as she had the intellectual ability to do anything she liked. While she didn't write for an academic audience, her work was highly respected in that arena too.

In terms of her own reading, it is hard to over-state the enormous amount of research behind each of the books. As well as the physical toll the trips took on her body and mind, the academic work behind the scenes was massively impressive. We can see this in the substantial bibliographies they contain. When I got to know her in her own environment, I saw the evidence of this. She lived in a library of well-used books, organised by geographical region. She estimated the number to be 8,000 but I would say more, and the piles just kept growing higher. She also had a strong interest in military technology and sometimes read the specialised military magazine *Jane's Defence Weekly*. She felt duty-bound to learn about it having seen, for example, the gruesome effects of cluster bombs in Laos and phosphorus gas in Gaza. Having an academic past, I can testify that each of her books took as much research as a Masters Degree, at the very least, and in some cases – like her books on race relations in England, on South Africa and on Israel/Palestine – a PhD. And she kept doing it over and over again. Relentless research, travelling and writing became her unique way of life, the mountain paths and roads of new countries constantly calling her.

She treated the writing as a serious *job*; she was extremely disciplined. She took copious notes each night, even after devastatingly hard days on the road. Each conversation was recorded verbatim. She very rarely took out a notebook during a 'chat-show' (her term for a conversation/interview) but wrote her notes afterwards. Many of these were very long indeed. While she often had fun along the way, of course, with a beer or three

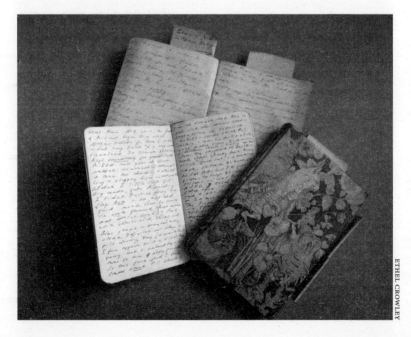

ETHEL CROWLEY

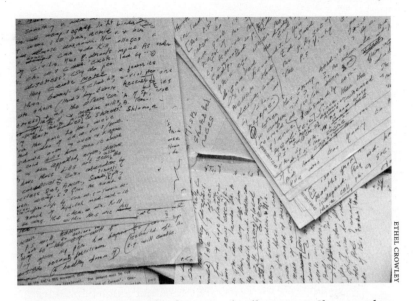

consumed, her sense of purpose was deadly serious. She spent her time well – she was so observant that she could get more out of one encounter than another writer could glean in a week. This shows in her lifelong prolific output. If she didn't get enough material on one trip, she would return for others. Her research for the books on Cuba, South Africa, Russia and Israel/Palestine all involved two, three or more fact-finding trips. These weren't dreamy enterprises. She was also a jobbing writer (and book reviewer) throughout her life; she produced a massive amount of material. She always loved to come back home to Lismore to finish the books, never hankering to go to live in another country. Her work is very different to other writers who have gone to live abroad, even for a while. She approached her travel writing as a job, as work to be completed at home on her return, so one wouldn't call her a nomad. The travelling and writing was *her work*. And unlike many travel writers, Dervla was never, ever – ever – sponsored by anybody.

It is possible that Dervla's relentless work ethic actually did her writing career no favours. Would her reputation have been stronger if she had been less driven throughout her long life? She wrote twenty-four travel books, as well as numerous other pieces.

Perhaps each new book distracted readers' attention from the previous ones, so she unwittingly became a victim of the sheer volume of material she produced. If she had written four instead of twenty-four books, people might have focused on each one better and the release of each might have been a bigger event. If Laurie Lee had written twenty-three more books as well as *As I Walked Out One Midsummer Morning*, would people still talk about that one in particular? Dervla could have 'dined out' on many, many fewer trips and books, picking a particular country or region and focusing on it, thereby becoming a recognised expert. Neither was she very fond of media interviews or being in the public eye. Her innate adventurousness and insatiable curiosity kept propelling her off to new places. The trapped air from one place was still in the pockets of her backpack when she set off for the next.

Most readers are more familiar with the earlier works, especially *Full Tilt*, than the later books, though, at the latter end of her career, the media was attracted to her two topical books on Israel/Palestine. Between these two 'bookends' are many that have been undervalued, like those on the Balkans, South Africa or Siberia. This collection includes them all, celebrating the long, full life that she lived and her oeuvre in its entirety.

Like others of her travelling predecessors, domestic life – with all that that entailed – was never going to be a priority because the siren calls of the next book and the next trip always beckoned. Her goal was always to uncover more about social and political change and to experience life from the perspective of the poorest people living in the most remote locations. She did this by choice, of course, because she loved travelling so much, rather than the involuntary movement of displaced persons and refugees. She was very self-aware about this, always stressing: 'But I just *enjoyed* myself!'

\*

Dervla was a unique thinker, a true original who could never tolerate an uncritical, preconceived philosophical formula. We can

see influences from socialism and environmentalism, of course, but each empirical situation was viewed anew, without bias. For example, while a huge admirer of the achievements of Castro's Cuba, she admitted that had she been born there, she would have sorely resented the curbs on her freedom to write and travel.

As Dervla cycled through Pakistan and Afghanistan in 1963, the leftist criticisms she made of the Western modernisation project were ahead of their time. Her ideas were prototypical for what became Dependency theory, the radical critique of the mainstream capitalist development model that emerged in the 1970s. She knew that imposing crude Western culture was wrong because it was destructive of local cultures and therefore ultimately unsustainable.

She had a strong anti-materialist ethic and put into practice what she believed. Throughout her life, she did without any modern conveniences and lived in a spartan fashion. She mused – tongue firmly in cheek – as to whether she lacked a gene for liking anything technical. In 2008 she said, 'My genes reject car ownership, TV, washing-machines, cell phones, computers, iPods and other such complex innovations. Were I a species rather than an individual

35

I'd be doomed to extinction as a creature unable to adapt to its changing environment.' In fact she did adapt somewhat in later years, getting quite attached to her computer despite herself. She began each day with news from BBC Radio 4, Al Jazeera and online newspapers like *Haaretz*. She told me that 'the Internet is a huge advantage for me now, when I'm so restricted in my movements. I can see the world through Al Jazeera's eyes'. She was open-minded enough to change when she saw the need to renew her approach.

She was at her happiest in the midst of unspoiled nature wherever she went – the wilder the better. She despised cities. Paul Theroux shares her opinion, calling them 'snake pits', full of people who want to part you from your money in one way or another. This was unlike her contemporary, Jan Morris, however, who wrote so vividly about them and whose paeans to Trieste and Venice are modern classics. Dervla couldn't wait to leave cities as dawn broke and get out into the open countryside. Not for her were strolling on city streets, sipping coffee in cafés or ambling in manicured parks. Cities were of use mainly for finding people to interview; she was always in the hunter-gatherer mode of the inveterate writer. Two cities that she found attractive despite herself, however, were Havana and St Petersburg.

Her worldview was based on an intense love of nature and animals. She was the deepest of Green in her orientation to the world. She had a profound sense that humans were just one type of creature among others, albeit with the enhanced ability to do harm to other species and the global environment. She often carried binoculars for bird-watching on her trips. The case, which sat under an arm, was sometimes mistaken for a gun holster. Her deep love of animals was shown in the huge number of pets she had – mostly dogs and cats – throughout her long life. She even brought a puppy called Tashi home from Nepal in the sixties, who lived with her for almost twenty years. She said she was a 'very special dog'. She appreciated the individual personalities of all her animals. We joked about trying to come up with a list of all their names, but time ran out.

She discussed spiritual and religious matters in many of the books. She was interested in what they meant to other people but never practised any faith herself. Her gentle approach to the world around her was akin to Buddhism in some ways, but she didn't need to practise it. She told me that the closest she would come to a label was a 'humanist'. She said, 'People are in control of the world and they need to behave responsibly when exercising that control.' She rejected the idea that she was an atheist: 'That's too aggressive a term. I'm not anti any religion. I just never felt the need to adhere to any. I don't condemn any religion; I only condemn extremism of any kind.'

Her campaigning side emerged in her activism against nuclear power in the 1980s, which she detested until the end. Following a visit to Three Mile Island in Pennsylvania, the nuclear power plant that had a partial meltdown in 1979, she wrote a critical book on it. Not long before she died, she told me, 'These days, climate-worried people are accepting the nuclear industry's propaganda that it's "clean" and the obvious energy solution. What about the miners of the uranium, and what's to be done about nuclear waste?' She continued, 'The younger generation don't know the basic facts about nuclear energy. Nothing has changed since I wrote the book, despite extra precautions taken now. Nobody still has a solution to the problem of nuclear waste. The essential hazards are the same. The hazardous conditions in the uranium mines are terrible – the workers suffer diseases from being irradiated.' She showed real pride in this book: 'The book took me ages – there was so much reading and research to do. And I'm still proud of the fact that not one nuclear scientist could contradict what I said in that book. And, you know, I had started out knowing about as much about nuclear power as a dog about a holiday!' She had also become overtly and publicly political in her very latter years as a proponent of the One-State Solution in the Israel/Palestine conflict.

She was completely untouched by academia, yet was an intelligent, iconoclastic free thinker who could hold her own in any company. She just blithely did (and said) her own thing. In my own not inconsiderable experience of academia, she was more erudite than most academics of long standing, and unlike most of them, was always willing to read something that might challenge her own point of view.

I'd like to suggest that Dervla was an 'active cosmopolitan'. Cosmopolitanism was defined by Ulf Hannerz as 'first of all an orientation, a willingness to engage with the Other. It is an intellectual and aesthetic stance of openness toward divergent cultural experiences, a search for contrasts rather than uniformity.' To say that someone like Dervla is cosmopolitan is to say that she is first and foremost a citizen of the world, over and above being a citizen of any state. In contemporary political philosophy, according to David Held, the principle of cosmopolitanism is based on the idea that every person in the world deserves equal respect and consideration, that everybody is treated impartially based on universally applied rules, and that these are acknowledged by everyone. The cosmopolitan can be in her comfort zone in many parts of the world and among many types of people. She can find some essential feeling of connection with people from cultures that are different to her own culture of origin. It is not the product of social class, status or formal education but is something to be worked at, invented and reinvented on a daily basis.

The active cosmopolitan challenges herself to develop a *cultural competence* in order to actively engage with people who are very different to her. She can adapt in different places and in different situations, developing a (perhaps happily imperfect) mastery over culture. While Dervla did not speak any other languages well, this didn't seem to be that much of an impediment. When you consider the places she went and the connections she made while there, it shows what a great communicator she was. When among people with whom she could not share language, she had little tricks – like showing photos of family and pets – to establish rapport.

Dervla had a strong sense of empathy with her fellow women and men, which is the key ingredient here. She focused on the essential humanity of others and trusted her well-honed instincts to get on as well as she could with people, in all sorts of circumstances. She followed her nose and her heart and it worked well, most of the time. In her dealings with people, she was openhearted, sympathetic and completely unconcerned with social status. She had an enormous talent for listening. Her long-term friend Hilary Bradt commented, 'When Dervla listens to you, you open up about aspects of your world that nobody else even thinks to enquire about.' She was insatiably curious about the world she lived in and wanted to contribute to people's understanding of each other. She was always willing to listen to different perspectives, to grasp the complexities of social life. She was empathetic enough to walk a mile in someone else's shoes, to try to see how they saw the world. She said, 'If I am to be remembered, I'd like to be remembered as someone who was interested in the ordinary people of whatever country I was in.'

*

I hope that this anthology will appeal equally to readers who have read all of her books, read some or read none. The chapters are organised by decade: from her childhood and younger years in the 1930s to the 1950s, to the 1960s, when she published her first books, through to the 2010s, when she finished with her books on the Middle East. The last chapter contains a small selection of her journalism.

Perhaps this collection might foster readers' dreams of more adventurous travel to new places. Those of us who read her books have thought, if she can do it, maybe we could too. Dervla was a role model in terms of encouraging her readers to be adventurous, and to get out into the world independently, simply and cheaply – and most of all, alone. She tried to keep her life as independent as possible and never accepted an advance for any book. She just quite literally got on her bike and went. She took a walk on the wild side – and she was Irish! As Mary Russell put it, the lone women travellers are 'society's square pegs: the guardians of our right to deviate'. Dervla was more like a trapezoid peg in a round hole, and we couldn't get enough.

To borrow what Alain de Botton said of Alexander von Humboldt, the needle of her curiosity followed its own magnetic north. She was most attracted to the uninhabited, wild places where industrial man had not yet left a mark – or a scar. These days, people use buzzwords like extreme travel, responsible tourism, slow travel, sustainable tourism, ecotourism and digital detox. Dervla practised all of those before the users of these terms were even born. She led the way.

On her return from her trips, she would, as she termed it, 'go into purdah' to write the books. This involved fully transcribing the forensic notebooks at her wonderful old desk overlooking the cobbled courtyard of the Old Market. Final manuscripts were produced on her electric typewriter, before being submitted to her publisher. Incidentally, the embroidered cover on the typewriter had been gifted to her by the Dalai Lama in the sixties. The only background sounds would have been birdsong and a dog snoring in its basket beside the wood-burning stove. She said that this enforced isolation kept the trip alive in her head long after she got home. Producing this anthology has in turn kept Dervla alive in my own head after she has taken her last journey.

When Dervla was made, the mould wasn't just broken, but pulverised into smithereens; she was such an original that it is hard to imagine a mould had ever even existed. She leaves behind a remarkable legacy of curiosity, compassion, adventure, bravery (she'd hate that) and bloody brilliant writing. That is the ultimate *raison d'être* of this anthology of extracts – to pay tribute to her and to place that brilliant writing in the spotlight once again.

ETHEL CROWLEY

### References

Allen, Benedict *The Faber Book of Exploration* Faber, 2004.

Bradt, Hilary 'Dervla Murphy at 80: Living at Full Tilt' *Wanderlust*, November 2011.
http://www.wanderlust.co.uk/magazine/articles/interviews/dervla-murphy-80th-birthday?page=all

Colegrove, Bill *Scraps of Wool* Unbound, 2017.

Conway, Isabel 'Murphy's Lore' *Business Post* 24 November 2019.
https://www.businesspost.ie/life-arts/murphys-lore/

Crowley, Ethel, *Your Place or Mine: Community & Belonging in 21st Century Ireland* Orpen Press, 2013.

Crowley, Ethel, *Irish Examiner*, 27 November 2021.
https://www.irishexaminer.com/lifestyle/artsandculture/arid-40752591.html

Frostrup, Mariella *Wild Women & their Amazing Adventures over Land, Sea & Air* Head of Zeus, 2020.

Hannerz, Ulf 'Cosmopolitans and Locals in World Culture' in M. Featherstone (ed.) *Global Culture: Nationalism, Globalization and Modernity* SAGE, 1990: 239.

Held, David *Cosmopolitanism: Ideals and Realities* Cambridge University Press, 2010: 44-7.

Kelly, A.A. *Wandering Women: Two Centuries of Travel out of Ireland* Wolfhound Press, 1995.

Luddy, Maria *Prostitution and Irish Society 1800–1940* Cambridge University Press, 2007.

Morris, Mary & Larry O'Connor *The Virago Book of Women Travellers* Virago, 1996.

O'Toole, Fintan *We Don't Know Ourselves* Head of Zeus, 2022.

Russell, Mary *The Blessings of a Good Thick Skirt* Flamingo, 1994.

Sheridan, Colette 'Travelling A Different Path' *Irish Examiner*, 26 November 2011.
http://www.irishexaminer.com/weekend/travelling-a-different-path-174952.html

Theroux, Paul *The Tao of Travel* Penguin, 2012.

Thomson, Hugh 'Dervla Murphy Interview: Around the World in 80 Years' *Telegraph* 1 July 2010.
http://www.telegraph.co.uk/travel/artsandculture/travelbooks/7865817/Dervla-Murphy-interview-Around-the-world-in-80-years.html

# 1930s–1950s

# GIRLHOOD

*Since Dervla was a small child, she showed a great sense of adventure, which was actively encouraged by her unconventional parents. First, she explored her own local area, taking great pleasure in cycling and swimming around west Waterford and south Tipperary. She then took cycling trips to the UK, France, Germany and Spain as a teenager and young adult. These were training forays for the longer, more challenging international trips she took later. She was a voracious reader and her greatest desire was to become a famous writer herself. Dervla wrote her autobiography* Wheels within Wheels *in the 1970s when her daughter Rachel was very young. This iconic work speaks for itself; it is among the best-known of her books.*

## Silverland: A Winter Journey beyond the Urals (2007)
## Russia & Siberia

An odd thing happened as our coach drove slowly along Cologne's Rhine embankment. I had been thinking about the immediate future, not the distant past, yet suddenly and vividly I saw an eighteen-year-old girl cycling along this same embankment displaying on her shirt front two badges – the gold and blue of the CTC (Cyclists' Touring Club), the green and white of An Óige (Irish Youth Hostels Association). The bicycle, named Cleopatra, was grossly over-loaded; this being my first tour abroad I hadn't yet learned how to travel light. In May 1949 much bomb damage remained visible and I marvelled to see construction workers active on a Sunday and to hear that most Germans were doing night shifts to put things together again as quickly as possible. When the cathedral appeared, almost intact though surrounded by ruins, its survival seemed proof that Europe's recent regression to barbarism had not been total. That evening, in a letter to my parents, I wondered, 'Is it silly or wrong to feel so reassured by a beautiful building's survival? The same air force that spared it killed thousands of civilians for no reason in Dresden etc.' I still haven't found an answer to that question. It doesn't go away. Was it silly or wrong of me to feel as distressed by the Taliban's destruction of the Bamian Buddhas as by the US air force's killing of Afghan civilians?

## *Wheels within Wheels* (1979)
## Autobiography

At 7.45 on the morning of November 28, 1931, a young woman in the first stage of labour was handed by her husband into Lismore's only hackney cab. The couple were slowly driven east to Cappoquin along a narrow road, in those days pot-holed and muddy. It was a mild, still, moist morning. During the journey a pale dawn spread over the Blackwater Valley, a place as lovely in winter as in summer – a good place to be born.

\*

Two days later I was christened in Cappoquin's parish church. At first the priest refused to baptise me, insisting peevishly that 'Dervla' was a pagan name and must be changed to something respectably Catholic like Mary or Brigid. My father, however, would not give in. He recalled that a sixth-century St Dervla was reputed to have lived in Co. Wexford and that from Ireland the name had spread throughout Europe. Then he carefully explained, to an increasingly impatient curate, that Dearbhail meant True Desire in Gaelic and that the English, French and Latin versions were Dervla, Derval and Dervilla. Finally they compromised: my birth certificate names me as Dervilla Maria.

*

When my parents arrived in Lismore [from Dublin] on their wedding day – being too poor to afford even a weekend honeymoon – they found a build-up of suspicious resentment. The previous county librarian had been a popular local figure since the 1870s. He had recently reluctantly retired, leaving nine books fit to be circulated, and the townspeople were furious when an aloof young Dubliner was appointed to replace their beloved Mr Mills. A secure job with a salary of £250 a year had slipped from the grasp of some deserving local and they smelt political corruption. It mattered not to them that no local was qualified for the job, and what little they knew of my father they disliked. His family was conspicuously Republican – a black mark, not long after the Civil War, in a predominantly Redmondite town.

*

In the spring of 1935 it was decided that for character-forming purposes I needed 'young friends'. My mother therefore arranged various juvenile social occasions and my most vivid memory from this period is a feeling of fury when other children disrupted the elaborate fantasy-world I had created in the orchard.

For my fourth birthday party cousins and an imposing cake were imported from Dublin. But at three o'clock, when the local guests began to assemble, I was missing. Nora quickly traced me to a derelict shed, overgrown with briars, at the end of the garden. My detested beribboned party dress of salmon-pink silk – I can see it still – was torn and streaked with green mould stains, and my back, in every sense, was to the wall. 'You should be ashamed of yourself!' fumed Nora. 'Stuck out here all mucked up with that *gorgeous* dress *rooned* an' your visitors waitin' inside an' even your blood relations down from Dublin!'

My reply was to become a clan slogan. 'I don't want any bloody relations,' I replied succinctly. 'I'm staying here.'

*

Not long after this I nearly joined the angels by drinking half a bottle of neat whiskey. Had I gone on a similar binge in Lismore I would almost certainly have died. As it was, an ambulance rushed me to hospital [in Dublin] where I recovered with a speed that ominously foreshadowed an infinite capacity for strong liquor.

*

Although our new home was very nearly a ruin we tolerated it for the next twenty-one years. My mother must have abhorred these slum-like surroundings but she refrained, as always, from complaining about the inevitable. For a rent of ten shillings a week one couldn't, even in Lismore in the 1930s, expect very much. The rent was so low not only because of the house's dilapidation but because of the previous tenant's suicide in the dining room. …

As a child I always knew there was nothing to spare for non-essentials. But I was never hungry or cold so it did not occur to me to interpret this condition as poverty. Nor did I ever long for the unobtainable, with one spectacular exception – a pony of my own. And since that desire so clearly belonged to the realm of fantasy it caused me no discontent.

*

One raw November noon, not long after my discovery of bigotry, I stood waiting for my grandfather outside Trinity College and as I watched the crowds hurrying across College Green I wondered, 'How important are all those people? Soon they will all be dead. And I'll be dead. What *is* a person? Do we really matter? Or do we only think we do? Why are we alive?' As they formed in my mind I was aware of the enormity of these questions. And I remember a detached, fatalistic acceptance of the fact that even as an adult I was unlikely to find coherent answers. But I was also aware that merely by asking such questions I had acknowledged the mystery at the centre of things and so perhaps had already found as much of the truth as was necessary for me. Oddly, I made no attempt to try to relate these speculations to the formal religion which was so much a part of my life at that time. They belonged to a category labelled 'Private Important Thoughts' – Pits for short – and nothing would have induced me to discuss them with any grown-up. Does every child have, as I had, an image of what adults expect children to be? And do they all courteously preserve this image, outwardly, lest their adults might be discomfited, while inwardly they are becoming something quite different, full of Pits that have nothing to do with Dr Dolittle or stringing conkers?

*

I went out one morning to fetch the newspaper and learned that war had been declared. Hurrying home, I relished the sense of crisis in the atmosphere and expectantly scanned a cloudless sky for the first bombers. But when I realised that Ireland was not going to be involved I lost interest in the whole distant drama. For me, its chief effect was to intensify the boredom of grown-up conversation; I regarded literature and theology as lesser evils than military tactics. Occasionally, however, I was diverted by Hitler's interminable monologues on the wireless. These I found irresistibly funny and I remember rolling under the dining-room table one day in an uncontrollable paroxysm of mirth. My parents, who both understood German, reacted otherwise.

*

Every summer Pappa [her grandfather] spent July and August with us. I would guess that my father was his favourite child though apart from their common bibliomania the two were alike in no obvious way. Pappa was not merely 'good with children'; he truly enjoyed them and his annual arrival by train drew not only myself but a score of other children to the railway station. Yet he never gave pennies or sweets or treats to me or to any of his young friends. Instead he played with us endlessly – our own games in our own favourite haunts. And always he brought from Dublin a battered suitcase tied with rope and bulging with dog-eared children's books bought for twopence a dozen on the quays.

*

There is a difference between the interest taken in books by normal readers (people like my parents) and the lunatic concern of bibliomaniacs (people like Pappa and myself). Everything to do with books mattered to me and I fretted much more over their wartime deterioration – that squalid gravy-coloured paper! – than I did over butter rationing or inedible bread. (Clothes rationing I of course considered a blessing in disguise.) After a quick glance at any open page I could by the age of nine have told you the publisher of most children's books – and often the printer and illustrator, too. One of my hobbies was rewriting blurbs which seemed inadequate and I collected publishers' lists as other children collect stamps.

*

A river shows different aspects to the fisherman, the naturalist, the trader, the artist, the soldier, the boatman and the swimmer. I formed my relationship with the Blackwater as a swimmer. Before I can remember, my father regularly immersed me in the cool, dark silkiness of its depths and I swam almost as soon as I could walk. It is a good thing to have had a river among one's mentors; its strength develops the body, its beauty develops the soul, its agelessness develops the imagination. Also, its moods teach respect for the mindless power of nature. The Blackwater is very moody; it has deep holes, sudden floods, hidden rocks, tricky currents and sly weeds. It claims at least three lives a year and I was not allowed to bathe alone until I was twelve. Although I could easily have broken this rule without being detected, it never occurred to me to do so.

*

My first appearance in print came a few months later. Mark [a treasured friend] had drawn my attention to a children's essay competition in a weekly provincial paper. Prizes of seven-and-sixpence, five shillings and half-a-crown were being offered for the three best essays submitted weekly. Competitors must be under sixteen and were free to choose their own subject. I had at once protested that I could not possibly win. 'Rubbish!' said Mark. 'Go home and try.' So I wrote five hundred words on 'Picking Blackberries', in prose as purple as blackberry juice.

The *Cork Weekly Examiner* came out on Fridays and I counted the days and then at last was standing in the newsagent's shop unfolding the paper with trembling hands. Looking down the pages I felt the nausea of suspense and could scarcely focus. Then I found the competition corner. My heart leaped like a salmon at a weir. The unbelievable had to be believed: Dervla Murphy had won first prize (aged twelve). And to crown her glory the other winners were aged fourteen and fifteen.

*

A grimly authoritarian regime would either have broken my spirit or provoked me to run away – probably the latter. But Waterford's Ursuline Convent allowed enough scope for me to lead my own kind of life without inviting disaster. (The Hat [the headmistress] threatened to expel me three times; but this, I now feel, was because of my private feud with her rather than because I had unforgivably challenged The System.) The atmosphere was relaxed without being permissive – to this extent, a replica of home – and I liked most of my schoolmates and all my teachers. Also, I greatly enjoyed disliking The Hat.

*

The train was full of children returning to Waterford schools in self-segregating groups. I joined the Ursuline coach and remained by the door to wave dutifully to my father. When he was out of sight I felt oddly *released*; yet I did not immediately merge with the rest, much as I had been looking forward to rejoining my friends. Suddenly, for the first time, I was aware of myself as an outsider. Neither at home nor at school did I quite fit in. That is one of the moments I remember with a vividness which has never faded. I was staring fixedly at the Round Hill – an ancient, tree-covered fortification from which Lismore takes its name – and I felt not at all upset by this recognition of my own apartness. Neither did I see it as anything to be smug about; but I was interested in it, because it seemed to presage numerous as yet indefinable threats and promises. Then as the train changed its tune, on the bridge across the Blackwater at Cappoquin, I changed my mood and went swaying up the corridor to join my classmates.

*

It never occurred to me to speculate about the effects of this decision [to give up school and stay at home to help look after her invalid mother] on myself at the age of eighteen, or twenty-five, or thirty. If I could have foreseen myself after the passing of another fourteen years, I would probably have refused to believe in the truth of my vision. Perhaps few fourteen-year-olds look far ahead, and even now, at forty-six, I feel foolish and futile if I try to do so. The present is enough. Attempts to control the future seem needlessly to limit its possibilities. If this view were general, anarchy would overtake the world. But one hopes there is room for a minority of non-planners.

That evening my immediate future, if far from ideal, looked quite tolerable. I would have ample time to read and write and cycle and swim. I would see Mark regularly – and he meant more to me than any number of school friends. Unlike many of my contemporaries, I had no interest in parties, clothes, films, dances, pop-stars (if such then existed) or boyfriends. In many ways, God had indeed fitted the back for the burden, in my case as well as my father's.

*

Were I asked to pinpoint the most exciting period of a life that latterly has been more eventful than most, I would say – 'The years from fourteen to seventeen.' But I must be careful here. How much do we romanticise youth and hope and energy, so that only their glory is remembered? Perhaps all I should say is that in retrospect those years seem to have contained much happiness and little unhappiness, despite a constant underlying irritation at having to waste so much time every day on tedious chores. And despite occasional brief – but intense – moods of depression caused by personality clashes with my mother.

*

Not until it [a story] was finished did I think of secretly sending it to a publisher – secretly because I wished to avoid parental sympathy when it was rejected. I felt very adult and earnest as I withdrew all my meagre savings from the post office, looked up the address of a suitable typist on the last but one page of the *TLS* and took down a list of possible publishers from *The Writers' and Artists' Yearbook* in my father's office. I was now actively engaged in the literary world, not just daydreaming about it. The most I really hoped for were some constructive words of advice to a fourteen-year-old from kindly publishers' editors. And that is exactly what I got.

*

I remember one very cold January morning standing in the kitchen by the turf-range (a wartime innovation) while eagerly opening a letter from [a pen-friend in] Malaya. As I slit the envelope I saw, just for an instant, the closeness of my mental relationship with Mahn Kaur as a measure of my closeness to Asia; and our whole correspondence seemed very much a preparation. Those rare moments when we apparently get a signal from the future do not affect the conduct of one's daily life. But they have their value below the level on which one feels impatient or thwarted – or even hopeless.

A few weeks later came Gandhi's assassination. I was in bed with tonsillitis and I shall never forget switching on the wireless to hear the news. During those years I was mesmerised by the writings of Gandhi and I regarded him with a rapture which has since been considerably modified.

*

I left Lismore on April 15, 1951, to spend three weeks cycling through Wales and Southern England – including, inevitably, five days in Stratford-upon-Avon. Some of the neighbours were aghast when they heard I had taken off, alone, on a bicycle, to travel through what was little better than a pagan land. And they were even more aghast when they realised that my parents had encouraged me to commit this outrage.

At nineteen I had never before left Ireland, apart from one Triple Crown excursion to Twickenham. ... I was fervently nationalist and anti-partitionist and therefore, in theory, anti-British. Honour required me to see Britain as a foreign country because my school history books had taught that the British were solely responsible for all Ireland's past woes and present handicaps. Thus I was shocked to discover, as I cycled through Wales and England, that it was impossible to feel 'abroad'. Half of me seemed 'to belong' in Britain.

*

Soon I was eagerly planning and reading in preparation for a Spanish tour in the following spring [1954] and it was on this journey that I first fell in love with a country. ... In Spain, at that time, there was an exciting sense of remoteness, both spatial and temporal. I pedalled as far off the beaten track as possible... George Borrow's *The Bible in Spain* and Walter Starkie's *Spanish Raggle-Taggle* were the books which directly inspired me to cycle around Spain. And the fact that I had done my homework so thoroughly – reading volumes of history, biography and travel, balanced by novels, plays and poems in translation – perhaps partly explains my feeling of instant affinity with the Spaniards. They seemed at once more comprehensible and more 'foreign' than the Germans or the French and I even found myself speaking a version of Spanish despite my notorious inability to learn foreign languages. ... At twenty-two I had reached my physical peak and could effortlessly cycle 120 miles a day through mountainous country on a heavy roadster laden with large panniers which were quite unnecessary for such a short trip. ... In Spain I kept a detailed diary for the first time, writing it up every evening, however tired I felt, and posting it to Godfrey [her boyfriend] once a week. On my return home he encouraged me to use this material and I sold a series of twelve articles to the *Irish Independent*, Ireland's most popular daily newspaper. [One of these articles is reproduced in chapter eight] Heartened by this success – I had for the first time earned a considerable sum of money, by Murphy standards – I began working on a travel book. ... I felt very hard-done-by when four publishers rejected it. ... To write successfully on Spain, I reckoned, one would need the ability of a V.S. Pritchett or an Arland Ussher – authors with whom I knew I could never compete. ... At twenty-three I felt increasingly conscious of the passage of time, of my own thwarted potentialities and of being trapped in a situation from which there could be no possible escape in the foreseeable future. My ambition to cycle to India now came more often to the surface of my mind and I tormented myself with thoughts of Afghanistan and the Himalayas. It had been established that I was physically equal to such a journey; all I needed was freedom.

\*

We had never agreed on the subject of housekeeping... The furniture was to be waxed on Tuesdays, the silver polished on Wednesdays, the hearths blacked on Thursdays, the shopping done at this hour and the ironing at that... I violently resented my mother's humiliating post-wash-up inspections; she was treating me now as though I were a fifteen-year-old skivvy. ...

My return to Spain in 1956 was not the anticlimax it might have been. I postponed my holiday to September, to enjoy the grape harvest, and in many ways found this tour even more satisfying than the first. Writing a personal travel book about a country brings one very close to it, for reasons that even now I do not quite understand.

*

On my way home I crossed the Pyrenees with twelve large bottles of Spanish brandy (bought for the equivalent of 25 pence each) rolled up in my sleeping bag and carefully roped to the carrier. This feat possibly constitutes a world record of some sort. But shortly afterwards Babieca's back wheel buckled irreparably so the effort may not have been the economy it seemed.

*

As soon as I was back into the rhythm of the treadmill I would again become impotent to assert myself. For a mad moment I thought of cycling away in the morning to take a boat to England and there finding a job – any job – and freedom. But of course it would not be freedom. While my mother lived I could nowhere find freedom.

*

During the winter of 1956–7 the rapid and conclusive disintegration of our house coincided with the maturing of my father's life insurance policy; so we decided to build a bungalow on the outskirts of Lismore. North, the site overlooked the Blackwater

Valley where wooded ridges rise from the river to the foot of the mountains; south, it overlooked placid fields, bounded by fine old trees, and against the sky lay another wooded ridge, the watershed between the valleys of the Bride and Blackwater. We were within five minutes' brisk walk of the town yet only one other building was in sight – the farm at the end of the long field that sloped down behind us to the river.

*

My father's was the first corpse I had seen, yet it left me unmoved. It was simply an irrelevant, impermanent piece of matter. As the funeral procession travelled to Lismore I sat by my mother in the ambulance behind the hearse, more conscious of apprehension about my new responsibilities than of grief.

My father was buried in Lismore on February 27 [1961] – the first of his family, for many generations, to be laid to rest outside Dublin. The town that had received him so coldly thirty years earlier closed its shops in mourning, and it comforted us that the phrases of praise and regret were uttered not only because convention prescribed them.

*

My long imprisonment, during those ten weeks of spring, completely broke my spirit. I ceased to fight, inwardly, and lived from day to day in a cocoon of resignation. I ate almost nothing, smoked far too many cigarettes and drank far too much whiskey. Yet I never got drunk; I was at the more dangerous stage of keeping my alcohol level up twenty-four hours a day. Finally Mark took action, when he was unable to endure any longer the change taking place within me. I can remember no details, but a responsible daily woman was installed, my mother was somehow persuaded of the urgent necessity of releasing me and on May 7 – that date I have never forgotten – I cycled down the road, feeling incredulous, with three hours of freedom ahead of me. This was to be the routine: Saturdays and Sundays excepted, I would be free from two to five every afternoon.

It needed only this break in the automaton rhythm of the past months to release a cataract of despair. I was nearly thirty and had achieved – it then seemed – nothing. As a daughter I was a failure, as a writer I was atrophied, as a traveller I had only glimpsed possibilities. But at least I was again reacting and feeling, even if all my feelings were painful.

*

On the evening of August 24 [1962] [her good friend] Daphne came to sit with me through the night and at twenty-five past one in the morning my mother died – as peacefully, in the end, as had my father. She had survived him by exactly eighteen months.

As my mother drew her last breath, peace enfolded me. It was profound and healing, untinged by grief, or remorse, or guilt, or loneliness. I thought of it as a gift from my mother's spirit – and then mocked my fancy, without quite discrediting it. For long I had suffered with her, and made her suffer, and been made to suffer by her; and of late I had mourned for her. Now I could only rejoice – and in Daphne's company I did not have to disguise my joy. A great burden was gone, the double burden of another's tragedy and my own inadequacy. I stood at the threshold of an independent life and I felt, that night, my parents' blessing on it.

*

It is difficult to convey my feelings when I woke next morning and realised that I was responsible to and for no one but myself – that I was free to do what I liked, when I liked, as I liked. For more than sixteen years every day had been lived in the shadow of my mother's need. Even on holidays, my movements had had to be exactly regulated so that I would unfailingly arrive home on a certain date. I remember sitting in the hot sunshine in the back garden with Daphne – surrounded by that untrammelled growth of nettles and thistles which proved me to be my father's daughter – and feeling currents of an appreciation of liberty running through my body like mild electric shocks. I was exalted by the realisation of freedom. When callers came to offer sympathy, Daphne received them and gave the necessary convention-soothing impression that I was too distrait to appear.

*

I have since realised that events and emotions which at the time of their happening were apparently destructive and enfeebling, in their enduring results were constructive and tempering. I had learned a lesson in humility that could not have been taught to anybody of my arrogant nature by less violent means. Without my friends I could not possibly have survived; their love had borne me to safety. ...

Many hours on the sand-dunes had been spent methodically planning my journey to India. Having for the past twenty years intended to make this journey, it did not strike me as in any way an odd idea. I thought then, as I still do, that if someone enjoys cycling and wishes to go to India, the obvious thing is to cycle there. Soon, however, I realised that most people were regarding me either as a lunatic or an embryonic heroine; in 1962 Western youth's mass trek to the East had not yet begun. When I went into a cycle shop to have Roz's derailleur gears removed, and explained that I was going to India and felt they would not be suitable for Asian roads, the mechanic looked at me very strangely indeed. After that I became a trifle inhibited about discussing my plans.

Several people suggested that the trip should be sponsored, perhaps by the makers of my bicycle – or by Guinness, since their product so habitually nourished the body that was to undertake this alleged marathon. Or even by a newspaper, to which I could send back dramatic stories from improbable places. But these suggestions appalled me. Any sponsor would have made of my private journey a public stunt and the very thought of the resultant limelight made me sweat with terror. ... It was planned as, and it proved to be, a happy-go-lucky private voyage to enjoy some of the world in the way best suited to my temperament. And, if the publishing trade winds were blowing my way, to provide material for a book.

\*

The winter of 1962–3 was Europe's most severe for eighty years and I shall never forget the agonising cold of that dark January morning when I began to cycle east from Dunkirk on an ice-bound road.

\*

Then, shortly before my return home in March 1964, I met Penelope Betjeman in Delhi. She had come to India to collect material for a book and when I confessed to literary ambitions she said, 'Of course! Marvellous journey! Marvellous book! You must send it to Jock Murray.'

We were cycling together through a crowded Old Delhi bazaar – Penelope with an accident-inviting load of firewood tied to her carrier – and I yelled above the blare of rickshaw horns. 'To *whom*?'

'To Jock Murray,' Penelope yelled back. 'You'll adore Jock – everybody adores Jock.'

'Do you mean Jock Murray in Albemarle Street?' I asked disbelievingly.

'Yes of course,' said Penelope. 'Jock will love it – just his sort of thing.'

I was so profoundly shocked by this irreverent suggestion that I almost ran into a sacred cow.

\*

When the manuscript had been typed I sent a copy off to each of the interested houses and circulated the third carbon copy among my friends. Then came a letter from Penelope: 'Have you sent your book to Jock Murray? If not, why not' – or words to that effect.

To me the idea still seemed preposterous, but I was in a mood to try any alternative to high-powered modern publishing – even at the risk of committing sacrilege. I parcelled up my faint, dog-eared fourth copy and sent it off to 50 Albemarle Street.

A few days later a telegram signed 'Murray' asked me to call when I was next in London. Was it possible...? Could it be...? I packed my saddle-bag, leaped on Roz and cycled to Cork to catch the boat.

Next day, quite unmanned by suspense and awe, I turned into Albemarle Street and approached the spot where, fifteen years earlier, during my first visit to London, I had stood on the pavement gazing respectfully at the door I was now so improbably about to enter. In reality No. 50 was not at all overwhelming. No efficient army appeared to organise me, the place smelt suitably of books, old and new, and Jock Murray's office was cramped, chaotic and almost as dusty as Clairvaux. At once I knew that I had arrived at the predestined end to a much longer journey than my cycle to India.

# 1960s

# FREEDOM

*Following the deaths of both of her parents, January 1963 saw Dervla fulfilling her life-long dream of cycling to India, which was immortalised in her first book* Full Tilt.

*The latter half of 1963 was spent working at a home for Tibetan child refugees in the Himalayan town of Dharamshala.* Tibetan Foothold *tells the story. Following her return, she had treatment for several months in the London Hospital for Tropical Diseases for a cyst on her liver. Difficult to diagnose, it appeared to have been caused by a sheep parasite carried by the Tibetans. She said that 'thanks to the good old NHS, I got treated'. She remembered getting a bone marrow test: they bored into the middle of her chest bone with a manual drill, without anaesthetic. She said the pain was excruciating, naturally enough.*

*Having become enchanted with Asia, she then spent seven months in Nepal in 1965. She had posted letters home during her time away to her friend Daphne, which doubled as her book notes. She then wrote* Tibetan Foothold *and* The Waiting Land *on Inis Oírr, off the west coast of Ireland. She remembered being cut off from the mainland for six weeks on one occasion, because of bad weather.*

*She then left for Ethiopia in December 1966, returning over three months later. Hiking across remote areas with her mule named Jock, she was robbed and truly thought she was to be murdered. It is the one incident (among so, so many) that she always quoted when asked whether she had ever been really afraid for her life.*

*During her pregnancy in 1968, she hiked through Turkey, against her doctor's advice. Later that year, she welcomed her baby daughter Rachel into the world.*

## *Full Tilt: Ireland to India with a Bicycle* (1965)
## Ireland to India overland

On my tenth birthday a bicycle and an atlas coincided as presents and a few days later I decided to cycle to India. I've never forgotten the exact spot on a hill near my home at Lismore, County Waterford, where the decision was made and it seemed to me then, as it still seems to me now, a logical decision, based on the discoveries that cycling was a most satisfactory method of transport and that (excluding the USSR for political reasons) the way to India offered fewer watery obstacles than any other destination at a similar distance.

However, I was a cunning child so I kept my ambition to myself, thus avoiding the tolerant amusement it would have provoked among my elders. I did not want to be soothingly assured that this was a passing whim because I was quite confident that one day I *would* cycle to India. That was at the beginning of December 1941, and on 14 January 1963, I started to cycle from Dunkirk towards Delhi.

*

I shall never forget that dark ice-bound morning when I began to cycle east from Dunkirk; to have the fulfilment of a twenty-one-year-old ambition apparently within one's grasp can be quite disconcerting. This was a moment I had thought about so often that when I actually found myself living through it I felt as though some favourite scene from a novel had come, incredibly, to life. However, within a few weeks my journey had degenerated from a happy-go-lucky cycle trek to a grim struggle for progress by *any* means along roads long lost beneath snow and ice.

At first my disappointment was acute, but I had set out to enjoy myself by seeing the world, not to make or break any record, so I soon became adjusted to these conditions, which led to quite a few interesting adventures. Also, I was aware of 'seeing the world' in circumstances unique to my generation. Should I survive to the end of this century it will be impressive to recall that I crossed the breadth of Europe in the winter of 1963, when every humdrum detail of everyday life was made tensely dramatic by the weather and going shopping became a scaled-down Expedition to the Antarctic. It was neat hell at the time – I cycled up to the Rouen Youth Hostel with a quarter-inch icicle firmly attached to my nose and more than once the agony of frozen fingers made me weep rather uncharacteristically – yet it seemed a reasonably good exchange for the satisfaction of cycling all the way to India.

\*

When I arrived on the outskirts of this town [Shahrud, Iran] a car overtook me and the driver (manager of a local sugar factory and reader of the daily paper) stopped and said, 'Dervla going to India, yes?' I blushed with becoming modesty at this proof of fame and replied that I was indeed Dervla going to India, so he invited me to spend the night at his home, where I now am, having had a shower and a huge supper. It's quite impossible to retain one's youthful curves in these countries; to refuse food is an insult so one merely unbuttons one's slacks in a surreptitious way and goes on and on eating. Before the meal everyone consumes a vast amount of biscuits, oranges, pastries, figs stuffed with almonds, toffees and bon-bons of all descriptions, pistachio nuts and endless glasses of tea. Then you're expected to welcome with a glad smile a mound of rice you can hardly see over and masses of meat and vegetables.

\*

Strolling through the bazaar [in Herat] I was delightedly conscious of the fact that when Alexander's soldiers passed this way they must have witnessed scenes almost identical to those now surrounding me – bakers cooking flat bread in underground ovens, having spread the dough on leather cushions stuffed with straw and damped with filthy water; blindfolded camels walking round and round churning *mast* in stinking little dens behind their owners' stalls; butchers skinning and disembowelling a sheep and throwing scraps to the yellow, crop-eared dogs who have been waiting all morning for this happy event; tanners curing hides, weavers at their looms, potters skilfully firing pitchers of considerable beauty, cobblers making the curly-toed, exquisitely inlaid regional shoes and tailors cutting out the long, fleece-padded coats which when thrown over the shoulders of an Afghan makes him look like a fairy-story king.

\*

The more I see of life in these 'undeveloped' countries and of the methods adopted to 'improve' them, the more depressed I become. It seems criminal that the backwardness of a country like Afghanistan should be used as an excuse for America and Russia to have a tug-of-war for possession. Having spoken to nine or ten young Afghans who have been exposed to Western influences, I notice an impatient feeling of contempt for their own country, an undiscriminating worship of everything American and a general restlessness, rootlessness and discontent. They repudiate their native culture yet cannot succeed in adopting an alien civilisation which they imagine is superior, though they don't understand the first thing about it. Give me the nomads' outlook every time – they haven't heard of America yet. I don't claim to know the right answer to the 'underdeveloped' problem but I feel most strongly that the Communist answer is less wrong than the Western; the

Communists have much more imaginative understanding of different national temperaments, as two Russians I spoke to here today revealed very clearly. They want to impose Communism as a way of life, but with the minimum of damage to the traditional foundations of the country concerned, whereas Westerners have told me repeatedly that they want to bulldoze those foundations right away and start a nice, new, hygienic society from scratch – an ambition that seems to me almost too stupid to be true.

*

Mohammed's mother is a tremendous character – one of those old people who make the young realize that old age is not something to be dreaded, when it can give such mellowness and balance and contentment to the human being. I would have readily forgiven her for being distant to someone who represented, according to her traditions, the complete negation of womanhood but, although she speaks no English, the warmth of her welcome has made me feel truly 'one of the family' this evening. Not for the first time, I am astonished and humbled by the tolerance of Muslims, who so easily accept the fact that my standards differ from theirs, yet give me no feeling of being regarded as inferior on that account. Even more remarkable, the liberty which they recognise as my inheritance does not deter them from treating me with a courtesy too rarely found in modern Europe; by this civilised fusion of our two cultures I have all the advantages and none of the disadvantages of their own womenfolk. I think it is fair to say the modern Muslim, even if he is an uneducated peasant, shows less prejudice towards other religions than we Christians do, with our persistent tendency to brand any religion not our own as 'ignorant superstition'. This Muslim tolerance makes it all the sadder that politicians so often artificially stimulate religious differences for their own ends.

*

[Bamian] I woke this morning, looked through my window and almost fell out of bed with excitement. This hotel is built on a 1,000-foot cliff rising sheer from the valley floor and across the valley, distinct in the brilliant, early sunshine, I saw a 120-foot-high statue of the Lord Buddha standing, as it has stood for over 2,000 years, in a gigantic alcove in the golden sandstone mountain – both alcove and statue having been carved with extraordinary skill out of the rock. The whole face of this mountain is pitted with the caves of Buddhist monks and another, eighty-foot, statue stands about a quarter of a mile east of the giant one. Quite apart from this unique spectacle the valley itself is superbly beautiful; a depression in the centre of the mountains, fertile and neatly tilled, dotted with tiny villages and criss-crossed with lines of silver-barked sinjit trees, whose diminutive rosy buds were glowing softly in the early light. Even though I was mentally prepared for those Buddhas the impact was tremendous when I actually saw them presiding impassively over the valley. ...

The statues, however, look far less impressive close-to than from the other side, or centre, of the valley. There the effect of so many centuries of weathering is not apparent, although, considering their great antiquity, the damage is very slight and much skilful restoring has recently been done; even the paintings executed on the arches of the alcoves and the caves are still traceable.

*

I slept very little last night and couldn't stand up without help this morning; I was in too much pain to eat an elaborate breakfast. While drinking my tea I coughed involuntarily and at once fainted clean away because of the agony. When I had come to, my host and I held an emergency conference and he advised me to go to the German-built hospital in the town, fifty-five miles from Doshi. I'll skip details of the journey – I did *not* observe the landscape and fainted twice more: I'm getting quite expert at it. A young Afghan doctor said that three ribs are broken; he plastered them and ordered me to bed and banned cycling for a month.

This hospital is exactly what you would expect an Afghan hospital to be – even one built by Germans. A male nurse undressed me and two police officers and three other officials stood by as interested spectators while I stood naked from the waist up being plastered. There are a few women nurses here – elderly widows without sons or husbands or fathers to restrain them from leading such immoral lives! A bathroom-cum-lavatory leads off my room but the water supply has been broken down since the Germans left in 1945. However, this doesn't deter everyone from using the lavatory: it would be so much healthier to have an Eastern one outside instead of a Western one, minus water, inside. I can't see myself escaping from this dive without dysentery – the room is *dense* with flies. Fortunately it opens onto a verandah and the bed is beside a big window with a wide view of the heavenly garden which is like a miniature forest, full of chestnuts heavy with blossom and Scotch firs and many other big trees, unfamiliar to me, in early summer foliage. There are also blazing flower-beds, smooth lawns and a little bubbling stream. Possibly I'll survive; a Czech doctor is going to re-examine me tomorrow. …A grim night, and now I know what it feels like to be a guinea-pig.

*

At midday I went asleep for about half-an-hour on a mountainside, having been up since 5.30 a.m., and woke to find myself in a *tent*. I had decided that I was still asleep and dreaming when a filthy old man of the Kochi (nomad) tribes appeared and explained by signs that they'd noticed me going to sleep with no shade, which they thought very bad, so he erected one of their goat-hair tents over me – without loosening a pebble, they move so stealthily. The moral here is that the basis of a successful psychological approach to Afghans is *not* to be afraid of them. Yet it's literally true that the same old man would think nothing of murdering his own daughter if she ran away and married into an enemy tribe. It does take a while to sort out the fact that such people don't want to murder *you*!

*

To be objective about the Indian subcontinent – discarding my inherited anti-colonialism, and a temperamental bias towards mediaeval Afghanistan – even two days in this one city [Peshawar] make nonsense of the argument that Britain exploited the country without compensation. Of course she exploited her, but in what city between Constantinople and Peshawar do you see good and plentiful schools, hospitals, homes for the blind, orphanages, clinics and Christian churches that are allowed to function? And where in the Middle East do you find efficient transport services, reliable communications, an army that *looks* like an army, well-trained civil servants, electricity plants that actually produce electricity and roads that *are* roads? Britain grew fat on Indian wealth, but enough was ploughed back to make the familiar picture of her as a heartless bandit look just plain silly.

*

Just before this I found the corpse of a young man – dead eight or ten days I should think. His skull had been bashed in so I've officially 'forgotten' the discovery as I wish to remain on good terms with *all* the local factions while trekking here. My nose led me to the poor devil, who was pushed into a crevice between two big boulders. I notice that rifles are not carried in this part of the [Gilgit] Agency but they evidently manage to liquidate each other without them. After investigating I was quite glad to immerse myself in the waterfall!

From the summit I had a magnificent view of a tumult of rough white peaks in every direction – including Nanga Parbat again, triumphantly conspicuous above the rest. On the way down I saw a couple of cave-man types, with long, tangled hair and beards, carrying ice from the glaciers to Gilgit Town. By following them my return was shorter – but much more hair-raising – and I got back at 5.20 p.m. utterly exhausted and ravenously hungry.

*

Then, as I stood looking pathetically around me, in the faint hope of seeing some nomads, a solitary black cow (for all the world like a good little Kerry) appeared some twenty yards upstream, walking purposefully across the meadow towards the torrent. There was no other sign of life in the valley, either human or animal, and in retrospect I tend to believe that she was my guardian angel, discreetly disguised. But when I first noticed her I did not pause to speculate on her nature or origin. She was obviously going to ford the nullah [river] for some good reason of her own, and we were going with her. I pedalled rapidly and bumpily over the grass to the point for which she was heading. There I hastily unstrapped the saddle-bag, tied it to my head with a length of rope mentally and appropriately labelled 'FOR EMERGENCIES', and was ready to enter the water.

The cow, when she joined us on the bank, showed no surprise at our presence, nor did she register any alarm or despondency as I put my right arm round her neck, gripped Roz's crossbar firmly with my left hand, and accompanied her into the turmoil of icy water. It had occurred to me that if I found myself out of my depth this could become an Awkward Situation, but actually the water was never more than four feet deep, though its tremendous force would have unbalanced me had I been alone. My friend, however, was clearly used to this role and we crossed without difficulty, unless the agony of being two-thirds submerged in newly melted snow counts as a difficulty. I felt that there was a certain lack of civility about our abrupt parting on the opposite bank, after such a meaningful though brief association, but our ways lay in different directions and I could do nothing to express my gratitude. So I can only record here my thanks for the fairy-tale appearance of this little black cow.

*

After the first few yards of carrying Roz up that gradient between those rocks my shins had been so badly banged about that I could have wept with pain, and Roz's back mudguard, severely injured while crossing the earlier nullah, was now completely torn off. Clearly this nonsense had to stop, for both our sakes, and the only alternative was to wear Roz round my neck. Thus arrayed, I proceeded upwards, still suffering from lack of oxygen, with my head sticking out of the angle between crossbar and chain and my vision obscured by the front wheel. Being in a weakened condition the ludicrous aspect of the situation struck me with special force and whenever I stopped to rest I wasted precious breath on giggling feebly at my own dottiness.

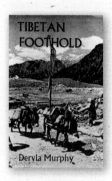

*Tibetan Foothold* (1966)
Dharamshala, Himachal Pradesh,
India

The Home [for Tibetan child refugees] overlooks an undulating
landscape, now shrivelled to dull dust. While waiting for lunch I sat
on a mud roof in the shade of a peepul tree and looked down on
the stagnant, scummy waters of a little lake into which emaciated
buffaloes were being driven for their daily splash. Near them an
equally emaciated Hindu was vigorously washing himself, standing
waist-deep a yard out from the shore and pushing the green scum
aside before plunging his head underwater. Above, the sky was like
a reflection of the landscape, colourless with heat, and kites and
vultures wheeled slowly around, ever vigilant for carrion. Below in
the compound, two women were quarrelling shrilly in Hindi and
their irritation communicated itself ridiculously to me. Clouds of
flies buzzed and tickled; the hot, greasy odours of curry and ghee,
rising from the kitchen, killed any flicker of appetite I might have felt.

\*

I got off to a gruesome start this morning. When we arrived at the
Dispensary at 5.30 a.m. my first job was to put two children, who
had died during the night, into the cardboard boxes which serve
here as coffins. They were both four years old but malnutrition had
left them as small as an average two-year-old; it's quite impossible

to cure such miserable scraps once they get measles, bronchitis or dysentery. To make matters worse, there is no possibility of notifying their parents, though the majority of the children have at least one parent living; so one often finds a mother or father wandering around the compound searching for their child, who has died perhaps several months ago, clutching the pathetic little bag of cheap sweets that was to have been their reunion present. Most of the parents are working on the roads in the Chumba or Kulu valleys, and they save up until they can pay the bus fare to Dharamshala and provide a few 'extras' for their children.

The Tibetans' religion says that the dead must be given to one of the four elements – earth, fire, water or air. In Tibet the custom was to dismember corpses on a 'cemetery' hill-top, where birds ate them in a few hours, bones and all. This was considered giving the dead to the air and the custom obviously arose because in Tibet the earth is frozen hard for most of the year, wood is too scarce a fuel to be used on funeral-pyres and indiscriminately throwing bodies into rivers is unwise. But now, in India, Tibetans are cremated like Hindus.

\*

Today the monsoon has gone mad and turned the whole world to a liquid turmoil – the mountain sliding and slipping in chunks with rumbling roars, cascades of water tearing by on all sides, the road a racing brown torrent, the paths, waterfalls and every roof in the place leaking like a sieve. At lunchtime our soup was diluted by raindrops sploshing down from the ceiling of this *new* bungalow and outside it was almost dark, with nothing, nowhere and nobody dry. The monsoon isn't fun at the best of times, but in a refugee camp it's hell. To go out on an evening like this and see rows of children lying on thin sacking laid over damp concrete under a leaking tin roof in a shelter open at both ends, and to listen to the pathetic coughing, would take a tear from a stone. On asking why these children were not in their rooms I was told that they couldn't sleep because of the hordes of vicious bed-bugs which attacked them nightly. Already

Juliet has a supply of Tik 20 ready for the anti-bug campaign – but this is a war that can only be waged in dry weather.

*

I woke this morning with mumps, an infection taken no more seriously around here than is a head-cold in Ireland: every week an ayah or a few children develop it – but they wouldn't dream of calling *that* an illness and carry on regardless. Irish women, however, are of inferior mettle, so after breakfast I shamelessly took to my bed – or rather to the wooden Tibetan couch on which Kesang sleeps at night, since I haven't got a bed proper. My eyes have been troublesome lately, and now Oliver thinks I've got a touch of trachoma – which is not surprising, as the majority of the children suffer severely from this infection. He has advised me not to read or write for a week, which fits in quite well with being mumpsical; I feel no great urge to do anything more than pity myself this evening. Yet you can't really resent a disease called mumps – it's such a *jolly* word!

*

Before breakfast today a message came from the Palace summoning me to that formal audience which His Holiness grants to all those who work with Tibetans. Inevitably, I spent the rest of the morning looking forward to meeting the man who represents that aspect of Tibetan life which most attracts, repels or bewilders foreigners.

The majority of Tibetans do not themselves understand why the Dalai Lama means what he does to them, yet their feeling for him is their strongest corporate emotion; he is more revered than was ever the greatest saint in Christendom and more loved and deferred to than the greatest king. This relationship between the man and his people, which has little to do with the personality of the individual Dalai Lama, is a singular development of certain Mahayana Buddhist beliefs and Tibetans never think of His Holiness as a mere man. ...

Where somebody of His Holiness's stature is concerned, there are probably as many different versions of the man as there are people who meet him; unavoidably one has one's instinctive personal reactions. One also has certain preconceptions and it would be untrue to say that I met the Dalai Lama with an open mind; all my conversations with those who knew him had led me to expect an outstanding individual – not necessarily likeable, but certainly a Personality. Instead I found myself talking to a simple, pleasant young man, who has the gracious manner and lively humour of the average Tibetan but who failed to impress me by any unusual qualities – apart from a total lack of egotism, which by our standards is remarkable enough in the circumstances.

On meeting some High Lamas one spontaneously recognises them as deeply religious men, yet with the Dalai Lama I had no awareness of being in the presence of an ascetic whose life is centred on things spiritual. This is not to imply that His Holiness's life is otherwise centred; it may merely be that he is as yet too immature to convey such a feeling to others.

However, half an hour's conversation convinced me that here was a ruler whose chief concern would always be the welfare of his people – though unfortunately he showed no sign of an intellectual ability equal to the enormous task of solving their present problems. But I was also becoming increasingly aware of a certain tension in the atmosphere. I felt that the Dalai Lama was constantly on his guard, that he was unsure of himself in dealing with foreigners and that he was continually attempting to gauge my reactions to him. One can only pity the vulnerability of this sensitive young man, who is so often exposed to the relentless scrutiny of a world either politely sceptical or impatiently contemptuous of the values which he represents. ...

*

The agencies' original assumption that Tiblets must be cared for in large centres is a classic example of the dangers of applying Western standards to Eastern situations. Life in the road-camps is undoubtedly arduous, and the children who remain in them are exposed to the occasional risk of being injured by falling rocks during the blasting operations. It is unlikely that the average Western child would survive such conditions for long, and so the relief workers raise their hands in horror and decide that as many Tiblets as possible must be rescued as soon as possible. Yet if one pauses to think the thing out it soon becomes obvious that what we regard as the insupportable existence of a road-camp community is not unlike everyday life in Tibet. Many of the refugees came from nomad tribes who habitually lived in tents, and all of them were accustomed to some degree of hardship. The Indian Government pays the refugees a slightly higher wage than that of the native coolie, to compensate them for having no little plot on which to grow food, so a husband and wife can earn between them Rs. 22.75 (about £1 16*s*.) per seven-day week. By local standards this is quite a good wage and should enable the parents to feed their children much better than they are fed here – especially if some of the Indian Government per capita monthly food ration were distributed among the camps rather than sent in bulk to Dharamshala and other centres. The children's health could not possibly be worse anywhere than it is here, and while it may be true that some of our Tiblets would have died if not brought within reach of Western medical aid this does not invalidate the argument that in general these children would be far better off, both physically and emotionally, if they had not been parted with their parents.

\*

It has taken us all day to realise that President Kennedy is dead [written on 23 November 1963]. We heard of the assassination at 8 a.m. on the Delhi news, and though India had her own national tragedy yesterday (when five of her senior army and air force officers were killed in a helicopter crash not very far from here) three-quarters of the bulletin was devoted to Kennedy. The Russian tribute struck us as being sincere, and if this impression is correct its sincerity is the best epitaph he could have. It is curious how hostile feelings to the American way of life and policies do not prevent most Westerners from involuntarily regarding the President of the United States as *our* leader – not merely the leader of a friendly power. At least that's how the four of us here – representing three European nations – reacted this morning. There was a sense of personal loss in our sorrow – and also an element of fear, at being suddenly deprived of a protector whose individual greatness had placed him outside the area of petty international antagonisms, while his humanity kept him within reach of the least of us.

*

This is my last day on duty in the camp and now I wish I was gone; within the last week my happiness, on going out each morning and being inundated by a wave of Tiblets, has turned to bitterness at the thought of leaving. It is difficult to understand, much less explain, what these children have done for me. All I know is that during the past four months they have caused a subtle but powerful transformation, so that I'm aware of taking something away from here that will be of permanent value. To those who have never lived through such an experience my words may sound like so much sentimental tommy-rot – yet they express a reality which others have already observed. Yesterday, Oliver slightly startled me by remarking on how much I had changed since we first met. When I asked him how this change looked to him he replied without hesitation, 'In some ways you're softer and in other ways you're much stronger and calmer.' I knew exactly what he meant and in fact I was able to return this compliment sincerely, for he too has been noticeably influenced by life among the Tiblets.

*

Christmas Eve in the Workhouse [reference to the nineteenth-century ballad] – scene as before – rancid butter and wood-smoke and eccentric porridge for supper. Fortunately I bought myself another Christmas present on the way back through Manali, which was a horribly extravagant thing to do – yet perhaps such extravagance is forgivable when there is no one else around to give me a present. Indian whisky is about the same price as Irish whisky, but that's the only point of resemblance between the two distillations. My plastic mug is showing signs of *melting* in a very odd way since it began to come into nightly contact with Indian whisky – which may account for the brew's curiously chemical flavour. ...What a splendid Christmas Eve this is – truly a silent night, and a holy one, in the shadow of these mountains.

*

A slight crisis occurred while supper was being prepared. As my hostess was making the chapattis her husband began to peel potatoes clumsily with his axe (!), because the household possesses no knife, and after watching this process for a few moments I could stand the sight no longer – partly for the poor man's sake and partly for my own, since I had eaten nothing all day. So I produced my own knife, having drawn it from its leather sheath. Suddenly everyone was motionless and in the tense little silence that followed I became guiltily aware of my *faux pas*. Fortunately I knew enough about Malani customs to react correctly; making the appropriate gestures of remorse I at once produced Rs. 10 – the price of the lamb which must be sacrificed tomorrow to placate the insulted Jamlu. And though cynics may here accuse me of being too naive, no-one who had once sensed the Malani atmosphere could doubt the use to which those rupees will be put: this family couldn't possibly consider going happily on with the daily round until their god had been propitiated for such an outrage on his territory.

After supper we had another slight crisis, when the election agent nobly tore himself away from his gambling to ensure that I was comfortable for the night. Admittedly the question of bedding did pose a minor problem; the family has none to spare and any blankets lent me from a 'caste' house would be so contaminated by my body that their owners could never use them again. Yet the solution seemed simple to me – a heap of hay in the corner – and the real complication was caused by my host's indignation at the idea of his guest being bedded down like an animal. However, he was at last induced to agree to this scheme by my emphatic assurances that *all* Irish people habitually sleep in hay.

\*

By 8 a.m. we were on our way. For a few miles the road followed the Sutlej before joining that famous Hindustan–Tibet highway which, north of this point, has been closed to all civilian traffic since the Chinese invasion in October 1962. At the junction a new signpost says 'Tibet 115 ms', and here I dismounted to stand for a moment looking longingly up that road. What I would have given to be allowed to follow it! But perhaps someday I *will* get to Tibet, however ludicrous the idea might seem at the moment.

From the junction our road climbed very steeply for about five miles, till the Sutlej valley looked like an aerial view beneath us. Then the highway penetrated the heart of this range, winding round and round the arid flanks of grey-brown, treeless mountains. For fourteen miles the ascent was gradual, though continuous, and I was able to cycle most of the way – again in shirt-sleeves, under a cloudless sky. This would have been another most enjoyable trek but for the incessant heavy military traffic going towards Tibet: to see it one would think that a full-scale war was in progress at the frontier at this very moment. Countless truck-loads of unenthusiastic-looking young troops were interspersed with truck-loads of arms, ammunition, pack-mules, fodder and general supplies. Watching these interminable convoys of mule-trucks and fodder-trucks I pitied India's present military plight; there can be no more difficult terrain in the world than the Hindustan–Tibet border area.

\*

## 1960s

I had an audience with His Holiness and found him much more relaxed and approachable than during our last meeting sixteen months ago. He seems to have matured a great deal in that brief time and to have gained in self-assurance, as though he has at last been able to come to terms with his strange situation. The impression I had today was of an astute young statesman in the making – yet when we came to touch on religion he spoke with an easy sincerity that was immensely moving and quite unlike his tense, watchful manner at our previous meeting. He looks considerably older now and a little thinner – but very much happier.

## The Waiting Land:
## A Spell in Nepal (1967)
## Nepal

At the Royal [Hotel in Kathmandu] I was also introduced to Peter Aufschneider and Sir Edmund Hillary. Sir Edmund looks and behaves exactly as one would expect a conqueror of Everest to look and behave, and on shaking hands with him I got a positively schoolgirlish thrill – though it is to be hoped that this was not apparent, since the unfortunate man must be bored almost to extinction by thrilled females. Peter Aufschneider (Heinrich Harrer's companion in Tibet) lives permanently in Kathmandu and now works for the Nepalese Government. He is very shy, modest and likeable – but unfortunately I'm invariably struck dumb on first meeting people who have long been admired from afar, so as a conversational unit we never really got off the ground.

*

There are many things that one 'should see' in this valley, but I secretly resent being bossed by guidebooks and am therefore a slip-shod tourist. To me the little statue that one unexpectedly discovers down an alleyway, and impulsively responds to, means much more than the temple one had been instructed to admire for erudite and probably incomprehensible reasons; so I just go wandering vaguely around on Leo [her bicycle] finding enough incidental entertainment in the three ancient capitals of Kathmandu, Patan and Bhatgaon.

These 'cities' (by our standards market towns) were for many centuries seats of the rival Newari dynasties who ruled and fought over this valley before it was conquered by the Gurkhas in 1769. As a race the Newari had an exceptionally developed aesthetic sense and the ordinary people of the valley seemed to have attained an almost freakishly high level of craftsmanship, most notably displayed in the bronze or stone temple sculptures and in those intricate weather-worn wood-carvings which adorn so many of the older buildings. If any European city had produced in the past such a concentration of artistic achievement it would long since have been demolished, bombed or self-consciously preserved – and whatever its fate the spirit of its craftsmen would have been well and truly exorcised. But here all this beauty is taken for granted, and its survival has been entirely a matter of chance. Some corners of the cities, where nothing has visibly intruded from another age or civilisation, seem quite powerfully haunted by the force and fervour of those nameless men whose work still lives on every side; and in such corners Time can occasionally slip into reverse, so that one is no longer deliberately reaching back into the past with one's imagination but actually *experiencing* it for a few brief, bewildering moments.

*

Before retiring I went out to the field and from there saw a vision of such supreme beauty that momentarily I wondered if it could be real. To the north, under a clear sky and a high-sailing moon, the whole Annapurna range stretched in one mass of white tumult and, dominating the range – seemingly dominating the world – was the sharp-peaked, austere and infinitely lovely Machhapuchhare, home of Pokhara's tutelary deity. One should not try to trap such splendour in mere words, but beneath the moon, in the utter stillness of the valley, all those silver snows burnt coldly with an overwhelming, undeniable life and spirit of their own. This silent, vital grandeur almost compelled me to kneel down and worship; and perhaps if no inbred self-consciousness intervened and it were possible to do so I would be all the better for it.

\*

Today I have had quite the most gruesome experience of a lifetime. Dolma, a forty-two-year-old Tibetan woman, died last night of debilitation (following prolonged dysentery) at the Military Hospital, where I went this morning to enquire about three other patients from the [Tibetan refugee] camp [in Pokhara]. On my way, while walking by the river, I rounded an outcrop of rock and found Dolma's severed head at my feet. I must confess that to come on such a sight unexpectedly, when less than twenty-four hours earlier this woman had been sitting with her head on my shoulder, receiving cheering-up treatment, gave me rather a shock. Nearby the four camp chiefs were dismembering the trunk with blunt little wood-axes, before throwing it into the water, and I left the scene as quickly as possible.

Here the Tibetans choose this method of corpse-disposal in preference to the chopping-up of bodies on a 'cemetery-rock' for birds of prey to eat – the most popular method in Tibet itself. Some Nepalese tribes, who live at high altitudes where wood is scarce, also use the rivers as graves, and I should think the bones are picked clean very soon after the dismembered body enters the water; at the moment I have a few open sores on my legs, and when I'm swimming these attract swarms of savage little fishes. In Tibet, the office of undertaker – or chopper-upper – belonged to a special caste who are shunned by the average Tibetan; but the camp has no member of this caste and the task is so unpopular that the chiefs are forced to do it themselves. However, it would be wrong to imagine that these nomads are averse to such a job out of our own sort of squeamishness; they decline to do it for superstitious reasons, not because the actual chopping up of a human body is repugnant to them.

\*

Already I can see that the worst side-effect of the monsoon is going to be a nightly insect-plague. Nepalese shutters have little square ventilation holes near the top and through these fly an inconceivable number of insects, attracted by my lamp. At present the table and everything on it are literally being made to move by the creatures; I have just stopped writing to count eighteen different varieties, from enormous, exquisite moths, bright green two-inch grasshoppers and horny russet beetles, to mosquitoes and winged ants and half-a-dozen weird objects that I can't even attempt to identify. The combination of buzzes and bangs and whizzes and whines and bumps and drones adds up to quite a din. What is worse, the floor is swarming with big black ants – in addition to my permanent army of tiny red ones – and with cockroaches. I must admit that when sleeping on the floor cockroaches seem to me expendable, though I'm not neurotic about them as I am about spiders. Luckily – almost miraculously – spiders seem to be the only form of insect life not represented in the room at this moment.

Incidentally my rats are becoming impossibly truculent – and obviously their mothers brought them up not to eat poison. Last night one of them knocked a zinc bucket off a tea-chest onto my head, so today I have a big lump above my ear; on moonlit nights it is positively depressing to see so many grey shapes scurrying around the room.

*

I sat on the bank to smoke a cigarette and de-leech my legs while waiting for the Tibetans. Surprisingly, most of the girls made quite a fuss about the fording and it was comical to see those tough nomad youngsters giving an excellent imitation of nervously giggling mid-Victorian ladies whose carriage has broken down on the way to a dinner party. Possibly this display was being put on mainly to attract the men's attention – though one can see that for non-swimmers such a crossing could be rather frightening. The ability to swim would almost certainly prove irrelevant if one were swept away by a mountain torrent but it does illogically give one an extra degree of confidence.

Chimba decided to call a halt here as many of the party were already 'creating' about being leech-infested; this was the Tibetans' first monsoon so these pests were unfamiliar to them. Foreseeing several septic legs by the time we got home I hastened to explain that never must a leech be forcibly detached from the skin; either salt or a lighted cigarette are the only answers. As we had nothing but rock-salt with us – and salt is in any case too expensive to waste on leeches – I went around from leg to leg with my cigarette, assuring the Tibetans that contrary to appearances they were not going to bleed to death within half-an-hour. Pasang, one of the more argumentative men, pointed out that he had already pulled his leech off and that his leg was *not* bleeding – nor did he appear convinced when I explained that this was exactly the point, and that bleeding was essential after the wretched creature had been removed. I didn't even attempt to explain that the bleeding was so copious only because leeches inject an anti-coagulant before beginning their meal.

\*

Perhaps a flight did go to Pokhara today, but this passenger was not among those present. By a painful coincidence I've done it again and fractured two ribs in a bus – though mercifully they are not the two that were cracked a couple of years ago in an Afghan bus. Yet I mustn't let this become a habit…

The misadventure occurred yesterday on the way back from the airport but, as sometimes happens with rib injuries, the extent of the damage was not immediately apparent. This bus had distinct affinities with Afghan models, and all our luggage was piled high in the centre of the chassis, between the two narrow wooden benches. The driver was little short of a lunatic, and when a sacred bull suddenly ambled into view from behind a line of grass-carrying porters we were going far too fast to cope safely with this everyday contingency. The sudden braking threw me violently against a tin of that dratted Multi Purpose Food but, though the pain was momentarily severe, I thought no more of the incident until I woke up in agony at midnight, about an hour after going to sleep.

Sigrid was still out at a bridge-party – as usual not knowing whether her guest was here or there – but she came in soon afterwards, made calming noises, bound me tightly in sheeting and, by administering three codeine tablets and a glass of neat brandy, convinced me that this was the most minor of injuries. Then, after a slight battle about the advisability of my annexing the bed upstairs, I again lay on my Tibetan rug, beside a most sympathetic Puchare, and was asleep within moments.

*

For the past eight days the whole country has been celebrating Dasain (also known as the Durga Puja) and by now we foreigners are really feeling the draught. The GPO has shut down completely; three days ago the electricity supply expired and we were informed that it could not be revived until the 6th of October; Singha Durbar has put up its shutters, leaving various Top Level negotiations in a state of internationally inconvenient suspension; and almost all servants, peons and chokidars are *chuti*, making communication extremely difficult – only now do we realise how much we depend on peons delivering chits when the telephones are unwell. The whole thing is irresistibly enchanting and I am particularly taken by the idea of a capital city where the GPO closes down uncompromisingly for days on end to give everyone a chance to say their prayers; one wonders if there is any other capital in the world so immune to the practical pressures of modern life.

*

Now that the so-called war is over tourists are again coming to Nepal, and almost every day during this past week a special plane has flown from Kathmandu to spew out on our airstrip a rigidly regimented group of 'Round-the-Worlders'. These groups of course comprise the bravest tourist spirits – the ones who have taken a deep breath and, against their friends' advice, decided to risk two or three hours in Pokhara, bringing hygienically packed lunches with them and drinking very little at breakfast-time because – 'My dear we were *warned*! There simply *aren't* any toilets in the place!' It is most unkind to laugh at such groups – but impossible not to do so, when they emerge from their planes wearing that same expression of bemused weariness, thinly veiled by a spurious joy at the excitement of 'exploring', which I have so often seen on the faces of similar groups being spewed out of luxury coaches in my own 'beauty-spot' home-town; and inevitably a regiment of Round-the-Worlders looks even funnier in Pokhara than it does in Ireland. I feel delightfully integrated with my neighbours when we stand in a row near the airstrip, being hypnotised by the latest Paris or New York fashions which, seen from a Central Nepal angle, appear even more grotesque than they actually are.

*

This morning I saw my first total eclipse of the sun, which lasted from about 8.15 until 9.30 – and in honour of which today is yet another public holiday throughout Nepal.

We left our hovel before dawn, since last night even Mingmar was unable to sleep for bugs, and by 8 o'clock we had reached the top of a 9,000-foot hill, after an easy climb through crisp, early air. From here we were overlooking a long, deep, narrow valley, and our path now continued almost level for some two miles, before plunging abruptly down to a small village by the river.

As we were scrambling down from the ridge-top to join this path I noticed something very odd about the quality of the light, and simultaneously I registered an unnatural drop in the temperature. Overtaking Mingmar I said, 'What on earth is happening? The light's gone funny, and it's so *cold*!' To this obtuse question a native

89

English speaker might have been forgiven for replying that nothing was happening *on earth*; but Mingmar merely said, 'The moon is having a meal.' I stared at him for a moment wondering if he were going dotty – and then I realised that the dottiness was on my side, for when he pointed to the sun I saw that about a quarter of its surface had already been obscured by the 'hungry' moon.

What an appropriate place this was for experiencing the eeriness of a solar eclipse! As we walked along that path so high above the valley, we could hear conches being blown wildly and cymbals and drums being beaten frenziedly, while all the lamas and priests of the little villages far below shouted and wailed and screamed in their contest with those evil spirits who, by attacking the sun, were threatening the whole of human existence. This extraordinary panic of sounds, combined with the 'evening' twitter of bewildered birds and a unique, greenish half-light, evidently aroused within me some deep racial memory, and for an instant, at the precise moment of total eclipse and estrangement from our whole source of life, I felt as my own that primitive fear which was then dominating the whole of Nepal.

\*

A seven months' visit is too brief for the development of a real understanding of any country as alien and complex as Nepal; but it is quite long enough for the visitor to come to love what has been experienced of both the virtues and the faults of this improbable little Kingdom. I am often asked, 'Did you like Nepal?' – to which I usually reply, 'Yes' and leave it at that. But no-one merely 'likes' Nepal; Nepal weaves a net out of splendour and pettiness, squalor and colour, wisdom and innocence, tranquillity and gaiety, complacence and discontent, indolence and energy, generosity and cunning, freedom and bondage – and in this bewildering mesh foreign hearts are trapped, often to their own dismay.

There is much to be censured in the Kingdom, and there are many institutions that do need reforming; but to reform them in the image and likeness of the West would be a subtle genocide, for there is much, too, that should be cherished, rather than thrown to the Lions of Progress. However, it is of no avail to think or write thus. The West has arrived in Nepal, bubbling over with good intentions (though the fire that keeps them bubbling may be fed on expediency), and soon our insensitivity to simple elegance, to the proud work of individual craftsmen, and to all the fine strands that go to make up a traditional culture will have spread material ugliness and moral uncertainty like plagues through the land. Already our forward-looking, past-despising 'experts' are striving to help Nepal 'to make up for lost time' by discarding the sound values that lie, half hidden but still active, beneath 'pagan superstition' – and that would provide a firmer foundation on which to build the new Nepal than our own mass-production code, which makes a virtue of unnecessary earning for the sake of unnecessary spending.

Perhaps nowhere in Asia is the contrast between a dignified, decaying past and a brash, effervescent present as violent as in Nepal; and one knows that here too, eventually, the present will have its shoddy triumph. Yet even when the Nepalese way of life has been annihilated the Himalayas will remain, occasionally being invaded by high-powered expeditions but preserving an inviolable beauty to the end of time.

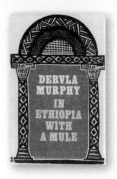

## *In Ethiopia with a Mule* (1968)
## Ethiopia

I set off at 7.30 a.m. and arrived here ten hours later, having ambled along happily for eighteen miles, seeing only five adults and a few young shepherds.

All day the track climbed gradually between ridge after ridge of low hills. For miles a narrow river ran beside it, the water moving clear and green among gigantic, rounded boulders – many of them looking remarkably like Henry Moore's reclining figures – and twice the temptation of deep, wide pools proved irresistible. Saying 'Hang bilharzia!' I turned Jock loose and jumped in, clutching a bar of soap.

At 11 we stopped for brunch beneath a grove of tall, wide-spreading trees, and here I saw my first African monkeys – a troop of capuchins racing and swinging through the branches above me. Also – walking with bird-book in hand – I identified today the Lilac-breasted Roller, Bateleur, Namaqua Dove, Purple Grenadier, Red-cheeked Cordon Bleu and Black-billed Wood Hoopoe. These birds were marvellously tame; as Jock and I plodded quietly through thick dust we were often within a yard of them before they moved – and even then many only hopped or flew a few feet further away.

During the afternoon we passed a herd of over a hundred camels, all purposefully chewing the highest branches of small thorny trees and big thorny shrubs. One was pure white – a rare and beautiful animal. Probably this herd recently brought salt from the Danakil Desert and is now being rested in preparation for the journey home. ...

This has been a day of deep contentment – wandering alone along a *makeena*-free [machine-free] track, seeing only hoof prints in the dust, with all around the healing quiet of wild places, unbroken save by birdsong. The loveliest time is from 4.30 p.m. on, when the light softens and colours glow. This afternoon, brown, red and yellow cliffs, flecked with white marble, were rising above dark green shrubs, and on every side the outlines of high mountains became clearer as the heat-haze thinned.

\*

Here we sat on the edge of the crater while Dawit's servant took part in a fascinating 'long-distance-call', which started when a minute figure on a hilltop far above us demanded information about the *faranj* [foreigner]. This figure proved to be the head-man of a nearby village and, on hearing that I was a protégé of the Tigreans' beloved Lielt Aida [Haile Selassie's granddaughter], he at once invited us to have *talla* [local beer] some miles further along the track. Then the hills and valleys began to echo and re-echo with haunting, disembodied cries, as his orders for our entertainment were relayed to the village by invisible shepherds. When using this rather public but very effective method of communication the highlanders employ a high-pitched voice and a peculiar rhythmic chant that carries for miles through the still, thin air of the mountains.

\*

For the next two hours I wandered around nearby, enjoying the swiftly changing morning colours, or sat in the shelter fraternising wordlessly with innumerable children and adolescents. Last night these youngsters were too scared to approach within yards of me, but this morning, overcoming their timidity, they edged closer and closer to the Strange Being – and eventually one little girl summoned enough courage to determine the creature's sex by poking at its chest. On discovering that breasts existed beneath my loose shirt this brave explorer rushed off to find her mother, screaming 'Set nat! Set nat!' (It's a woman!) However, her companions could not easily credit this improbability so now, emboldened by her example, they proceeded to remove my shirt – which led to further exclamations of wonder when they saw the colour of untanned *faranj* skin.

*

Then an odd thing happened. All the morning I had been aware of the extreme tiredness of hunger and every slight climb had felt like an escarpment, but I hadn't been conscious of making any extraordinary effort to keep going. Yet here I was suddenly stricken by what cyclists call 'the knocks', and for ten minutes I had to sit on the roadside, struggling to summon the strength to walk *down* that final slope. The extent to which those knocks may have been fostered by Ethiopian brandy in a vacuum remains a moot point; but the psychology of the incident is curious for had Gondar been ten miles further away my knocks probably would not have developed until another ten miles had been covered.

I had planned to stop first at the Post Office, but now even letters mattered less than food. Wobbling into the respectable Fasil Hotel I sat in the bar-restaurant, on a blue tin chair at a blue tin table, begged the startled barman to give me something – anything – edible, and within half an hour had put away a mound of pasta and *wat*, five large rolls, an eight-ounce tin of Australian cheese and six cups of heavily sugared tea.

Standing up from this banquet I saw a fearsomely repulsive figure behind the bar; it is a strange experience to stare at one's own reflection for some moments without recognising it. When I did recognise myself I no longer wondered at the unfortunate woman fleeing last evening. If I saw any such apparition coming through the bushes in the dusk I too would flee, fast and far. The combination of ingrained dirt, sun-blackened skin, dust-reddened eyes, sweat-matted hair, height-stiffened lips, blood-caked chin and sunken cheeks really did have an unnerving effect. I had been aware of losing weight, but I hadn't realised just how emaciated my body was. At once I booked in here for a week, to fatten up before the next lap.

When Jock had been stabled I went up to my room – preceded by a pair of servants solemnly bearing my dusty sacks – and the next two hours were spent in three successive hot baths. I had no clean clothes to put on, but as I went downstairs the mere fact of having clean skin made me feel positively chic.

The news of our arrival had already spread and quite a crowd was awaiting me in the bar – which embarrassment became understandable when I learned that Leilt Aida had recently been telephoning the Chief of Police every evening, to enquire if we had yet arrived in Gondar. One member of my 'Reception-Committee' was the Director of the Gondar Bank, who kindly offered Jock the hospitality of his back garden during our stay here; and he also promised to organise a daily supply of grain.

When I went to the Post Office to telephone Makalle I collected a belated Christmas mail; so the rest of the day was spent 'attending to my correspondence'.

*

The quartet sat beside me and for the next ten minutes we chatted as civilly as the language barrier allowed. ... Meanwhile I was listening to the remarks being exchanged by the priest and the older man; the words for mule, money, medicine and clothes were disturbingly comprehensible. The priest then declared that I must spend the night in their compound, and his expression was tense as he watched for my reaction. I smiled, bowed gratefully and declined the invitation – which was perhaps a foolish thing to do, but at that stage my nerve was going and I only wanted to get away.

Standing up, I started to move towards Jock – and at once the four surrounded me. The laymen were holding their *dulas* [walking sticks] rather obviously, no-one was smiling anymore and I could feel myself going white. As he spoke shrilly to his companions, the priest's eyes were bright with greed; he used his cross to gesture towards me – and then towards the lake. Immediately an argument started, the stocky youth supporting the priest, the slim youth siding with the older man. I lit a cigarette.

During those brief, long moments I was reacting on two levels, for beneath the seething terror was a strange, indifferent acceptance – a feeling that gamblers can't always win and if this was it, it was it.

The argument only lasted for the length of a nervously smoked cigarette, but before it ended I had an odd experience – so unfamiliar that it is difficult to describe, yet so real that it cannot honestly be omitted. While the priest was shaking his fly-whisk angrily in the older man's face, and before it was possible to judge who was winning, I suddenly knew that I was safe – as surely as if a platoon of police had appeared to rescue me. For an instant I was aware of being protected by some mysterious power; and to a person without definite religious convictions this was almost as great a shock as the unpleasant encounter itself.

A moment later the argument was over. The older man ran to Jock, took up the halter and turned towards the compound. The priest caught me by the arm – he was smiling again, though his eyes remained angry – and pointed after Jock, while the youths stood close behind us. But now I, too, was getting angry. Eluding the priest's grasp I pursued Jock, grabbed the halter and waved my *dula* threateningly. At this stage my fear was of being injured, which is quite a different sensation to the fear of death and doesn't deter one from trying to defend one's possessions. However, my ridiculous *dula*-waving was ignored. Within seconds the four were around us again, the youths had seized my arms and the men were unloading Jock.

They took my sleeping-bag, torch, spare Biros, matches, camera, insecticides, medicines (including a packet of Tampax, which amused me even at the time), two books (*Ethiopian Birds* and W.E. Carr's *Poetry of the Middle Ages*), Jock's bridle and a hundred and twenty Ethiopian dollars – about eighteen pounds sterling. My

Huskies went unnoticed, being wrapped in the old pack-saddle, and neither cigarettes nor *faranj* food interested them, though these must be saleable commodities in Gondar. However their oddest omissions were my watch ... and Jock himself, who is worth another hundred dollars. Possibly they considered that in this region, where mules are uncommon, he would be an imprudently conspicuous acquisition if his owner were still alive.

When the quartet left us my knees suddenly went soggy, and as I began to reload Jock my hands were so shaky that I could scarcely tie the ropes. However, this was no time or place for indulging in the tremors – I wanted to be far away from that priest by sunset.

*

There are two phases of enjoyment in journeying through an unknown country – the eager phase of wondering interest in every detail, and the relaxed phase when one feels no longer an observer of the exotic, but a participator in the rhythm of daily life. Now I am at ease among the highlanders, for wherever I go, in this static, stylised society, everything seems familiar. Not only the graceful formalities – significant though minute – but the long lean faces and the clear brown eyes, the way men flick *atar* [peas] from palm to mouth, the movement of settling *shammas* [robes] about their bodies when they sit, their stance as they stand and talk, leaning their hands on the ends of a *dula* that rests across their shoulders, the harsh, staccato language, the expressive gesticulations, the sudden bursts of apparent anger that can quickly change to laughter. All this makes up a world which only two months ago seemed puzzling, amusing and sometimes a little frightening, yet which now seems as normal as my own far world away to the north.

*

A few moments ago two shepherds drove the family's wealth into the compound – one sheep, two lambs, a billy-goat, three nannies, two kids and five cows. All looked dreadfully emaciated. This is the edge of the Lasta famine-area, which has been afflicted by drought during the past several years, and tonight Jock has had only half an armful of straw and I am on emergency rations. One of the shepherds, aged about fourteen, has limbs so frail and a head so disproportionately big and eyes so sunken that he seems to epitomise all the starvation in the world. Nor is his younger brother much better. There is a harrowing difference between sitting beside human beings in this condition and seeing Oxfam pictures of famine victims. Both boys, and the three younger girls, are clad in scraps of worn cow-hide. As I write, two older girls are coming into the compound, bent double under huge water-jars; they must have had to carry these from some distant well or river, for they looked near collapse. One of them has a gruesome leg, covered from knee to ankle with suppurating sores. Yet she seems quite cheerful, so now I feel ashamed of the fuss I have been making about my knee. Here medicine is not in demand – a sign that these people have had little or no contact with *faranjs*.

*

From Lalibela we descended to a white, hot, arid valley and during the next two hours I found myself becoming depressed by my surroundings, for the first time in these highlands. This valley is still inhabited and we passed several settlements, two small herds of emaciated cattle, and a few neglected, unploughed fields from which the last thin *teff* crop has long since been harvested. Yet I saw not even one shepherd-boy, and as we walked between endless low, grey-brown hills, disfigured with dead scrub, the whole sun-plagued scene reeked of misery. The junipers, which somehow contrive to look freshly green everywhere else, were withered here and even the cacti hung limply. One felt that the remaining population had accepted the nearness of death and were sitting dully in their *tukuls*, not trying anymore. Deserted, uninhabited landscapes delight me but the memory of that still, suffering valley will haunt me for a long time to come.

*

While Jock grazed I sat on a rock and looked with joy at all this loveliness; but soon after we had begun the descent I was regretting not having looked more intelligently at the precipice and less ecstatically at the loveliness.

This 500-foot escarpment provided a new kind of wrack for my nerves. It was almost sheer and it jutted out over the valley – which lay another 1,500 feet below, with nothing but good fresh air in between. Even Jock took a pessimistic view and had to be led. Then, a third of the way down, I lost my nerve and we got stuck. Looking about in wild surmise I saw that we had taken the wrong route, for directly below the top there had been no definite path. Now, however, the correct route was visible – two hundred yards away, separated from us by a wide, perpendicular crack in the cliff-face.

When I decided to return to the crest to make a fresh start I discovered that Jock couldn't turn. Never before have I been so near to panic. This was completely irrational, as a drop of 2,000 feet is no more dangerous than one of 500, but I shuddered at the sight of the ground so very far below and at the extreme insecurity of this friable precipice; and Jock's trembling appeared to justify my own jitters. Yet we couldn't spend the rest of our days like carvings on a cliff-face so I set about regaining my nerve by gazing steadily down at the valley floor, in the hope that familiarity would breed sufficient contempt for me to be able to continue calmly. Then I moved forward, and Jock reluctantly followed. For the next forty slow minutes we were descending – with occasional ascents, necessitated by deep gullies or insurmountable outcrops of rock. Half the stones I trod on went hurtling into space: the loose clay crumbled at every step: a minor landslide started if I leant on my *dula*: the thorny scrub 'came away in me 'and' if I despairingly grabbed it. And all the time I was waiting for the worst to happen to Jock.

*

By this time Assefa and I had but a single thought and, as we searched for *talla*, a cheerful man emerged from a mud shack and invited us to help celebrate the christening of his fifth son. In the dark, straw-strewn room about forty men sat on mud benches around the walls, fondling rifles, while a minstrel played in the centre of the floor and a tall, elderly woman sang and danced with strange, fierce gaiety.

This invitation was providential, as no-one could long remain sad at a highland party. After an enormous meal, accompanied by much *talla*, I found myself holding a half-pint tumbler brimming with *araki* [liquor], which normally is served in tiny vessels. I sipped the burning liquid slowly, but was soon cut off from reality by a sentimental haze through which I regarded myself, my host, his fifth son, all his other sons, my fellow guests, all highlanders, the world in general – and even the prospect of arriving in Addis – with benevolence.

At seven o'clock Samuel, the Director of the school, waveringly led Assefa and me towards his home. Evidently I was then at the maudlin stage; on looking up at the brilliance of the storm-cleared sky I wanted to weep because in comparison Irish skies seemed to have so few stars.

# 1970s

# MURPHY PLUS ONE

*Dervla published four books in the 1970s. Her autobiography* Wheels within Wheels *appeared in chapter one. She wrote this primarily for Rachel and never really intended it to be published, until her publisher came across it by accident. Rachel was a small child in the early seventies, so Dervla stayed at home, mainly producing* Irish Times *book reviews as well as miscellaneous articles wherever she could.*

*She brought Rachel on her first big trip – to South India – in November 1973.* On a Shoestring to Coorg *is the story of getting to the idyllic region in the Western Ghats and settling in there for some months.*

*The second book,* Where the Indus is Young, *is the report of the hard winter they both spent hiking in the mountains of Baltistan, Pakistan with Hallam, a packhorse. This was a massive endurance test for all three of them.*

*The third book here,* A Place Apart *on Northern Ireland, was Dervla's attempt to get under the skin of that region so close geographically yet so far in terms of understanding. She took enormous risks there, whether or not she quite realised it at the time. As a result, however, there are some brilliant observations and conversations in the book that show how great Dervla was at connecting with people of all hues, during some of the hardest years of the 'Troubles'.*

## *On a Shoestring to Coorg* (1976)
## South India

The deck-area of our steamer is not too crowded and after Bombay one appreciates sea-breezes, even when adulterated by clouds of hash; forty or so of our fellow-passengers are hippies on their annual migration from Nepal, or the North of India, to Goa.

In affluent Europe I find it easy enough to understand an individual hippy's point of view, but on seeing them massed against an Indian background of involuntary poverty I quickly lose patience. Several of those within sight at this moment are emaciated wrecks – the out-and-outers, travelling alone, carrying no possessions of any kind, clad only in tattered loincloths, their long *sadhu*-style hair matted and filthy, their bare feet calloused and cracked, their legs pitted with open scurvy sores, their ribs and shoulder blades seeming about to cut through their pallid skins, their eyes glazed with over-indulgence in Kali-knows-what and their ability or will to communicate long since atrophied. This is dropping-out carried to its terrible conclusion – but dropping into what, and why? Certainly these wrecks will soon drop into a nameless grave, and for their own sakes I can only feel the sooner the better. One agrees when hippies criticise the essential destructiveness of a materialist society, but what are they offering in its place?

\*

This afternoon we passed first between newly harvested, golden-brown fields where pillars of blue-grey smoke marked bonfires of burning maize stalks. Then for miles our road twisted through lonely mountains covered in dense, shadowy jungle, or plantations of teak or eucalyptus – the last popular as quick-growing firewood. A few brown rhesus monkeys sat or sauntered by the roadside but Rachel missed them. In buses I refrained from pointing out things of interest, feeling she must be left to observe and absorb at her own pace. There is so much – details I take for granted – to delight and amaze her: full-grown bulls gently wandering between the benches in a bus stand waiting-room; cows with brilliantly painted horns wearing silver necklaces or garlands of flowers; flocks of bright green parakeets flying parallel with the road, racing the bus and, not surprisingly, overtaking it; petite women-coolies carrying great loads of earth or bricks or timber beams on their heads and babies on their hips; elaborately carved wayside temples; gigantic banyan-trees like bits of architecture gone wrong; cascades of bougainvillaea and poinsettia; demented-seeming, nearly naked *sadhus* moaning *mantras* as they hold their begging-bowls under one's nose.

*

This evening I think I can identify one of the things that went wrong during my first stay in India. After a slow journey through the Middle East, and through places as gloriously un-Westernised as Gilgit and the Hindu Kush, I found the degree of apparent Westernisation anti-climactic. Now, however, having flown direct from London – and perhaps having in the intervening decade become a little less obtuse – India's Westernisation seems to me very superficial: though that is another too sweeping generalisation, since even Hinduism has been modified by industrialisation. Yet only slightly, so far. On the whole, the British influence, like that of many earlier conquerors, is being inexorably assimilated into India's *dharma* [law or doctrine], which eventually will be a little changed by this contribution as by all the others – though the changes will not necessarily be those the British will have wished to effect.

*

Mercara's average temperature is 66°F and as we trotted downhill the sun was warm, the breeze fresh and the sky intensely blue – an almost incredible colour, to northern eyes. At intervals, in the cool depths of the forest, we saw sudden, glorious flourishes of colour – tall trees laden with pink or cream or red flowers; and blue-jays, hoopoes, mynahs, weaver-birds and subaltern's pheasants were all busily breakfasting, and we chased gaudy butterflies as big as sparrows, and once Rachel came within inches of treading on a small snake. Probably it was harmless, but at the time my maternal blood ran cold. One is a much less light-hearted traveller with foal at foot.

*

Mysore City is said to have deteriorated since the British left but I find it most attractive. It is small enough to be tackled on foot and there are few motor-vehicles on the wide, straight, tree-lined streets, most of which run between solid, well-kept, cream-washed buildings with terraced roofs and spacious gardens. The traffic consists mainly of horse-gharries, pedal-cycles, bullock-carts and multitudes of wandering cattle, many of whom lie complacently in the middle of the main roads chewing the cud as though the internal combustion engine had never been invented. One has to like a city in which the cow still takes precedence over the car.

*

This afternoon, as I walked alone, I thanked Fate for having guided me to Coorg. With a five-year-old fellow-traveller I cannot seek out those remote areas which most appeal to me and it is rare indeed to find a 'developed' region free of brash advertisements, domineering pylons, strident petrol stations, abundant litter, synthetic building materials and hideously artificial colours. But here, in this 'finest of the kingdoms of Jambudwipa', a civilised harmony still exists between landscape and people. So perfectly do the artistry of nature and of man complement each other that one feels miraculously restored to the Garden of Eden, to the world as it was before Eve ate the apple of technology.

\*

We next found ourselves in the Jewish Quarter, which consists of a long, narrow cul-de-sac with India's most famous synagogue at the closed end. A few of the tall, whitewashed, green-shuttered houses have antique-cum-junk shops at street level, run by mild, gracious men who would not dream of pestering the tourist but are happy to talk knowledgeably about their wares, or about the history of the Malabar Jews. We chatted for over an hour to a pale, sad character with a long chestnut beard who was thirty-five years old but unmarried because, being a White Jew, he could only marry a White Jewess and there are few of those left in Cochin. (Thousands of Indian Jews have migrated to Israel.) I was not in the least surprised when he explained that White Jews, Black Jews and Slave Jews (the three 'castes' of Malabar Jewry) cannot intermarry, and that the Slave Jews are regarded as outcasts by the others and up to a few years ago were forbidden to enter the synagogues.

\*

This evening I have come to the conclusion that India – the whole Indian *Dharma* – is peculiarly tourist-proof. By which I mean it is too individual, to absorbent, too fortified by its own curious integrity, to be vulnerable to those slings and arrows of outrageous vulgarity which have killed the loveliness of so many places since tourism became big business. I had expected to find Cape Comorin despoiled, yet it remains first and foremost a place of pilgrimage:

a holy place, as it has been for centuries beyond counting. Like so many of Hinduism's less accessible pilgrimage sites, it is marked by an extraordinary atmosphere of quiet excitement, of devout gaiety; and added to this is its own unique flavour. From the bus one suddenly sees the sea – or rather, three seas – and a temple on a rock about half a mile offshore. And that's it. One has reached the end of India.

\*

I used to assume vaguely that Indian spitting was simply a consequence of Hindus being inexplicably chesty and peculiarly devoid of any spark of Civic Spirit. Recently, however, I have discovered that the habit is closely linked with their pollution laws, which are complex beyond anything a simple Western mind could imagine. To us many of them seem outlandish, though others contain obvious elements of common sense. For one thing, all bodily discharges are regarded with extreme horror and fear; and saliva, phlegm and mucus, which are believed to be 'spoiled semen' (even today semen is popularly supposed to be stored in the head), are thought of as having an especially powerful polluting effect. Therefore the body must be cleared of these ghastly menaces at the first possible moment, and it doesn't matter a damn where the discharge lands or who else is polluted in the process.

\*

By 11 a.m. on the twenty-sixth I had realised that if I were not to die of neglect some action must be taken. Leaning on the wall I made it to the veranda and tried to persuade three passers-by that I genuinely and urgently needed medical attention; but they all insisted that I must go to a clinic or hospital as no doctor would come to me. However, I knew it would be suicidal to go doctor-hunting in a steady downpour of cold rain with a high temperature, so I tottered despairingly back to my sweat-sodden bed.

Then Rachel appeared beside me, in a rather genie-like way. 'I'm better,' she said, 'and I'm hungry. May I go out to look for food? Why don't you get a doctor? You look terrible. Have you no medicine? Why am I better?'

I mumbled that no doctor was available, whereupon Rachel said, 'Why don't you write a letter to a doctor and get a servant to take it?'

'What doctor? What servant?' I muttered muzzily.

'Any doctor and any servant,' said Rachel, impatiently.

I raised my head and began to take her seriously. She brought me a pen and paper and in shaky capitals I appealed to a 'Dear Doctor' while she trotted off to fetch 'a servant'. Moments later she was back with a young cycle-rickshaw-wallah she had found sheltering on the veranda. His English was unintelligible but he seemed to understand when I explained that if he returned with a doctor I would give him Rs.5 before I left Madurai. Pocketing my note he disappeared and less than fifteen minutes later showed an elderly Indian woman doctor into the room. She was from a Christian maternity hospital scarcely five minutes' walk away and she assured me that had we gone there on Christmas Eve we would have been given a very warm welcome and appropriate treatment.

But what was 'appropriate treatment'? Despite heavy doses of fabulously expensive British-made drugs my temperature remained between 101° and 104° for the next few days, while my headache resisted every available painkiller and I developed a strange racking cough – quite unlike bronchitis – which almost caused me to faint with exhaustion.*

*

In Indian cities, a foreigner might now live for weeks amongst Westernised Hindus without realising there was such a thing as a caste-system; yet one cannot live for twelve hours in rural India

* Some time later, routine malaria blood-tests incidentally revealed that we had both had brucellosis: so Rachel was lucky to have recovered within three days.

without having to accommodate it, and in the cities it has merely been modified – not abolished. Few 'twice-born' Hindus – however Westernised, aesthetic, socialistic or liberal they may profess to be – will feel completely at ease sitting in a bus beside a latrine-cleaner.

As aggrieved Sahibs used to point out, when accused of maintaining a colour-bar, the interracial barriers in India were first erected by Hindus. (Though it is true the British did eventually become as socially exclusive, in their way, as any Brahman.) What I tried to convey to Rachel today is the strange fact that the majority of Hindus value the caste system just as much as we in the West now value the ideal of social equality. It is not an affliction they helplessly endure but an institution which gives an essential cohesion to their unique and otherwise disparate society. Hence the declaring illegal of Untouchability by the Indian Constitution can at present be little more than a formal salute to an alien concept. Many criticised Gandhi's singling out of Untouchability for abolition, leaving the rest of the caste structure intact, but the Mahatma well knew that the caste system could not exist without a foundation of Untouchables to take upon themselves those impurities which otherwise would pollute the whole of society. Although Hinduism is renowned for its ability to absorb outside influences, and change them more than it is changed by them, it may now have reached a crisis point at which its genius for assimilation can no longer operate. Richard Lannoy has suggested 'institutionalised inequality' as one definition of the caste system and it is hard to see how the official Indian government policy of social equality can either be absorbed into Hinduism or democratically imposed on hundreds of millions of citizens to whom it is repugnant. Something, it would seem, has to give – and this time it may be Hinduism. But not yet.

At present, especially in South India – a man's caste, rather than his personal talents, determines the degree of political power he can obtain: and this is having a disastrous effect on the national morale. India's parliamentary democracy has of course given the uneducated but numerically more influential sub-castes an unprecedented opportunity to dominate their local scene; yet this opportunity is often wasted because caste still matters more than the interests or opinions of the individual voter.

\*

I found the unpredictability of caste attitudes well illustrated the other day by Mrs Machiah, when she and Rachel and I were walking back from the Ayyappas' house. Ahead of us on the road Rachel saw one of her favourite playmates – an enchanting five-year-old Harijan girl, who admittedly is always filthy – and immediately she ran to her and slipped an arm through hers. Away they went, skipping together in a continuation of some game started that morning, and I turned to Mrs Machiah, about to remark on the little girl's charm. But my companion's expression silenced me. She called Rachel, and I hesitated, caught between the devil of offending our friend's susceptibilities and the deep blue sea of allowing my daughter to be polluted by caste consciousness. Then before I had resolved my dilemma, came the final twist to the situation. Suddenly the little girl's mother appeared out of the forest, with a load of firewood on her head, and shrieked angrily at her child not to touch the *mleccha* [person traditionally seen by Hindus as a polluting foreigner or outcaste]. Why? Surely the most uninformed Harijan is aware that *mlecchas* have no place – do not count, even as outcastes – in the world of caste?

\*

Coorg hospitality seems not merely a social duty but part of the people's religion. On each veranda – presided over by innumerable ancestral photographs – we had to partake of coffee, biscuits, savoury scraps with unpronounceable names, papaya knocked from the tree for us, yellow, red and green bananas, supportas, and delicious bulls-hearts, which look exactly like ox-hearts and have sweet, creamy flesh and many large, flat, shiny black seeds. At the end of all this I wondered where I was supposed to fit an Indian lunch for an honoured guest, but when I saw and smelt the meal my appetite revived. There were two sorts of rice – steamed and fried – curried sardines, salted raw shark, omelette with onion and exotic spices, pickled oranges, dahl, dhosies (delicious rice-flour pancakes) and fried cabbage. Jagi's mother hovered anxiously while we ate, obviously on tenterhooks lest her efforts proved unpalatable to the guests, and thus I was compelled, by politeness as well as greed, to overeat grossly.

\*

Incidentally, Aunty wordlessly registered disapproval today when she saw Rachel dressed for the occasion in that Madrassi outfit made for her by the Ittamozhi tailor's apprentice. This baffled me, until I realized that the outfit is typical of what little Harijan and low-caste girls wear, not only in Tamil Nadu but here in Coorg. Little high-caste girls, before they graduate to saris at puberty, wear European-style clothes, usually beautifully tailored by mother, aunt or grandmother but modelled exactly on Marks and Spencer's children's garments. So poor Rachel's glad rags – of which she is so proud, and in which she looks so attractive – were today a *faux pas* of the first order.

\*

Occasionally, in India, the sheer weight of tradition overwhelms and our Western concept of time becomes meaningless – a disturbing and yet exhilarating experience, offering a glimpse of possibilities discounted by logic and modern science, but not by the immemorial intuitions of mankind. And so it was this morning, as I watched the Brahman making his oblations, ringing his bell, wafting incense, presenting garlands, cupping his hands over the flame of the dish-lamp and gravely reciting Sanskrit formulas the exact words of which he may or may not have understood.

I despair of conveying, to those who have never seen it, the eloquent gracefulness of a Hindu priest's hand-movements as he worships. All his oblations and recitations are accompanied by these intricate, stylised, flowing gestures which symbolically unite him to the object of his worship and are of surpassing beauty. At the end of this morning's *puja* [ceremonial worship], as the Brahman withdrew from the temple – moving past the *mleccha* with downcast eyes – I could not at once emerge from the state of exaltation into which he had unwittingly drawn me.

\*

The excitement spread and, with typical Coorg spontaneity, many of the crowd surged onto the maidan to give their own performances – including General Cariappa and Rachel, who went stamping and leaping through clouds of dust, hand in hand, beaming at each other and waving gaily in response to the cheers of the delighted crowd. I shall not quickly forget the tall, slim, military figure of the General, contrasting with the small, sturdy, suntanned figure of my daughter as they cavorted improbably together by the light of mighty plantain-stump torches – held high with rosy sparks streaming off them in the night breeze, by a dozen laughing youths on the periphery of the crowd.

## Where the Indus is Young:
## Walking to Baltistan (1977)
## Baltistan, Pakistan

In my first book, *Full Tilt*, I described Peshawar as being 'like an English city with a few water-buffaloes and vultures and lizards thrown in'. Those words were written the day I came over the Khyber Pass, after months of cycling through the remoter regions of Persia and Afghanistan. But in 1974, having come straight from the fleshpots of Karachi, Islamabad, Pindi and Saidu, I found this 'Paris of the Pathans' – Lowell Thomas's phrase – a very special place. It seemed less a city in the modern sense than an agglomeration of medieval bazaars inhabited by attractive rough diamonds of many races. It is one of the three Pathan cities – the others are Kandahar and Jellalabad, in Afghanistan – and since my first visit it has become one of the hippies' main junctions.

In 1963 the great eastward Hippy Migration had not yet started and *Full Tilt* has frequently been accused of increasing its momentum, which suggestion troubles my conscience more than it flatters my vanity when I see groups of drugged wrecks dragging themselves around Asia. However, Peshawar's attitude to strangers has been only slightly modified by the hippy influence. Pesh Awar means 'Frontier Town' and for at least 4,000 years this city has been dealing with invaders of many types. The hippies are merely a source of local amusement – and of course profit, for the many drug-peddlers in the bazaars.

*

The change in Pakistan's mood that struck me most on this return visit was not very positive. It has come about through the growing-up of a generation with no lingering shred of affection for the rest of the subcontinent, nor any awareness of being linked to it by countless bonds forged through centuries of shared history. I met many members of this first-born generation of Pakistanis – doctors, farmers, lawyers, merchants, teachers, bank clerks, journalists, civil servants – and the majority seem to feel for India only a contemptuous, uncomprehending hostility. Unlike their parents, they have no memories of growing up with Hindu neighbours, taking part in Hindu festivals, seeing pictures of Hindu gods and goddesses in the bazaar. I found them disquieting, for they represent a considerable increase in the world's sum of hate. They were enormously disconcerted when told that we had spent the previous winter in India and met there with nothing but kindness. They did not really want to know that beyond the border were other ordinary men and women, as generous and helpful as themselves.

*

Haji Nasir had invited us to call on him after breakfast 'for more talk of religion and insignificant refreshments' – an irresistible invitation! As it is difficult to find individual houses in Gilgit I asked a youth in the bazaar where Haji Nasir lived and he promptly replied, 'Follow me! I am his son!' We were led up a narrow, winding passage, between the smooth grey mud walls of many compounds, until we came to a double-door of weathered and warped wood, leading into a neat little compound with rooms opening off a verandah on two sides. Our guide took us straight to his father's study-cum-prayer-room, where Haji Nasir was sitting on the floor, on a red velvet quilt spread over cushions, reading a superbly illustrated and illuminated seventeenth-century Persian manuscript. We sat on the edge of a charpoy and Rachel drew pictures while the Haji and I talked about Buddhism. Then I was shown his latest Karachi publication, a slim volume of religious poetry written in Persian to commemorate a double family tragedy – the death of his eldest son in an air-crash between Pindi and Gilgit, and the death of his favourite nephew, a few months later, in a jeep crash between Gilgit and Skardu.

\*

On a wide, sunny terrace stood three primitive mud buildings, amidst apricot and walnut trees. We were greeted by five women – unveiled, uninhibited and handsome, in total contrast to the hidden, tongue-tied, pallid females of Gilgit town. Unwashed within living memory, they wore elaborate but clumsily made silver ornaments on their foreheads, over heavily embroidered brocade caps. Three were suckling fly-blown babies of indescribable filthiness, normally kept under Mamma's ragged cloak but proudly displayed for our benefit. While I made admiring noises over these infants a little girl was sent to fetch a dozen walnuts. As we walked on I reflected that this gift meant more than all the lavish hospitality of our down-country friends, who are endlessly kind but so rich their generosity could never have the significance of that fistful of nuts.

\*

I doubt if Rachel will ever experience an odder Christmas Day. At sunrise the band of the Northern Scouts (whose parade-ground was nearby) began to play *Auld Lang Syne* very loudly and quickly and continued to play it for half-an-hour without pausing to draw breath. Whether this was a sentimental salute to the memory of Christian officers, or a military way of celebrating Id, no-one seems to know. It was a dark, cold morning, with a low cloud, and at 7.30 a sudden thundering of hooves, accompanied by blood-curdling war whoops, brought us rushing to the restaurant door. Twenty fast little polo-ponies, wearing gay, tasselled saddle-cloths, were charging past like the Light Brigade in fancy dress. Their riders – the Northern Scouts polo-team – wore mufti but carried long lances with pennants. Nobody else took the slightest notice of the team, or knew where they were going, or why, and quickly they disappeared into the foggy greyness of the morning.

*

I have my own system of grading poverty and today I concluded that the local level is not 'acceptable'. I don't at once deduce poverty if I see people studying the sun because they have no watches, or drying their hands at tea-house fires because they have no towels, or staring at themselves in jeep mirrors because they have no looking-glasses. But I *do* deduce poverty when almost everybody is obviously permanently underfed. I have to admit, most reluctantly, that the opening-up of this area may be a good thing. If only that process didn't always involve the destruction of local traditions, the debasement of taste and stimulation of greed. It is tragic that living standards in remote regions cannot be raised without drawing people into the polluted mainstream of our horrible 'consumer society'.

*

As we were debating where to stable Hallam, our landlord Sadiq Ali arrived and suggested the kitchen. So I coaxed our *ghora* in, tethered him to a rafter and here we all are, very cosy and snug, our oil-stove boiling a kettle for *chai*, the window blocked with an old exercise-book lent by Rachel and the chimney-hole also papered over. Outside the window is a snow-filled orchard of apricot saplings and beyond that a mighty display of mountains, less than two miles away. I fetched water from the stream near our neighbours' houses: it is unfrozen at only one point, where housewives repeatedly break the ice. We shall continue to use candles. In theory Skardu is electrified but in practice the current flows only rarely and weakly despite – or because of – the many wires that drape the town.

These run from tree to tree like tropical creepers, at just the level to strangle or otherwise dispose of unwary riders. Indisputably this is an endearing capital.

*

Sadiq Ali visits us regularly every morning, often accompanied by one or more friends, relatives and neighbours. The locals say we are the first foreigners to have wintered here for over forty years, which may or may not be true. Certainly we are a novelty, the more so as we do not live aloofly in our own camp or in the Rest House, but are available for inspection at all times. Our door can be bolted from inside as well as padlocked from outside, but I have never yet used the bolt, even at night. (What greater tribute could be paid to the essential friendliness and goodness of the Balti atmosphere? One feels completely safe going to sleep at night in an open house.) In such places as this a foreigner must choose an extreme: either to live in the sort of isolation traditionally associated with Western travellers or to integrate and forget about privacy. In Hindu communities the latter course is difficult because of caste taboos, as I found in both Nepal and South India, but in Muslim lands there are no such barriers. The prolonged and often silent scrutiny of unknown chance callers can be very trying, yet it would be churlish to begrudge these wide-eyed visitors the pleasure they get from watching me washing-up, or brushing my teeth, or polishing the tack, or reading to Rachel, or peeling onions to give some air of reality to our packet soups.

*

We got home at 2.30 and as I was unsaddling Hallam Rachel gave a gasp of horror and pointed to his near flank: an abscess the size of a tea-plate had just burst and pus was oozing hideously through his thick winter coat. I pointed out to the stricken Rachel that the worst was now over, from Hallam's point of view, and while

117

she gave him love and apricots I got the stove going and cooked a hot barley mash. Then Sadiq arrived and assured me that there is a good horse-doctor here, which information I received with some scepticism, remembering the quality of the human hospital. I'm not sure that a *ghora-hakim* can do much good at this stage – presumably one waits for nature to heal the wound – but I would like an expert's opinion on what caused it.

*

Our boy attendants were on their way to school and one of the senior students, who spoke scraps of English, invited us to visit their 'College'. We were conducted to an old two-storeyed house, the ground floor of which was a stable, ankle-deep in dried dung. A shaky, almost perpendicular ladder led to a landing from where, on our approach, three women fled in a flurry of shawls over faces. This floor was littered with fresh poultry-droppings and having negotiated these we went through a low door in a thick stone wall and found ourselves in the open air. Threadbare goat-hair rugs had been laid on stony ground swept clear of snow, and here Gol's scholars sit in rows imbibing what passes locally for education. Each child brings his own wooden writing board but no other equipment is used; no abacus, no books, not even a homemade blackboard. An undersized twenty-two-year-old with a lean, pallid face and shifty eyes came forward to greet us. 'I am passed Matric. with Skardu College,' he introduced himself. 'Please you draw picture of me with your camera? What is your town in America? Please you take rest on this stone. What is your business here? I am Principal teacher in this school. I teaches this boys Urdu, English, pysix, matmatix and the good history of Pakistan.'

By speaking very slowly and repeating each question at least three times I elicited from this teacher of English the information that Gol's school was founded in 1947 and now has 140 pupils and two teachers. Possibly it makes its pupils barely literate in Urdu, but even this seems doubtful.

A group of small girls had gathered beyond a low stone wall to stare shyly at us, their tattered shawls covering the lower halves of their faces. When I provocatively asked the Principal, 'Do you have no girl pupils?' he gazed at me for a moment in astonishment, then glanced contemptuously towards the group and said, 'Women cannot learn! We will not have them here!' In reaction to his glance the little girls giggled, completely covered their faces and scuttled away. 'I have one wife, two sons,' continued the Principal, 'but I will not want her if she read.'

\*

At noon we came to one of those intimidating stretches where the track has been built up on stakes driven into a rocky wall rising sheer out of the Shyok, which swirls rapidly past, hundreds of feet below. Here a jeep came over the highest point of the track, some twenty yards above us, without warning. (We had been unable to hear it over the roar of the river.) Hallam snorted with terror and reared up and I looked around to see him on his hind legs with Rachel poised over the water far below. Even to recall that vision now makes me feel sick. There has been no nastier moment in my entire forty-three years. As the jeep-driver jammed on the brakes Hallam recovered himself, Rachel dismounted and I beckoned the driver to help me unload, since a loaded animal could not pass the vehicle. Then I slowly led Hallam – still trembling and with ears laid back – along the edge of the precipice and over the top. There the track mercifully widened, allowing us to reload in safety. Meanwhile Rachel had dissolved into tears of fright and if ever an occasion called for loving maternal reassurance this was it. But I am deeply ashamed to relate that I rounded savagely on the poor child and told her to stop behaving like a baby. Human nature can be very unattractive.

\*

At about 2.30 a piercingly cold gale sprang up, mercifully behind us. It powerfully swept the dry, fine snow into drifts and then shaped them – like a restless, invisible sculptor – into countless ever-changing, elegantly curved mounds.

Where the Shyok swings south we climbed high above the river-bed and the surface again became hideously treacherous. Rachel cheerfully remarked, 'If Hallam slipped over the edge here, we'd both be drowned. Would you try to rescue me or would that be a waste of time?' The other day's terrifying experience has not spoiled her nerve for these perilous paths, as I greatly feared it would. Perhaps when I treated her so unsympathetically afterwards I did the right thing for the wrong reason.

*

Then suddenly, as we sat on a rock amidst all that brilliance and stillness and changeless beauty, I thought for some inexplicable reason of 'Outside'. And I felt an absurd spasm of disbelief in the existence of that busy, noisy, ever-changing turmoil from which we have now been completely cut off for two months. Never before have I felt so detached from the rest of the world and from my own past and future. Here the present is so simple and satisfying and undemanding – and so full of peace and beauty – that one is more than willing to pretend nothing ever has existed or ever can exist. Each day I seem to feel more deeply content and inwardly stronger, as though the uncomplicated joy of travelling through these mountains were a form of nourishment. If we settled here I suppose I would eventually become restless and anxious to be reinvolved with all the people, places and activities that make up my normal life. But as yet I feel only enrichment.

*

At noon, when we were within hailing distance of Khapalu's Rest House, we turned west down the right bank of the Shyok. Until we get back to Gol we will be on an old pony-trail which was the main trade route before the building of the left bank bridle-track (recently converted to a jeep-track) in the early 1920s. Soon we came to another footbridge, only about two feet above the Shyok. Here I had to adjust the load again, before Rachel rode Hallam through belly-deep water, and the next stage was a toilsome trudge over a mile of soft, dry sand where ravenous and wildly irritating sandflies followed us in clouds – the first insects of any kind that we have seen in Baltistan. Near the unlikely-sounding village of Youski we picnicked by a sparkling stream in the shade of stately walnut-trees and within moments were surrounded by excited, smiling women, carrying manure-baskets and/or babies. As we ate they squatted in a row in the sun to watch us, and the nursing mothers took advantage of this lull in fertilising activities to produce breasts for the refreshment of avid infants, most of whom had infected eyes.

*

Life in Baltistan certainly teaches one to adapt a few possessions to many uses: I can think of no better antidote to the West's gadget-demented subculture. Our sack, for instance, is officially a sack – if you follow me – but in its off-duty hours it becomes, according to prevailing conditions, a window-curtain, a tablecloth, a mattress, a pillow, a horse-blanket or a floor-covering to protect new Rest House carpets from my culinary activities. Similarly, the lid of the old Complan tin, used as a tea-caddy, also serves as a mirror (the inside), and a candle-holder (the outside), while our frying-pan serves as Hallam's grain-dish, and our kettle as teapot, and our nailbrush as clothes-brush, saucepan-cleaner, boot-brush and potato-scrubber, and our *dechi* [handleless saucepan] as wash-up basin and, *in extremis*, as chamber pot. Possibly the time is nearer than we think for the Western world to learn how expendable are most of its newfangled gadgets.

A Place
Apart

Dervla
Murphy

## *A Place Apart* (1978)
## Northern Ireland .

The North's towns and villages seem unnaturally subdued. There are so few cars, so many lines of concrete-filled barrels down the main streets to prevent parking near shops, so few people about and such grim police barracks – fortified, inside giant wire cages, against bombs and machine-guns. These jolt one, in prim-looking little towns, after cycling for hours through tranquil countryside. We are used to thinking of the village police station or gardaí barracks as a place into which anyone can wander at any hour, without even knocking, for advice and sympathy about a lost cat or stolen bicycle. It is very much part of our way of life that the police should be acceptable and accessible, not driven to defend themselves from the public like an army of occupation. Until the policing problem has been solved, how can normality be restored anywhere in Northern Ireland?

\*

This afternoon, in a small Bogside pub, I met two young men who were obviously longing to talk to someone new. (Many young Derry people tend to be wary of strangers though their elders have more than their share of informal Irish friendliness.) They introduced themselves as Sean and Liam; both are philosophy graduates of Queen's [University Belfast] and have been on the dole, living with their working-class families, for the past year. I asked could they not get jobs across the water and they said, 'Only on building sites, or driving buses.' Besides, they don't want to be too far away from their families at present. Sean's mother is a widow and as he has two younger brothers and three younger sisters he reckons she needs him around to help her impose discipline. I would reckon so, too. Liam's father is a semi-invalid (a TB leg was removed), and his mother's nerves have gone since 1969, when a gang of RUC [police] men on the rampage badly beat up her three sons in her presence. Liam said that his family had always been moderate Nationalists, totally opposed to the IRA in all its manifestations, and there was no conceivable excuse for the RUC's invasion of their home. ...

Neither Sean nor Liam needed much prompting to reminisce about the heady days when this part of Derry became 'Free'. As teenagers they went out to watch the rioting, as their contemporaries elsewhere might go to a football match, and they often became hoarse through cheering the rioters on. 'From a safe distance', they added wryly. They had grown up very aware of the importance among their peers of physical skill and courage but obviously they were philosophers before ever they went to Queen's. Liam said his most sickening memory was of three small boys hysterically seeking the autograph of a Provo [Provisional IRA] who had just killed a Brit [British soldier]. That quenched his enthusiasm for cheering. Sean's worst memory was 'The day an eighteen-year-old on the dole showed me ten £10 notes – his fee for shooting a Brit – and said "Easy money!" He didn't even pretend to give a damn about Irish freedom or civil rights. Maybe at the time I was a wee bit inclined to join the lads but that put me off forever.'

Until the ages of seventeen and eighteen, respectively, Sean and Liam had never once conversed with a Protestant; and this was normal for boys of their generation. As students at Queen's they at first felt themselves to be in an alien world; segregation was spontaneously kept up despite the liberal academic atmosphere. This was not through overt hostility or bigotry but because it seemed the natural thing to do. 'I'll never forget the sense of jittery isolation,' said Liam. 'There are thousands of Catholics at Queen's, but somehow knowing 75 per cent of the population of Belfast is Protestant got me all unnerved. During my first year I came home as often as I could. Yet I was ashamed of myself for feeling like this in my own country. It seemed so absurd. I saw then how you could trace it straight back to separate schools. Not to bigotry in my home – there wasn't any. And apart from that we're not sectarian-minded here in Derry, the way Belfast is. Derry is different.'

*

All Derry's social workers are deeply worried about a problem to be found now in cities all over Europe – the psychological effects of uprooting slum communities and re-housing them in comparative luxury. People who have been 'dropping in' on each other all their lives no longer visit, or depend on each other in emergencies, though they are still neighbours. Keeping up with the McCanns has suddenly replaced the old values and countless respectable families, who before always managed to pay their way, are in debt. During times of tension neighbourly support becomes more important than ever and its weakening here has contributed to a spectacular increase in mental illness and alcoholism among women.

Des and I talked at length to an elderly widow in a hideously carpeted little room strewn with expensive broken toys and crammed with shoddy new furniture; the large television, on spindly legs, supported a variety of seaside souvenirs. Annie lives with her married daughter who works in a factory and the five children are at school all day and the son-in-law 'had to go across the water because when he was out of a job for a long while he got tangled with the UVF [Ulster Volunteer Force, Protestant paramilitaries]. They pay regular like the Provos. Then the RUC was after him and he'll hardly come back – 'twouldn't ever be safe.' Annie is very fond of her son-in-law and was most upset when she accidentally discovered his connection with 'that lot'. She began to take a drop more than she should and when he went off and she was alone every day she only had the drop to cheer her up. 'Everything got worse for us all when there was no string on the doors.' She meant that in their new housing estate you could no longer put your hand through a letter box, pull the key out on a string and enter a friend's house without knocking. 'No one ever needed to be worried or lonesome or in want in my old street. Now it's gone – all pulled down.' And what to some town-planner is a triumph – one slum less – to her is a disaster.

*

Imagine a London in which the inhabitants of Kensington are afraid to visit old friends in Chelsea; in which nobody from Camden Town dares to drink in Hampstead pubs; in which a youth from Wimbledon would be risking his life by strolling through Green Park; in which a change of taxis is sometimes necessary between Putney and Richmond because few drivers are willing to venture outside their native borough. A London suffering from an acute housing shortage though row after row of solid spacious dwellings stand empty with bricked-up doors and windows. A London where policemen are likely to be shot dead within moments of entering certain districts – and so never do enter them – and where large buildings are frequently razed by uncontrollable swarms of small boys. A London in which only the West End is comparatively safe for all Londoners to shop in, because it has been securely barricaded off from the rest of the capital and is constantly patrolled by large numbers of heavily armed troops. Such a London could happen only in science fiction – we hope. Yet all the world knows that one city in the United Kingdom has been reduced during the past decade to this almost unimaginable way of life.

*

When I crossed the River Bann – broad and brown between flat banks – it seemed much more real, as a frontier, than the border between North and South. It divides the western, more Catholic and more economically underprivileged region of Northern Ireland from the predominantly Protestant counties of Antrim and Down. Antrim is Paisley country; when I stopped at a crossroads petrol station to ask the way a young attendant abruptly (and absurdly) said, 'Don't know.' Further down the road, two youths curtly gave directions while eyeing me with a mixture of suspicion and derision. On the outskirts of Ballymena I cycled between rows of preternaturally clean bungalows with shining windows, fresh paint, gleaming brass ornaments on gleaming tiled mantelpieces, washed and ironed curtains and not the tiniest weed visible in any garden. An hour later, on a quiet country road, an overtaking car slowed and began to follow me. My heart lurched, as it would not have done west of the Bann, and the next few minutes seemed long. When the ancient Mini overtook me, the passenger door was opened by one of the two youths to whom I had spoken earlier and I was treated to an indecent gesture. This was such a relief, when I had been half-expecting a bullet, that I almost said 'Thank you.'

*

I was advised to study the religious geography of the city before cycling around it and a friend lent me his detailed British Army Tribal Map of Belfast, which marks the ghetto areas orange and green [unionist and nationalist]. Then my host introduced me to the Catholic ghettos. With a prominent DOCTOR notice displayed on his windscreen he was less likely than other motorists to be delayed at security checkpoints, hijacked by bombers or stoned by gangs of bored boys who for the moment could find no more exciting target.

Perhaps because I never see television, and so was quite unprepared, those ghettos really shattered me. Yet I have known far worse slums in Asia. But Belfast is in affluent Europe and why should large areas of it be swarming with undernourished wild children and knee-deep in stinking litter, and strewn with broken glass glinting in hot sun under a blue sky – all on a summer's day

... So many bricked-up houses, reminding me of dead people with their eyes shut – some of them fine substantial buildings from which Protestants had had to flee in terror taking only their resentment with them. So many high brick, or corrugated iron, barricades between identical streets of little working-class homes, to prevent neighbours from seeing and hearing each other, and so being provoked to hurt and kill each other. Sometimes, over the barricades, I could glimpse Union Jacks flying from upstairs windows. And I remembered a friend of mine in another part of the North – a retired naval officer – saying how much he resented the British flag being abused as a provocative sectarian symbol.

*

Ian Paisley's Martyrs' Memorial Free Presbyterian Church on the Ravenhill Road is the third most expensive ecclesiastical edifice to have been built in the British Isles since the Second World War. ... I entered the building one very hot Sunday morning in July, perfectly prepared to find that Mr Paisley, too, has a good side – reserved for his congregation, so that I hadn't been able to see it before. Yet when I left the place an hour and a half later I knew that I had been in the presence of pure evil. ...

Paisley's pulpit is in fact a small stage and while preaching he strides up and down, gesticulating, shouting, grimacing – and, on this Sunday, waving a huge Bible above his head and declaiming, 'This is not a book of peace! This is a book of war! War against Christ's enemies, against the deceits of the Devil, against the snares of ecumenism! We must listen to the call to arms and not be afraid! And Christ will fight with us, as he overturned those tables, and will be proud to see us as we go forth bravely to attack for him!'

I was aware of blasphemy being committed as this demented creature paced from end to end of his pulpit-stage, flourishing the Bible and repetitively – almost hypnotically – insisting on the need to defend, to fight, to do battle, to vanquish, to conquer, to assert, to unsheathe the sword, to show no mercy to the enemies of God ... The

cunning with which he used an aggressive, militaristic phraseology
– all culled from the Bible – was literally blood-chilling. At a certain
point it brought me out in goose-flesh though Belfast was in the
middle of a heatwave. I longed then to get away, somehow to escape
from this man's powerful emanations of evil. But I was afraid to
move lest I might be pursued by some young man anxious to secure
his salvation by putting a bullet in my irreverent back.

*

It is tempting to condemn those who are so readily swayed by Mr
Paisley. But the Loyalists to whom I talked in the ghettos of East
Belfast, when I returned there in mid-September, did not seem
blameworthy. To them there is a war on and they feel for the Peace
People that scorn which the average stout-hearted Englishman
or woman felt for pacifists during the world wars. I particularly
remember one small neat parlour where Queen Elizabeth and Ian
Paisley were grotesquely improbable companions on top of the
television set. A pale little woman with lank black hair, whose UVF
husband had been 'in' [in prison] for the past two years, told me
that a friend had urged her to march [with the Peace People] – 'for
the sake of the children, to try to stop it all before they grow up'.
But how could she betray her husband – he who was doing time
to preserve Ulster for the Queen! – by 'walking in the street with
Papist harpies and viragos?' (A verbatim quote.) To this woman,
as to thousands of her neighbours, Fenians [Catholics] represent
a threat to *their* state, *their* jobs, *their* religion. So they are easily
persuaded that to support a movement which opposes all violence
including anti-Fenian violence, is treachery. Mr Paisley's party
proclaims itself interested only in Peace through Victory, by which
it means a return to pre-1969 days with the Protestant majority
firmly in control and no nonsense talked about power-sharing.

*

Visitors to South Armagh are comparatively rare in mid-winter – or at any season, for that matter. I was therefore welcomed as a novelty and also, when it emerged I was writing about Northern Ireland, as a possible mouthpiece for the Republican cause. (This is not necessarily the same thing as the Provo cause; some of those men were very anti-Provo.) But my companions found it hard to believe that an English publisher would bring out a book not loaded in favour of the Brits. And they considered my ponderings and probings a gratuitous complicating of a perfectly simple situation. They had the answer: BRITS OUT! TROUBLE OVER!

A grey-faced man of about fifty sat in a corner saying very little; he was introduced to me as the father of two boys, aged fourteen and sixteen, who had been killed not long before by a booby-trap bomb left near their home – for the benefit of the Brits – in a wrecked car. The boys had been trying to remove a door-handle when the bomb went off, instantly killing both. Their father, however, seemed to feel no bitterness against the Provos; or if he did he was prudently concealing it. He blamed himself, he said, for not having sufficiently warned the lads to keep away from wrecked cars, abandoned refrigerators or cookers or inexplicable milk-churns. To the company in general those two boys were war casualties, not victims of terrorism. Had they been looking for someone to blame they would certainly have chosen the Brits, arguing that only their presence makes it necessary to plant bombs around the countryside.

Tentatively, I confessed to feeling a certain amount of sympathy for the ordinary British soldier, who is only doing his job by patrolling the fields and air-spaces of South Armagh. At once three men replied simultaneously that the Brits are legitimate targets. They are volunteers, not conscripts, and when they join the British army they know they will be sent to Northern Ireland where there is a war on and they may be killed. From the point of view of the speaker, to whom the Provos are a morally defensible army fighting for a just cause, this was sound reasoning. The whole concept of an 'illegal organisation' is utterly meaningless in certain areas under certain circumstances. To the people of South Armagh the Brits are the illegal army, occupying their territory against the will of virtually the entire population.

*

The only way in which the battle for the extremists' minds can be won is by overcoming one's repugnance for their ideas and actions and communicating with them simply as other human beings. Instead of opposing violence to violence, tolerance must be opposed to intolerance and reflection to hysteria. But to achieve anything worthwhile this communication must be based on sincere efforts to understand. Condescending media interviews, with the Orange or Green extremist being kept emotionally at arm's length, have for years been a common feature of the Northern scene. One has to struggle to remember that the extremists *do* have a point of view which to them is valid, however absurd or debased it may seem to us. It is hard to be convincing, in the abstract, about such matters. Yet when one is actually talking to 'the men of violence' it is surprisingly easy to understand the workings of their hearts, if not of their minds. And once some understanding has been gained, it becomes possible to differ from them without despising them. I have made valued friends among both Orange and Green paramilitaries; few are so extreme that they refuse to respond to the concern of a non-extremist.

We all need to change gear mentally, as it were, and to approach the Northern problem at a different pace. Instead of compulsively and impulsively abusing the paramilitaries as gangs of thugs labelled IRA, UVF – and so on – we must focus on the fact that each group is made up of individuals most of whom have been born into the spiritual and intellectual equivalent of a Calcutta slum. Many paramilitary deeds are revolting crimes but the paramilitaries themselves are not, usually, revolting criminals. I have made this point before but I am not apologising for repeating it. We *must* peel off the terrorist labels and look at the individuals underneath and try to understand why they are what they are – and ask ourselves what we would be had fate arranged for us to be born into an extremist family down a back street off the Falls or the Shankill.

*

*12 July* At 9.10 a.m. I was introduced to the Loyal Orange Lodge that had adopted me for the day. It was a Primary – as distinct from District, County and Grand – Lodge in rather a 'deprived' area. Around the Orange Hall little tables were laden with beer bottles and whiskey glasses, and scrubbed-looking Orangemen, in their Sabbath suits, were drinking and smoking and quietly chatting. Each had his sash to hand, carefully wrapped in brown paper or a plastic bag, and at the back of the Hall the first relay of banner-bearers were adjusting their leather harness and fixing bouquets of Sweet William and orange gladioli to the banner poles. I had scarcely crossed the threshold when I was being offered 'a wee one'. At the risk of seeming effete I chose beer. It was, as I have said, 9.10 a.m.

A year ago I would have felt a little uneasy at this gathering but by now I have reached a certain understanding of the Orange psyche. However much the Orange leaders may rave and rant against Papists and Southern Irish knaves, your average Orangeman is prepared to be a good host to everybody. If the Pope himself had appeared on the Field today I do believe he would at once have been offered 'a wee one' by men who last evening were kicking his effigy down Sandy Row. The Orangeman's ferocity is in the main a herd thing; given the wrong sort of leadership (which he always has been given) he can be very dangerous indeed. Left to himself he is as friendly and generous as any other Irishman.

*

Only one sure prediction can be made about the present Irish Troubles: they will not go away tomorrow, or the day after. No political initiatives or emended legislation or constitutional juggling can bring true peace to Northern Ireland until its people have changed within themselves. Some experts like to tell us that the problem is mainly, or entirely, an economic one. But when talking with the Northern Irish – in their farmyards or shops or pubs or rectories or slum kitchens or country-house drawing-rooms – it seemed to me primarily emotional/ethical/psychological. Therefore the outlook is depressing if one thinks exclusively within the timescale of individual lives; only the passing of generations can bring about the profound changes that are needed. Yet depression is curiously inappropriate to Northern Ireland today; although it should be a gloomy place it is not. (Often it can be heartbreaking but that is something different.) Amidst all the physical destruction and mental distress there is an enormous amount of creative energy at work. The essential changes are unmistakably under way and there are exciting vibrations of hope in the atmosphere. Increasingly I tend to view The Troubles as a painful purge that had to be endured by a diseased society as a prelude to a happier era than the North has ever known before.

# 1980s

# BEARING WITNESS

Dervla's first book of the 1980s was her condemnation of nuclear power. She became animated about this issue as she had passed near the site of the Three Mile Island nuclear reactor in Pennsylvania half an hour before its accident in March 1979. She conducted an enormous amount of research for this work, of which she was very proud until the end. She saw this period as her watershed point, after which her writing became more political. This changed her normal publishing schedule.

Dervla's book on Peru was published in 1983, though she and Rachel, who celebrated her tenth birthday there, did the trip in autumn 1978. At the time, she regarded this trip ('this Andean frolic') to be probably the last one with Rachel. That was not to be, however.

The next book, on Madagascar (1985), was based on a trip taken by them both in summer 1983. Madagascar is well known for retaining some very rare species of flora and fauna because of its isolated position. Dervla enjoyed seeing rare lemur species there and used the time to investigate her own position on ecology. She considered the loss of a single species, no matter how apparently ugly or useless, as an enormous loss to humanity. She was very fearful of the effects of the twin dangers of mineral exploitation and tourism there.

Her next book was published in 1987. In 1985, Dervla stayed in flats in Manningham in Bradford (predominantly South Asian) and Handsworth in Birmingham (predominantly Black) for about three months each. She was interested in troubled race relations in these cities. In autumn 1966 Dervla had cycled from London to Edinburgh and met lots of people from ethnic minorities in English cities. The idea to write about this lay dormant until January 1985. In the book, she tiptoed lightly between ethnography, sociology and journalism, sharing conversations with people she met in local bars and in their homes. She was also caught up in riots during her time there. What 'side' was she on? The side of unadulterated honesty.

Her trip through Cameroon with Rachel (ably assisted by Egbert the horse) was in 1987, with the resultant book published in 1989. The main memory Dervla retained in her vast memory bank was the agony of a tooth abscess she got while there. I still have my copy that my college friend Katie gave me back then – inscribed 'To all your future adventures' – and we are, happily, still close friends.

*Race to the Finish?*
*The Nuclear Stakes* (1981)

The nuclear threat has already been defined by many competent experts but few of these are established authors. Therefore their books are not as well known as they deserve to be and the need to reach a wider readership inspired some of my friends to drive me into the arena. At first this seemed a nutty idea, given my peculiarly unscientific and untechnological make-up. However, it was argued that that apparent handicap might prove an advantage: anything scientific, written in language simple enough for *me*, must be generally understandable. Also, an anti-nuke book by a travel writer might lure into the debate certain readers who had never previously concerned themselves with such issues.

My publisher, being a fair-minded man, longed for an 'objective' book. In the 1980s this is rather like looking for an objective book about White Slavery or the heroin trade. The nuclear weapons/power industry is capable of exterminating all life on earth: so one tends to write about it with a certain lack of detachment. However safely nuclear power stations may be designed, built and operated, there is no possibility of halting the spread of nuclear weapons while commercial nuclear technology is being vigorously marketed all over the world. Hence the majority have by now come off the fence and those who are not pro-nuke are 'anti' – and proud of it.

The matter is urgent. This unique danger presents a unique challenge to human wisdom. A new technology has never before been abandoned and of course it goes against man's exploratory nature to seem to *retreat* by turning away from the Fissile Society just because novel difficulties have arisen. But the nature of those difficulties makes retreat essential.

\*

On 6 August 1945 I was thirteen and bored by war-talk. For almost as long as I could remember people had been killing each other in vast numbers all over the globe. Bullets and bombs – at a safe distance – were part of my mental furniture. And Japan was *very* far away.

Yet I do remember Hiroshima. I remember it as something peculiarly dreadful, though not personally frightening. From my parents' conversation I extracted an awareness that this was not just another lethally brilliant military invention like V2 rockets. They seemed to regard the Atomic Age – headlined inches high in every newspaper – as presenting an altogether novel philosophical challenge to mankind. According to my father (something of a scientist *manqué*) this new era was *essentially* unlike all those preceding tens of thousands of years of human history and pre-history. His reasoning was beyond me, but the turbulent atmosphere of that week has remained in my memory ever since.

There were conflicting emotional currents. On an official, political level ran the grisly exultation of the Allies, who had 'Beaten Germans in Battle of Science', as one headline declaimed – quite forgetting that such names as Niels Bohr and Hans Bethe were not particularly Anglo-Saxon. On another level there was quick remorse. Eisenhower declared: 'It wasn't necessary to hit them with that awful thing.' And of course there was fear. At a press conference in the White House, less than three hours after the bomb was dropped, President Truman announced: 'British and American scientists, working together, have harnessed the basic power of the universe.' But: 'Further examination is necessary of possible methods of protecting us and the rest of the world from the danger of sudden destruction.' It was explained that the implications of this harnessing, for both good and evil, were still hidden. (The thousands who, as the President spoke, lay dying in agony amidst the rubble of Hiroshima would scarcely have agreed.) The 'swords into ploughshares' theme was also introduced by Mr Stimson, US Secretary of War, who referred to means that had been found to release atomic energy 'not explosively but in regulated amounts'. With those words, he had announced the birth of the nuclear power industry.

My father was not among those impressed by this harnessing of the basic power of the universe. The Greeks, he recalled, had intuited the atom. And Prometheus didn't do too well after stealing the fire of the gods – so maybe the Greeks had a message for us. But I was much too young to worry about the future of mankind. Soon I had dismissed the Atomic Age. To an unsophisticated adolescent, growing up in the happy depths of the Irish countryside, it seemed for quite a while supremely irrelevant. But during those years its relevance was rapidly increasing in the US, where the Manhattan Project, while producing the Hiroshima and Nagasaki bombs, had laid the foundations for both the nuclear arms race and the world's nuclear power programme.

*

It was 2.30 p.m. on Tuesday, 27 March 1979. Within a few miles of my Greyhound bus, as it sped along the Pennsylvania Turnpike, the free world's most serious commercial nuclear reactor accident was about to happen. My companion noticed the signpost leading to Three Mile Island (TMI) but I missed it. We had left Chicago at 8 p.m. the previous evening and the undulating Pennsylvanian countryside was having a soporific effect.

Beside me sat a retired high school teacher from Ohio with the curiously unwrinkled, lard-coloured, rectangular face of a certain type of elderly American male. Earlier he had glowered at my anti-nuke badge – 'Better Active Today Than Radioactive Tomorrow!' Plainly he deprecated such symbols of shallow romanticism about the environment, or paranoid nervousness about health, or lack of sympathy for the energy needs of an advanced society. He said, rather truculently, 'So no nukes – then what do we use for power? Anyway, coal's worse – a *lot* worse. Gives people bronchial troubles and kills miners. And if we release much more carbon dioxide into the atmosphere we'll destroy the global climate. But anti-nuke freaks can't think straight.'

Nobody likes to be classified as a freak, least of all those with tendencies that way. I replied crisply that an awareness of coal hazards partly explains the anti-nukes' support for alternative energy research, which could by now have contributed significantly to our needs had it received even a fraction of the billions of dollars invested in nuclear energy over the past thirty years. Afterwards I wondered if the events of the next week did anything to modify my acquaintance's fissile enthusiasm.

\*

Millions vaguely assume that after a nuclear war people would still have food and shelter, a normal environment, secure social structures and medical problems no different in type and amount to those that had existed before the bombings. Here ignorance is a perilous form of bliss. The longer we live in his cloud-cuckoo-land, the more likely is nuclear war. ... We need to be told repeatedly, in simple language, about the burns, trauma, radiation sickness, leukaemias, solid tissue tumours and birth defects that would result from even the most 'limited' nuclear war – afflictions which could not possibly be treated in a post-nuclear-war society that had disintegrated under the stress of unprecedented devastation, terror and despair. In any first world country, the medical profession could cope more or less adequately with the *immediate* effects of a major reactor disaster but they could not even begin to cope with the results of a nuclear bombardment.

\*

The argument for nuclear power is invariably obscured by a fog of statistics, predictions, diagrams, estimates, charts, extrapolations, graphs, forecasts, calculations, feasibility studies – and a few extra statistics. But if we ignore the fog and focus on the foundations we find an assumption that man *must* continue to live the way he lives now – only more so. Pro-nukes cannot see that to do this will prove ecologically impossible, leaving aside other considerations. It may be that future generations – if there are any – will see the great nuclear adventure as the climax to an era. We cannot guess how the transition to the next era will take place. Only the inevitability of change is certain, because our planet's limitations dictate it. We are not, after all, the Lords of the Universe.

Now my friends are asking: 'So what are you telling us to *do*, at the end of your book? How do we go about *stopping* nukes?' Happily, not being a leader, planner, organiser, crusader, ideologist or orator, I feel no obligation to tell anybody to do anything. My value as an anti-nuke is strictly limited to communicating on paper the reasons why we should do something. Others must advise *what*...

*Eight Feet in the Andes: Travels with a Mule in Unknown Peru* (1983)
Peru

Outwardly Cajamarca is classic Spanish colonial: slow, tranquil, unspoiled. At noon the sun pours gold into narrow, quiet streets where the complacent carved façades of only slightly decaying mansions seem unaware that the Spanish Empire is no more. In the several market places rickety stalls sell a contrasting array of goods ancient and modern, including dried llama foetuses for use in magical rites. The air is pure, clear, invigorating: never too hot or too cold. Across the intense blue of the mountain sky high white clouds occasionally wander, their shadows seeming to alter the textures and colours of the nearby ranges. Long centuries before the Spaniards arrived – or indeed the Incas – this valley was settled and cultivated. And somehow one is aware of the tentacles of its experience stretching back through millennia of unwritten but not unimportant history. It has an old and secret soul; the colonial mansions seem quite modern.

\*

When Nature called me at midnight the surrounding glory, beneath a flood of silver radiance, kept me sitting entranced on a rock for over an hour. Beneath our ledge the river bed glimmered pale. Near and far, dark mountain silhouettes stood out against a royal blue sky, faintly star-sprinkled. There was no stirring of a breeze, no whisper of running water: the stillness was so unflawed that it seemed the sovereign moon, floating high, must have put a spell on our whole world. To me that perfection of stillness is the grace of the mountains, poured into one's soul. There is more to such experiences than visual beauty; there is also another sort of beauty, necessary to mankind yet hard to put in words. It is the beauty of freedom: freedom from an ugly, artificial, dehumanising, discontented world in which man has lost his bearings. A world run by an alliance of self-hypnotised technocrats and profit-crazed tycoons who demand constant, meaningless change. A world where waste and greed are accepted – even admired – because our minds' manipulators have made frugality and moderation seem like failure in the Acquisition Game. A world where *deliberate* cruelty to each other, despite a proliferation of 'humanitarian' do-gooding agencies, is tolerated – because who can stop the multinational conquistadores? What I'm trying to express is scoffed at nowadays — or simply not recognised — or if recognised made into an off-putting cult. But I *know*, and have always known, that we 20th-century humans need to escape at intervals from that alien world which has so abruptly replaced the environment that bred us. We need to be close to, and opposed to, and sometimes subservient to, and always respectful of the physical realities of the planet we live on. We need to receive its pure silences and attend to its winds, to wade through its rivers and sweat under its sun, to plough through its sands and sleep on its bumps. Not all the time, but often enough for us to remember that we are animals. Clever animals, yet ultimately dependent, like any other animal, on the forces of Nature. Sitting there in the moonlight, it frightened me to think of the millions who have become so estranged from our origins that many of their children believe architects make mountains and scientists make milk. These are people who live *always* with artificial heating, lighting and transport. People who have never *used* their bodies (is this why sex has become such an obsession?) but use only their minds. And often not even their own minds, but the minds of others who have produced the goods that make it unnecessary for individuals fully *to live*. The Box epitomises it all – millions passively absorbing misleading oversimplifications and being artificially stimulated by phoney emotions. Where are we at? The end of the road perhaps … For we have travelled too far and too fast from the life the *campesino* [peasant farmer] still lives. And it may be that we are now meeting ourselves coming back – never a healthy encounter.

*

These Andean days tempt one to disregard all literary propriety and let loose a flood of superlatives: the highest, deepest, broadest, longest, narrowest, steepest, wildest, most precipitous, most rugged, most exhausting – and most beautiful. Undoubtedly today was the most superlative-provoking of all; at 8 p.m. I'm still 'high' on the glory of it. During our ten-hour walk we saw three people ('most isolated'). At one point my nerve almost failed me on Juana's [their mule's] behalf ('most difficult'). And all the other 'mosts' may be applied, freely and literally, to various stages of the day's progress.

*

This new valley soon became domesticated, with intensively cultivated slopes beyond the Rio. The *carretera* [road] remained high above the widening valley floor and we were looking down, as we walked, on a microcosm of *campesino* life. Red-roofed adobe farmsteads were scattered at either side of the river, very far below. Men and oxen were struggling to plough near-vertical fields which looked as though they might at any moment slip off the mountain. A couple were flaying a sheep that hung from the eaves of their home. Women were spinning while tending their flocks. Toddlers were playing with kids and lambs, cuddling them and tumbling with them on the green turf. Older children were chivvying a turkey flock away from the river's edge. Girls were fetching water in battered kerosene tins. Youths were unloading burros just back from the market. Pairs of old grannies were weaving poncho-cloth. Sleek horses were grazing on lush pasture. About this pastoral pageant – observed from a thousand feet up, so that one felt ridiculously like a spy – there was an aura of permanence, order, peace, security.

\*

Our dottiest day had such happy consequences that last evening I was, regrettably, in no fit state to write my diary. Pomabamba celebrates its annual fiesta at this time (St Francis of Assisi is the patron saint) and it would have been churlish of me not to participate. So yesterday was spent in a haze of nameless alcohol. The occasion had something in common with an Irish wake, to the extent that during fiestas the *campesinos* see drunkenness not as an extravagance, or a joke, or a vice, but as – in some obscure way – part of the religious ceremony. This is an ancient and worldwide primitive tradition; at the dawn of Hinduism Aryan priests newly arrived in Northern India got ritually smashed on soma. I don't know what I got smashed on last evening but throughout the day I was given so many powerful potions that I ended up dancing with the *campesinos* in the Plaza – though dancing is not one of my skills. The fiesta spirit(s) so envelope(s) everyone that even the Indians, now thronging into Pomabamba, forget their 'thing' about gringos. This uninhibiting effect of alcohol is the main reason why, for millennia, unsophisticated peoples have used drink and drugs during religious ceremonies; these free the soul to establish contact with whatever form of the immaterial is believed to exist beyond the confines and conventions of mundane life.

\*

Nobody could accuse me of being either conventional or teetotal, yet I'm slightly shocked by the *campesinos'* drinking hours. This is Sunday and when we reached Acollo Marco at 8 a.m. there were more men lowering beers in the cafés than there were women emerging from the pleasingly simple 17th-century church. The *campesino* who starts drinking at sunrise is unlikely to stop until he falls into the arms of his wife, usually to be found somewhere nearby awaiting this outcome. He will by then have spent enough to feed his children well for a week; at 70 soles a litre *cerveza* is expensive even for us. Chicha [home-brewed beer] however costs only five or ten soles a litre, depending on its quality, and it would make sense for the government to encourage more home-brewing, if necessary by restricting the *cerveza* supply. But the fat-cat brewers would not approve of that; starving *campesino* children are no concern of theirs.

While Juana breakfasted off freshly cut Alf [alfalfa] we each devoured a mound of fried potatoes mixed with onions, tomatoes, chopped goat-meat and peas, and topped with two fried eggs. As we ate, the standard debate about my gender took place among staff and customers. The longer this trek goes on, the more disinclined are the Peruvians (especially the women) to believe that I am Rachel's *mother* rather than her father. And this evening, when I confronted a mirror for the first time in months, I could see their point. By now I scarcely looked human, never mind feminine, with hideously bloodshot eyes (dust and wind), a dirt- and sun-blackened face, thick cracked lips and hair like a gorilla's mane. Add to that my Peruvian army boots, bulging bush-shirt, ragged jeans, broad shoulders and deep voice – it's no wonder I'm addressed more often than not as 'Señor'.

\*

Animals are sold on the edge of the town where we saw four young *mestizo* [of mixed Spanish and indigenous heritage] women sitting by the roadside, looking festive in elaborately embroidered bodices, long multi-coloured and multi-layered skirts and brilliant, hand-woven shawls. Each had a hairy brown piglet and this porcine quartet was tethered together, happily rooting on a patch of grass. When Rachel stopped to scratch their backs one woman jokingly urged me to buy a *cerdo* for my *hija* [pig for my daughter]. We sat beside them and the usual questions were asked; most women register bewildered sympathy on learning that I have only one child. These four already have several children each and thought the Pill a good idea, even if the padres are against it. But three out of the four said their husbands disapproved, many children being needed to make the most of one's land. Of course you need less if you have fewer children. Yet every good farmer's instinct is to make his land as productive as possible and hereabouts no couple can do that without several pairs of helping hands and feet. There is also a deep-rooted fear of children dying and aged parents being left uncared for and homeless. It ill-becomes us who are State-pampered to criticise the 'fecklessness' of those whose only security, now and for the future, lies in a sufficient number of able-bodied offspring.

*

From the courtyard we followed a broad, tree-lined track – part of the Camino Real. Rachel was leading and I was walking level with Juana's rump. Suddenly I yelled – 'Rachel! STOP!' She had been staring up at a flock of parrots, swooping noisy and green across the now-blue sky, and had almost trodden on a tarantula. The full significance of this encounter will be appreciated only by those who know that I am mortally afraid (it's a true phobia) of the tiniest spider. Even to write the word makes me shudder slightly and to come face to face with a tarantula early in the morning, on an empty belly after a bad night was almost too much; one relishes local colour but there are limits … The creature was unbelievable, walking slowly across the track from left to right; the size of a rat – but a rat with eight legs – so huge and hairy and malevolent-looking that when I realised the implications of our tent having been open all night, in this monster's territory, I nearly fainted. On reaching the right-hand verge it had second thoughts, turned and went back to base more quickly, then crouched in the dead leaves with glaring eyes, looking like all the nightmares I have ever had come true … But then, as we hurried past, I suddenly felt non-phobic; precisely *because* this thing was so enormous it seemed more a beast than an insect. (Or, as Rachel would have me call it, an arachnid.) This does not of course mean that I would ever happily share a tent with it.

*

Towards sunset we came upon this wide ledge, close to a summit, which offers lush grazing, a miniature well of bubbling fresh water and scrub firewood – a rare bonus at this altitude. As for the view, it ranks among our Top Three. The eastern snow-peaks are on a level with us, across a narrow gorge too deep for its floor to be visible. Far below, to the north, the river gorge lies at the base of that grey rocky range we crossed yesterday. Beyond are many other lines of peaks and one perfect powder-blue triangle stood out against a blood-orange sunset. For half an hour the western sky was such a glory of changing colours and cloud shapes that we couldn't concentrate on fire-making.

At dusk we were joined by a ragged twelve-year-old shepherd boy. He warned us that tomorrow's *redura* [short cut] is very difficult, then produced from amidst his rags eight boiled potatoes; having watched us climbing for hours this afternoon, he thought we must be very hungry. One remembers such kindness long after the elaborate hospitality of elegant friends has been forgotten. Ten minutes later José's father and small sister arrived to pay their respects; they live in a hovel around the nearest corner. Father endearingly insisted on leaving one of his three large Heinz dogs tethered nearby to guard us against thieves – as though we were his precious animals!

I'm writing outside the tent, lying on smooth turf beneath a full moon. Often I pause to gaze at the nearby snow-peaks, radiantly silver above the ebony abyss of the ravine. It saddens me to think that this is our last Andean full moon – but that's ungrateful. We are fortunate indeed to have lived for so long with so much beauty.

*

Here sentiment prompted us to leave the *carretera* and enter Cuzco by the *ruta de la conquista*, a rough track preserved as it was when Pizarro led his men along it into the conquered capital – to lay the foundations for almost 300 years of colonial rule. At 1.15, as we approached the Plaza de Armas – in Inca days the great Square of Aucaypata, larger than St Mark's Square in Venice and the very heart of the empire – Rachel did a quick sum and announced that the conquistadores had beaten us by a week. They left Cajamarca on 11 August and arrived in Cuzco on 15 November. We left Cajamarca on 9 September and we have arrived in Cuzco on 20 December. The Spaniards' progress was of course slightly slowed by their having to fight four major battles en route. But we had no Indian guides and one member of our expedition was aged nine/ten. I looked past Juana to Rachel in the lead, her short legs covering the last stage of (for her) a 900-mile walk. And then – why deny it? – I felt very proud of her. Especially because there was never once, through hunger, thirst, heat, cold or exhaustion, a whimper of complaint. Rachel would not wish me to say so, but as mini-conquistadores go, she's done pretty well.

*Muddling Through in Madagascar*
(1985)
Madagascar

Malagasy exiles call their capital 'Vohitsara' (City of Beauty) and truly Tana is a wondrous place. It has grown on the sides of a Y-shaped rock-mountain as vegetation grows on an embankment, the houses finding spaces where they could – balancing on ledges, clinging to precipices, tucked between boulders and trees, peering down onto each other's red-tiled roofs. Around the base of this granite rock lie flat paddy-fields, now slightly encroached on by a new district, Ampefiloha, where the alien Hilton towers over jerry-built government ministries that have aped its incongruous functionalism.

*

By eight o'clock it was difficult to squeeze between the stalls and, being taller than the average Malagasy, our eyes were perilously within range of protruding umbrella ribs. Few shoppers were buying in bulk and Rachel noted that those few had the air and apparel of servants from rich households. The Friday Zoma is, it seems, as much a social occasion as a shopping expedition. And for the *vazaha* [foreigner] it is total immersion in Tana life. Every sense is engaged – by a swirl of unfamiliar smells; by the bold colours of exotic merchandise and tribal fashions; by the musical surging of the Malagasy language as buyers and sellers haggle, discuss, advise, tease, condemn, laugh, protest; by the textures of home-spun silk *lambas*, scaley tree-barks, dried shreds of animal skins and feathery bunches of freshly picked herbs; by the weird flavours of spicy titbits hot off charcoal and containing God-knows-what.

Suddenly my mind leaped to a typical Western supermarket: neon-lit, sterile, odourless, computerised, TV-guarded, its chemically sprayed fruits and steam-scoured vegetables bred to standardised shapes, sizes and shades, its shelves shiny and bright with slick deceptive packaging, its wan and bored checkout staff scarcely acknowledging the customer's humanity. Surely the Zoma way is better than our way? Is there not a value beyond calculating in the links between producer and consumer, seller and buyer, Nature and Man?

*

A semi-Western lifestyle, such as the French imposed on Malagasy towns, cannot be maintained without a modicum of organised work on the part of the administrators and their staffs. But the Malagasy are amenable only to those outside influences which they deem benign – and which include neither the 'Work Ethic' nor the 'Save and Prosper' ideal, not to mention their decadent child the 'Rat Race'. Many Malagasy seem indifferent to comfort, convenience, cleanliness and efficiency, yet this does not mean that Madagascar is hopelessly corrupt or unable to run itself. The Malagasy have their own set of priorities, among which kindness, good manners, tact, generosity, fortitude of spirit and family loyalty rank high. By our standards their country is at present falling to bits, literally as well as metaphorically. Yet if they can avoid being blackmailed, bullied or otherwise lured into an alliance with either bloc, the Great Red Island may still be in harmony with its ancestral spirits as it enters the twenty-first century. And to the Malagasy this harmony is what matters most of all.

*

Conservation is low on the list of official Malagasy concerns. Repeatedly we got the impression that it is seen as another form of Western exploitation, a leftover from colonialism which brings well-paid *vazaha* experts into the country to lecture the natives on how they should use their meagre resources. If drought or floods have reduced an area's food supplies, why not catch as many lemurs as possible for the pot? If I were the mother of hungry children, would I not urge my husband to hunt anything edible? It is easy to be a committed conservationist on a full belly.

*

Without fluency in the language, and years of study, no outsider could hope to understand the whole *fady* [taboo], *sikidy* [divination], *ody* [charms] conglomerate. ... If we did give offence this would be no trivial matter. The whole terrified community would feel obliged to organise expensive and inconvenient rituals in an attempt to undo the damage.

It helps to enquire about particular local taboos. In the Ankaratra we might have caused panic by taking from our rucksacks a tin of ham or sausages, or a pack of salami – not that any of these was available in Tana. The Ankaratra ancestors send crop-destroying hail and thunderstorms in response to pork's polluting presence: a *fady* doubtless inherited from the Vazimba. Imerina's first settlers are said to have been implacable pork-haters and those who worship at their graves, as some still do, must avoid all contact with pigs. A pig-herd's first duty is to keep his charges away from such graves; this is even more important than keeping them out of the precious rice-fields. Elsewhere however pork is much relished by the Malagasy and pigs are among the commonest domestic animals; they even share their owners' homes at night should there happen to be a pig-napper in the area. (There are baffling regional *fady* associated with them, as with all animals and birds; a typical example is the taboo on stub-tails because a pig without a curling tail brings poverty on its owner.)

\*

Winter is also the corpse-turning season and there was much activity around two large tombs, built on scrubland not far off our track out of sight of any dwelling. The men and women thronging around their *razana* paused to gaze at us and a few called friendly greetings. I longed to snoop but good manners prevailed. Although there were no warning-off vibes, it would have been crass to intrude on any stage of the profoundly significant *famadi-hana* ritual.

During these exhumation ceremonies corpses are removed from their tombs, wrapped in new shrouds and often made guests of honour at jolly parties in their descendants' homes, before being returned to the spring-cleaned tombs with gifts of money and alcohol. This custom may startle when first encountered, yet to condemn it as 'morbid' is to miss the point. The Malagasy experience such a vivid sense of unity with the dead that maintaining contact with their corpses seems only natural – a recognition of their being alive and well and very powerful in the *Ankoatra*, 'the Beyond'. This view of physical death as a transition to another form of life, in which one enjoys increased wisdom and power, is not a million metaphysical miles from the Christian concept of unity with God in Heaven and participation in the Beatific Vision. To the Malagasy our apparent forgetting of dead relatives after the funeral, while we concentrate on how to live happily without them, is incomprehensible. Thus they appreciate the Catholic custom of celebrating memorial Masses on death anniversaries, and setting aside one month of the year during which the dead are specially remembered.

\*

This being a volcanic lake the cold clear water is instantly deep; one can dive in from the grassy bank. Between long swims we lay reading and writing for hours in not-too-hot sun on the fringe of a pine forest so far (but for how much longer?) spared the axes of the poor. At intervals two chatty little cowherds came to sit close beside us – dark-skinned and bright-eyed and clad in what seemed to be the ragged remains of nightshirts. They scrutinised with amusement and amazement our white skins and my diary-writing. Hilarity took over when we tried to teach each other how to count up to ten. A fisherman then intervened, under the mistaken impression that they were being a nuisance to us. Soon after they realised that their zebu [type of humped cattle] had wandered too far into the pines and away they scampered, waving their long sticks and yodelling weirdly – evidently a satisfactory method of communicating with zebu, for the animals at once returned to the grass by the water. I thought then how horribly different our encounter would have been in a 'tourist spot' – how these boys would have begged instead of chatting, and whined instead of laughing, and sniggered at our scantily clad bodies instead of stroking my bare white shoulder wonderingly with small black fingers. The distortion of human relationships, rather than the building of Holiday Inns or the sprouting of souvenir stalls, is the single most damaging consequence of Third World tourism. And let no one believe that these children's families would be better off if Antsirabe were 'developed'. They would not. But a lot of already rich Malagasy would be even richer.

*

Early on our second morning the whisper of distant water led us through a maze of free-standing cliffs – all grooves and cornices – to the edge of a sheer-sided, winding canyon miles long and 300 feet deep. Ribbons of short green grass accompanied a clear stream along the canyon floor. ... Here and there amidst that lush growth we glimpsed the sparkle of a waterfall. 'That *could* be lemur territory,' I said – and before Rachel had time to reply I saw a flash of white between two trees high on the cliff directly opposite our own.

Exulting, we flung off our rucksacks and settled down with our binoculars, legs dangling over the abyss. Soon we could see five lemurs: but for me there remains an incomparable magic about that first glimpse of white. All were sitting upright on the branches of small trees growing from the precipice; and all were facing east, to catch the first warmth of the sun which moments before had reached their cliff top. The Malagasy believe these sifaka lemurs to be sun-worshippers, because of this morning ritual, and for centuries to kill them was *fady* [taboo]. But alas! the *razana* [ancestors] rescinded this taboo more than a generation ago when a rapidly increasing human population began to cause seasonal food shortages.

Our ecstatic study of the sifaka continued all day, facilitated by their thick, silky, pure white fur (apart from a red-brown 'cap'). They needed no protective colouring before man came to Madagascar. While feeding, resting or grooming they keep their very long furry tails curled between their legs. But when they leap – covering enormous distances with arms outstretched towards their branch-goal, as in a gesture of welcome – those tails plume out like horizontal parachutes. ...

Soon three of our Antandroy sifaka – found only in southern Madagascar – were again visible, just below their cliff top, awaiting the first warmth. I focused on them with affection; in that arid world of warped stone and hostile plants, of utter silence and immobility, those cheerful lively little creatures, in their lush inaccessible oasis, by now seemed close friends. Rachel was perhaps a trifle disappointed that the gorge always separated us, but I craved no greater intimacy. It was good that they slept and played and fed and sun-worshipped beyond the reach of man, as their ancestors had done for countless millennia before man existed.

*

Mario and family insisted on our lunching with them in a small restaurant near the market-place... But during the meal my appetite was taken away by an item of news casually mentioned – the possibility that the multinational company, US Steel, might soon show renewed interest in the extraction of titanium north of

Fort-Dauphin. This element is found in the territory of the mouse-lemur, the smallest of all primates.

None of the Malagasy understood my distress – nor, indeed, did Mario. If US Steel brought dollars and jobs to Fort-Dauphin, and improved roads and communications, was that not the most important thing? Why fuss about a minute animal that no one ever saw, a creature not even useful – like its bigger cousins – as a tasty dish or a tourist attraction?

I said nothing: the argument is too complicated for such an occasion. And ecology is so new as a set of ideas that we are all easily confused, in our different ways, by its psychological spin-offs. Some people, myself included, are more *genuinely* upset by the extinction of a rare reptile, bird, mammal or plant than by news of a major earthquake in Turkey, or a famine in Ethiopia, or a cyclone in Bangladesh. The destruction of something irreplaceable, a product of Nature's genius working over millions upon millions of years, can arouse an angry, helpless grief far more intense than any emotion provoked by human tragedies in far-off places.

This is an uncomfortable fact to think about, let alone discuss. Yet it *is* a fact. And it needs scrutinising. And Madagascar, more than anywhere else I know, forces one to scrutinise it. What is this feeling? Is it sheer muddled sentimentality? Or is it linked to that First World callousness which allows us to support the nuclear arms race and the global arms trade with our taxes and votes while millions throughout the Third World needlessly suffer and die? I used to feel guilty about my own apparently disproportionate reaction to news of yet another ecological atrocity in Amazonia or New Guinea – or Madagascar. But for me Alison Jolly has sufficiently explained and justified that gut-reaction in the concluding words of her superb book [*A World Like Our Own: Man and Nature in Madagascar*]:

'The conservation of nature is not simply the conservation of our past – that which we did not create. It is also the conservation of our future. It is the conservation of all the forms of life that have not yet evolved, and of the understanding that we have not yet achieved, which may one day become mankind's reality.'

\*

On the outskirts of Andalatanosy we crossed a dried-up river bed where a mother and her two small daughters were filling buckets from another 'well', this one a pool some six inches deep so their task was comparatively easy. But the water looked feculent beyond belief – really it was thin mud. One hopes the sediment is allowed to settle before use, since this is our *hotely*'s well. Watching the little girls dipping their gourds I thought how miraculous, to them, would seem the taps we so casually turn on twenty times a day. We say 'flowing like water' to extravagant or careless use of something. It's a phrase I dislike. Anyone who has ever suffered – even once, even a long time ago – from real tongue-swelling thirst can never again take water for granted.

\*

Nobody realised that Minnie [the minibus] was totally out of control until the grinding smash came.

Thus far we'd all been admirably restrained, our protests never exceeding muted exclamations of terror or condemnation. But now we'd had it. Everyone tumbled out, shouting and screaming and abusing the drivers. We were badly shaken, in more senses than one; that crescendo jolt had unmended my ribs. Torches were produced and when we saw what had happened we were even more shaken. Curiously, a sudden silence fell. Minnie's right wheels were suspended in the air over a gully – the drop scarcely nine feet, but onto sharp rocks. She was jammed on the concrete parapet of a bridge – a typical French parapet, just high enough for us to have sliced off the top six inches (as we saw later) by the force of the impact.

\*

My hand/wrist is now so painful that my ribs can't compete. ... Studying it, Rachel...said, 'You *must* go to a doctor!' So I did, with a Malagasy interpreter and private misgivings. Why should one expect Malagasy hospitals to be any more efficient than Madagascar's other postcolonial institutions? But I at least might be able to get hold of some painkiller less deleterious than hooch.

The doctor sat white-coated behind a fine wide desk – a self-important young man, slim and trim and dictatorial. My interpreter pointed out that the cut [deep gash to the bone] had healed well and never been infected, that the burns were to be regarded as an unfortunate ancillary misfortune, but that the pain was severe, persistent and might have been caused by a sprain. The doctor examined the cut, felt my wrist, nodded knowingly and wrote out a prescription for antibiotics. He then summoned a nurse, gave her instructions and despatched me to have the wound 'dressed'.

My interpreter was not allowed into the small cramped untidy treatment-room where another nurse was sitting cross-legged on a stool eating a sticky bun. The waste bins were overflowing and a Geiger-counter for calculating bacteria would have gone off the scale. After a moment's consultation the bun-eater wiped her hands down the sides of her uniform, picked a sharp instrument out of a bowl of cold water and before I had registered her purpose was *reopening* the closed wound. I began to protest – then gave up. Fatalism took over; it is one of my strongest characteristics. The bun-eater was very gentle and, surgically speaking, skilful; the pain she caused was nothing to what I'm now used to. She made soothing noises as she worked away, while her colleague stood by patting my shoulder. Then the bun-eater stood back and surveyed her achievement, looking puzzled. I gazed gloomily at that bone that I hadn't expected to ever see again. There was of course no trace of pus or any foreign matter. The bun-eater shook her head, laughed, dabbed some purple lotion on the new wound and rebandaged it. I thanked her, went to the office to pay the bill, refused to use the prescription for antibiotics and tried unsuccessfully to buy pain-killers – the supply had run out five months ago.

Back in our room I lay down, with my left hand up on the bed-head, and gave my ribs a chance to begin their re-mending before we take the train to Tana tomorrow morning. I'm sorry if this sounds racist, but in Tana I'm looking for a *French* doctor. Madagascar may have no man-eating beasts or poisonous snakes, but judging by results it's the most dangerous country I've ever travelled in.

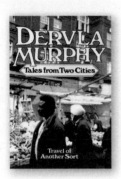

*Tales from Two Cities* (1987)
Bradford & Birmingham, England

I awoke before dawn and for an instant fancied myself back on the Indian subcontinent. Small sounds, like fleeting scents, can have powerful associations; and a yard or so from my head, on the other side of the wall, a woman (or child) was rhythmically pounding spices. ...

I drew the curtains on a reluctant dawn: cold grey light seeped through low clouds. The squally north wind carried a red and blue sliced-pan [bread] wrapper past my window; it swooped and soared like a stringless kite, trapped in the narrow area between my row of back-to-backs and the row opposite – twenty yards away, beyond a rough wall of concrete blocks. Some houses had been expanded by the addition of attic rooms and brightly painted dormer windows broke the symmetry of a long dark line of slate roofs.

Eager to explore, I hastened out. A cheerful milkman greeted me, then asked a question. He repeated it twice but to his huge amusement I couldn't understand a word he said. It seemed my local language problems would not be confined to the Browns; West Yorkshire's accents are attractive, but you do have to work hard at some of them.

Beyond the covered passage (six foot six inches wide and eight foot high, in obedience to an 1860 bye-law) I was on the dog-shitty pavement, surrounded by frozen mounds of soiled snow and looking up a long steep street of back-to-backs in various states of disrepair.

Opposite my pad a dozen new brick bungalows for OAPs overlooked a humpy patch of wasteland. Nearby, at the foot of the hill, several houses had recently been demolished and the quarter acre of rubble was strewn with squashed tins, broken bottles, old shoes, battered saucepans, two dead television sets and a stained mattress.

I walked uphill – as yet no one else was astir – pausing occasionally to look down at an uninspiring cityscape of gawky mill-chimneys dominating colossal factories and warehouses, the majority now disused. On the far side of the valley a sprawl of buildings, old and new, covered the lower slopes of a long, high ridge. Above them were snow-flecked fields; Bradford is a small city.

*

### A Note on Terminology

Within days of arriving in Bradford I realised that terminology is the first and not the lowest hurdle for any writer on race relations in Britain. If you are 'politically aware' there is of course no problem; everyone who is not White is Black, matter-a-damn if they are magnolia-coloured Vietnamese or fairer-than-Italian Pakistanis with green eyes and brown hair. But writers are by nature distrustful of usages that tend to muffle thought or conceal facts. In Britain there is quite enough ignorance and confusion about Browns and Blacks without increasing it by applying the same label to two totally different branches of the human race. Moreover, most Asians are proud of their distinctive cultures and resent being described as 'Blacks'.

Several anti-racists warned me that if I did not use 'Black' as a political statement I would be signalling a lack of support for their cause. Since I do not see myself as an anti-racist warrior, this left me unmoved. However, my choice of 'Black' to describe West Indians is itself imprecise. Because of genetic contributions from Europe, and to a lesser extent from India and China, most West Indians are not African black. Yet among the younger generation many who are almost white choose to be described as Black – this is *their* choice, which celebrates the fact that the Caribbean's dominant genes are *African*.

In Britain, 'Asian' is popularly used to describe Indians, Pakistanis and Bangladeshis. Yet many other Asians are also present in varying numbers – for example, there are some 122,000 Chinese, as compared to 99,000 Bangladeshis. Therefore I refer to people from the Indian subcontinent as 'Browns', while aware that this too is imprecise because they range in colour from white Pathans to black Madrassis. Finally, I was told that 'immigrants' can no longer be used, since by now some 50 per cent of Britain's Black and Brown communities are British-born.

\*

I deeply respect Islam for its influence on the character and behaviour of sincere believers. (When all the theological and metaphysical arguments are over, taming human nature is, as far as I can see, the main function of the world's great religions.)

In Bradford, as elsewhere in Britain, most Muslim boys (and some little girls) go regularly to their mosque school to learn the Qur'an by rote. Whites often comment 'Poor kids! Never given time to play or watch telly – bullied off to sit on the ground learning mumbo-jumbo!' Such remarks make one question the efficacy of multi-faith RE programmes. How do you convey to those Whites who have completely lost touch with the Christian roots of their own civilisation that for devout Muslims (or Hindus or Sikhs) life really does have a spiritual dimension? How do you explain to people who are indifferent to all forms of religion that Islam is the pivot of a believing Muslim's daily existence? It is not a separate mental area that you move into when you go to the mosque but a way of being, just as Catholicism still is for many in Ireland, especially among the older generation. The Mirpuris' [from the Mirpur District of Kashmir, Pakistan] religion provides a steadying sense of communal identity and pride, useful in times of adversity or stress and extremely important when individuals feel rejected, despised or threatened. There is a popular theory that Browns would make better citizens (i.e. more British-like and therefore better) if they gave up all that 'mumbo-jumbo'. People seem not to know that at mosque schools children are also taught the code of conduct by which, as good Muslims, they are expected to live. In Britain their *maulanas* [Muslim scholars] lay special emphasis on the immorality of hooliganism, vandalism, mugging, theft, laziness at work. To suggest that the abandonment of this training would make them 'better citizens' is ignorant nonsense of a particularly irritating kind.

\*

As a newcomer to England's North I was awed by the sheer size of mills, warehouses, furnaces, pit-heads – and by the soaring factory chimneys, some quite beautiful but few still smoking. The End-of-an-Age aura is overwhelming. Everyone knows that whatever the future may hold there cannot be a revival of traditional industries; if no one wants your steel or your woollen goods you can't go on producing them. However, this grimly simple fact is not always accepted by redundant workers who feel both personally devalued by unemployment and conscious of the whole framework of their community having been smashed.

On the return home from Sheffield a fifty-eight-year-old man seated himself beside me; he was clutching a large parcel and anxious to talk. A redundant steel-worker, he had been to his first grandson's christening. Traditionally, in Sheffield, the paternal grandfather tears a corner off his own apprenticeship papers and, after the baptism, puts it into the baby boy's tiny fist. His son, also recently made redundant, wanted him to follow this tradition but he refused. 'I told him – "That was a custom that meant something, it wasn't like kissing under the mistletoe. Now it means nothing and we mustn't pretend. This baby has to fit into a new world, we can't help him the way we always did before."' He unwrapped his parcel – it was the family Bible – and showed me the entries, going back 208 years, of the generations of his family who had worked in the steel-mills of Sheffield. 'We were craftsmen, all of us,' he said.

'You wouldn't last long working furnaces and tempering blades if you didn't know what you were doing.' Together we gazed silently at those pages of carefully inscribed names and I realised that my companion was very close to tears. So was I.

\*

Invitations into Mirpuri homes did not come readily; patience was needed. … Most of the homes I visited were well kept, sparsely though adequately furnished and luxury-free – apart from the now obligatory television set, video machine and transistor-cum-tape recorder. A few elderly women eventually let their hair down with the aid of a granddaughter interpreter, and spoke wistfully of the good old pre-television days when their husbands took them out, suitably veiled, to see Asian films at the Mirpuri-owned cinema. This was always a monthly treat and given an indulgent husband could be weekly. Now many of that generation never go out.

The purdah-quarter is usually the back room of a terrace house, which may also be the kitchen – or the living-room if a kitchen extension has been built on. In back-to-backs the situation is more complicated and wives may have to retreat to the bedroom when non-kinsmen call. The front parlour is reserved for menfolk and their visitors, in winter frequently to be seen sitting wrapped in blankets before a puny one-bar electric fire while their women (who are not in every respect oppressed) enjoy sub-tropical heat from the main stove in the *zenana* [women's part of the house]. As in their villages, the wife serves her husband, and any guests he may have, and then waits to eat with the children when he has finished – not before. Even in a few households where the husband seemed outwardly westernised, meals were never family affairs. When a husband rather than a wife had invited me to eat I was treated as an honorary male and fed in the front parlour. The families on my visiting list varied in the strictness of their purdah-observance. In some homes pre-puberty daughters, or sons of any age, brought the food from the kitchen to non-related male visitors; in others the wife did appear, her head always covered, and laid the dishes on a low table before silently and swiftly withdrawing, leaving the host to serve his guests. I was relieved to note that in Bradford, as in Pakistan, not a few husbands – when unprotected by the presence of sons or other males – were well and truly henpecked within the privacy of their homes.

*

Every day heightened my awareness of the extent and intensity of local animosity towards 'them'. If I were to extract from my Bradford diary all the anti-Brown remarks I chanced to hear, and all the impassioned accusations I listened to, those passages alone would add up to a stout volume. But is all this true 'racialism' in the dictionary sense – 'belief in the superiority of a particular race'? Or might it be more accurate to describe it, in many cases, as 'xenophobia' – 'a morbid dislike of foreigners'? It can often seem that working class Whites are reacting against Browns and Blacks, as they once reacted against the Irish, because they are *different* – and now, increasingly, are seen as threatening competitors on the schooling, employment and housing schemes. … There is some jealousy too, interwoven with *inferiority* feelings because so many Browns have done so well in their little businesses (a few of which by now have become quite big businesses), though starting from the same base of economic disadvantage as their White neighbours. All these negative emotions are understandable, though it is hard on one's tender liberal sensibilities to have to listen to so much violently expressed hatred every day of the week for months on end.

Word-juggling with 'xenophobia', 'ethnocentricity' and 'racialism' may seem a mere game for onlookers, irrelevant and indeed irritating to the victims of prejudice. But not so. The future of Britain's ethnic minorities depends on which of these reactions to outsiders is in fact predominant.

*

The current notion that racialists dislike coloured people and anti-racists like them has added to the confusion of the race relations debate. Liking or disliking is not the issue. I like my dog, my cats and even my goats much more than I like most human beings. However, my relations with them are quintessentially different from my relations with even the least likeable representatives of my own species. Yet in Britain now it often seems that Whites (anti-racists no less than racists) are so 'Race Aware' that they relate to ethnic minorities almost as though they belong to a different species, who deserve better or worse treatment (depending on which camp you're in) because 'they're not like us'. This is the attitude which most travellers don't have. They recognise but are not uptight about the barriers that do exist between people of different colours, creeds and cultures. They know that these barriers must be negotiated, that the differences are important. But they also know that whether we are vegetarians or will only eat halal meat, whether we insist on arranged marriages or don't bother marrying, whether we believe in one god or eight thousand gods or no god – none of these differences is significant beside our common humanity. Some will say, "That's pie in the sky!" Yet it is not an ideal to be striven for; it is an objective biological and psychological fact. And, if clearly perceived, it should make us all much more laid back about race relations: which could only do good. The cultivation of 'Race Awareness' tends to blur 'Humanity Awareness' – to obscure the simple, central and immutable reality that we are all human beings.

\*

My first fortnight in Handsworth [Birmingham] was well spent lodging in a Black-run hostel for the homeless. Most of those young people had big problems. At best they were estranged from their families, at worst just out of prison; in between they had experienced every other sort of misfortune you could think of – and a few you couldn't. With three exceptions they were disinclined to communicate with the White woman who had so inexplicably

pitched up in their midst. Nor indeed did they communicate much
with each other. That worried me, when I pretended to long for
telly and joined them in their large, bleak sitting room – minimally
furnished with uncomfortable chairs, its pale green walls bare, its
plastic-tiled floor chilly. The majority looked withdrawn, apathetic,
mistrustful, hurt. Already life had defeated them; perhaps they
were defeated the day they were born. They dreadfully contradicted
the stereotype of ebullient, extrovert, noisy young Blacks.

*

Birmingham's post-war reincarnation has obscured its interesting
past. The newcomer, arriving at New Street station, can only feel
shock/horror. That vast, ill-lit, grimy, low-ceilinged subterranean
cavern seems to have been modelled on a Victorian coal-mine.
Ascending to daylight via several escalators, one emerges into
Britain's second city hoping for better things. But one doesn't find
them. When Birmingham was redesigned in the 1960s it boasted
of being 'The Car City' and so it is. If cars could speak they would
no doubt tell us how much they enjoy scorching along the myriad
wide motorways that make most of the city unliveable in for anyone
who wants to stay even half-sane. Those roads go around and over
and under the most repellent conglomeration of architectural
aberrations I have ever seen concentrated in a city centre. To
survey Birmingham from the top of a double-decker bus induces
incredulity; it seems all this ghastliness can't be *true*…When you
look up the sky is blanked out by brash metallic circular towers
and immense angular blocks of post-war commercial buildings,
interspersed with the decaying corpses of Victorian industrial
triumphs. Weirdly coiling concrete car-parks also loom overhead;
and when you look down hundreds more cars are parked in sinister
shadowy areas between monstrous concrete struts upholding the
motorways. The buses swing round and round in circles amidst a
crazy confusion of other roads – above, below, beside – and the
effect of so much traffic speeding on various levels in different

directions is curiously menacing. One feels the heart and soul have been torn out of Birmingham (presuming it ever had either) and a few relics of its nineteenth century splendour – like the Corinthian Town Hall – are so overwhelmed by the surrounding ugliness that they seem to accentuate rather than relieve it.

*

When new to Handsworth, it hurt me to be hated, despised, feared and suspected by many of my neighbours. At first I tended to react with confused, almost small-child indignation – This isn't *fair*! I'm *me*, an *individual*, someone who wants to listen to their point of view! Why must they treat me like an enemy just because of the colour of my skin? Just because I'm White! But I soon turned that around. Why do so many Whites admit that if a Black man overtakes or approaches them on a quiet street they tense up, half-expecting to be mugged? Because most Whites don't think of Blacks as *individuals*...

To a Heathfield Road resident, 'The Blacks' very quickly comes to seem meaningless. *Which* Blacks? The devoutly busy Pentecostalists, mapping a route to Heaven? The employed younger generation, drinking moderately with White and Brown friends in the Grey Dove? The friendly older generation, drinking immoderately in seedier pubs because they have lost their jobs and cannot resign themselves to the boredom and indignity of life on the dole while their wives are still working? The tiny minority of successful big businessmen who are never seen in Handsworth and if they were would probably be pelted with half-bricks? The defiant, despairing younger generation who have never had a job and use gradations of Rastafarianism to disguise their shame and express their anger? The genuine Marcus Garvey militants, who scorn ganja-smoking Rasta drop-outs and both practise and preach constructive 'Self-Help' and not-so-constructive anti-Whiteness? The middle-class intellectual feminists who half-want to be on the militants' side but are rejected by them? The many hopeless young who have allied themselves with no group or cult but live quietly and sadly in pads or squats, tacitly admitting defeat at the age of twenty?

Blacks, like Whites, come in all shapes and sizes; it would be odd if they did not but as a minority they seem even more tragically disunited than the Brown communities.

\*

Suspicion of my real purpose was, naturally, at its most intense in the Villa Cross pub – undisputed Rasta territory and at that time Handsworth's (perhaps Birmingham's) main ganja-dealing centre. Within days of my arrival in Handsworth, several people of all colours warned me never to attempt to drink there. ... I cannot say how I might have reacted to my neighbours' warnings had the Villa Cross not been my geographical 'local', two minutes' walk across the road from my pad and therefore the pub I would in any case have used most regularly, irrespective of its Rasta ethos. That greatly interested me, but I was not going there merely to 'study the scene'. As a resident of No. 45 Heathfield Road the Rastas were my neighbours, their local was my local and I felt *entitled* to drink at the Villa Cross. To have avoided it would have seemed cowardly; in such situations one instinctively resists intimidation. ...

No-one had specified what form Rasta harassment might take and I felt mildly apprehensive on first approaching my local at 8pm one damp, chilly June evening. ... It was a Wednesday evening and the enormous, high-ceilinged bar was only half-full but still redolent of ganja and vibrating with reggae. In its Edwardian youth the Villa Cross must have been quite magnificent. Standing at the semicircular mahogany counter, I could feel everyone's attention concentrated on the unescorted stranger. ... I took my pint to a corner seat between two high, wide windows, one facing Lozells Road, the other overlooking the forecourt and Villa Road. ... A large Black and White group in the opposite corner studied me briefly but intently, before forming themselves into a tight circle for trading purposes. I got out my jotter and settled to my usual evening task of note-taking. All the tables were badly knife-scarred: a result of the cutting of countless bars of cannabis resin. Business was slow that evening; in Handsworth there is very little money around by Wednesday and most of the action was centred on the pool-table. I left after about an hour, feeling elated. My reception could scarcely be described as cordial, but neither had there been any harassment. I assumed that no-one had offered me ganja because of my advanced years.

The atmosphere was different on my next visit, two days later. ... I had to queue at the crowded bar and there was much excitement in the air. Single men and pairs of men were closely watching the door (and each other), awaiting their weekly customers. Already, at 7.30, the air reeked of hash. Two pallid but bouncy little White boys, aged 9 or 10, were doing a roaring trade fetching supper from nearby Take-Aways for hungry drinkers/smokers. Several Rastas were dancing solo around the floor, shaking their locks and shouting as they leaped in the air. Three teenage prostitutes were being wanton with Black youths in 'my' corner, but there was a vacant seat between them and a short-haired dealer. He was having trouble with his tiny silver ganja-scales and paid no attention to me when I sat beside him.

Placing my pint amidst a clutter of bottles, I took a tin of ten mini-cigars from my shoulder-bag and left it on the table while rummaging for my jotter and pen. Then I became aware that half a dozen Rastas had gathered around the table and were staring down at me saying nothing. Their united, silent, unsmiling concentration was absurdly unnerving. I reached out for my cigars, intending to offer them round by way of breaking what felt uncommonly like a spell. But one of the men quickly seized them and shared them among his friends before throwing the empty tin to the ground near my feet with an extraordinarily eloquent gesture of contempt. It seemed my first visit had been in effect a surprise attack and no-one then present had known what to do about it. But now the heat was on. ...

Next morning I had an inspiration, took a bus to the city centre and was fortunate enough to find one paperback copy of my own book on Ethiopia. … Even among pseudo-Rastas, there is a powerful mystique about the word 'Ethiopia' – a mystique which long predates the founding of Rastafarianism in 1930. …

To this day many Rastas are ignorant of Ethiopia's geographical location, but this does not diminish the 'power of the word'. Therefore when my book was observed beside my pint on the bar many guards were lowered and many questions asked. Soon the news was spreading that I, personally, had lived and travelled in Ethiopia during the Emperor's reign. Then it emerged that I had also been the guest and protégée of one of Haile Selassie's granddaughters – after which my Villa Cross tribulations were over. The Rastafarians, after all, believe Haile Selassie to have been not a mere prophet like Mohammed but God himself. And you can hardly name-drop more effectively than by recalling your friendship with God's granddaughter and producing photographs to prove it.

After that I was accepted as a regular. Not as a friend (apart from four young men), but as a tolerable acquaintance who was certainly not a police informer and could even to some extent be trusted. I never asked questions about anything, yet people talked more and more openly as the weeks passed, telling me when Red Leb was scarce, Pakistani Black plentiful or a new consignment of Moroccan Kief expected. Prices too were discussed in my hearing, and worried suspicions about spiked resin – but never, of course, sources.

\*

A Black Pentecostalist friend…told me of her brother Daniel's experience as a police victim. When aged nineteen, he travelled to a Birmingham soccer match with his Youth Club, led by a White teacher…Walking down Digbeth, Daniel fell behind to buy an ice-cream and was set upon by five White youths. The police quickly arrived, pulled the Whites off Daniel and charged *him* with causing a breach of the peace – on such occasions this is a common police reaction. In court two police witnesses contradicted each other's evidence. When Daniel's lawyer asked how the police knew who had started the fight, one PC replied, 'He was the only Black there.' Several solid citizens, including White and Black clergymen, testified to Daniel's good character. Yet he was fined £400 and when his appeal had been quashed he had to pay an extra £200 in costs – presumably to teach Blacks *not* to appeal.

[Such] examples of police misconduct are so 'typical' that similar incidents fill pages of my journal. ...Those experiences generate the enraged feeling that just because you're *Black* you're perceived as *bad* and so *your* word will never be accepted against the word of a policeman.

*

People find it quite hard to believe that the Soho Road – Handsworth's 'High Street' – is in Europe. It was my favourite Birmingham shopping street and at its liveliest and most colourful on Saturdays. On first walking down it I was overcome by nostalgia for the sub-continent. Countless details combine to create the authentic aura of an Indian/Pakistani bazaar – window-wide displays of multi-coloured sweetmeats, carefully built into pyramids; lengths of richly shimmering materials and elegant saris and *shalwar-kameez* (worn by dummies with the palest of pale brown skins); toy shops crammed with cheap plastic junk; jewellers' windows glittering with gold bracelets and anklets; tantalising curry aromas; greengrocers stocking what looked and smelt like every known fruit, vegetable and herb. I even saw bulls' hearts, for the first time since leaving Coorg – I sentimentally bought one, though this odd fruit is an acquired taste which I have never really acquired. My euphoria was such that on entering a Sikh-run pub I blurted out to an elderly White man at the bar, 'This is a fabulous street! It's like being in India!' The man looked at me sourly and said, 'Bloody right it is – who'd think that this was Chamberlain's city?' I wondered then if perhaps there is something wrong with my territorial instinct; it would delight me to have a Soho Road equivalent in an Irish city.

*

The next ninety minutes felt so weirdly unreal I could scarcely believe it was all happening. During that extraordinary interlude I watched the Have-nots running riot, systematically looting and burning shops without any apparent risk of police intervention. Although started by Blacks, this was certainly no *race*-riot. Within a quarter of an hour many Browns and Whites had zestfully joined in the plundering, some hurrying from nearby areas when the local media news-flashed: RIOTING IN HANDSWORTH! Prim and proper White women from little terrace houses off the Lozells Road – houses with sparkling windows and neatly pruned roses in their front garden patches – came rushing to load up prams, baby-buggies and wheelbarrows. Motor-vans and car boots were being frenziedly stuffed with goodies. And the Blacks were in a sharing mood. I saw many come leaping out of smashed shop windows to throw armfuls of loot on the street – or *lay* it on the street in cases of delicate electronic equipment – while inviting all and sundry to help themselves. It was quite clear at this early stage that many looters regarded the operation as something more than a conventional criminal exercise in 'gain for me'. I have a most vivid memory of one elated Black youth, his face copper-coloured in the glow of flames, inviting a White woman to choose from his pile of shoe-boxes – while the emptied shoe shop blazed in the background. 'What do you need?' he asked her – shouting above the roar of the new fire. Has anyone seriously heeded this aspect of Handsworth's riot – '*What do you need?*' – and recognised its implications for the future?

Another memory is of laughing looters being cheered by onlookers as they pushed heaped supermarket trolleys down the middle of the road between high sheets of flame: I couldn't have believed those trolleys were capable of such speed. The atmosphere was totally free of any threat of interpersonal violence, racial or otherwise; it was not even a quarrelsome – far less a 'murderous' – night. Aggro was confined to the Rasta versus fuzz battle, still in progress outside the Villa Cross. There was of course a slight risk of injury from the combustible environment as car-engines, petrol-pumps and domestic gas-cylinders in the burning buildings exploded – and some of the buildings themselves began to collapse. Yet during those chaotic twelve hours only *seven* civilians were injured: a figure which tells more about the nature of the riot than any number of 'Reports'.

To compound the unreality one pub – the Lozells Arms – stayed open while the shops all around it were going up in flames. Outside the door stood a group of Black, White and Brown men, calmly swigging their pints and viewing the riot as though it were some form of street entertainment. Another pint of cider was just what I needed but had not, in the circumstances, expected to find. Half a dozen customers still sat in the pub; as the barman drew my pint I suggested that it might be time to clear the place. Then I joined the drinkers on the pavement.

In a bizarre way the feeling was of a perverted lunatic carnival rather than a riot. But the heat was intense; now all the multi-racial looters looked the same copper colour in the glow of towering flames. And still more shops, having been swiftly stripped of their stock, were being set alight with manic glee. Providentially the evening was windless. One felt sick with fear to think of the consequences should a breeze spring up and take the flames down the many little nearby streets of crowded houses. ...

By ten o'clock there wasn't much left of the Lozells shopping area; some £16 million worth of property was burning. In harrowing contrast to the carnival spirit of the looters was the dazed, incredulous grief of the traders – the majority Brown. Most were as yet too shocked to be angry; rage came later. At the end of Lozells Road I found a group sitting on the edge of the pavement near an expanse of wasteland, opposite their burning premises, weeping like little children. An elderly Pakistani man stood alone, slightly apart from the rest, sobbing and repeatedly mopping his tears with his shirt-sleeve. A passing Black youth – empty-handed – paused and crossed the road to put an arm around the trader's shoulder. Then he offered him a cigarette and a moment later they walked away together, round the corner into Wheeler Street – where shortly before I had seen the Midland Bank being ransacked. ...

At about 7 a.m. I was devastated to hear that firemen had found two bodies in the Post Office. The Moledina brothers had been immensely kind and helpful to me – among the most welcoming Browns in Handsworth when I was a newcomer.

That was a most dreadful dawn, made inexpressibly more so by groups of jubilant Blacks celebrating their 'achievement' – their destruction of an area of Babylon – by singing and dancing in the streets while dazed Brown traders (many of whom live elsewhere) arrived to face the negation of decades of hard work and sobbed in each other's arms. At that stage it felt very like a Black versus Brown race-riot. One could understand why so much media instant-comment misinterpreted it as such, yet there had been many Brown looters and some of the Lozells Road few Black business premises were also destroyed. ...

After that it felt like time for a pint. I hurried through back streets – littered with half-bricks and broken glass – to a Soho Road pub that was being used by the national and international media as their Handsworth base-camp. At 2.15 a.m. I stumbled in, speechless (I thought) with exhaustion, my jacket reeking of human shit picked up behind the nettles. As I took it off by the door I was converged upon by five gentlemen of the press, all stylishly clad in sweaters, silk cravats, neatly pressed slacks – and all eagerly asking, 'What's going on out there?'

I had then been in action almost continuously for thirty-two hours and something snapped. 'You fucking lazy bastards!' I snarled. 'You only have to walk fifty yards from here to find out for yourselves!' Then I turned my back and ordered my pint, feeling rather self-scandalised. This was the first time in my life I had ever used the word 'fucking', which just shows how corrupting riots are. Or perhaps it was simply the baneful cumulative effect of eight months' exposure to inner-city speech.

*

Yet as I read the (Dear) report, and thought of all the individuals I knew who had been involved in that truly barbarous attack on the police, I found myself questioning the word 'crime'. It somehow seems inadequate for the events of 9 September. For the events of the following day and night, yes. But the riot itself was more and less than 'crime'. More because it was, in intent and execution, a savage declaration of war. Less because it was, in inspiration and impetus, a reckless gesture of desperation. There is no excuse, in the general view, for such behaviour. But on what is that view based? On security, comfort, prospects, the esteem of our neighbours – *some* position in the world, whether cabinet minister or office cleaner. You take a different view if you have nothing and are seen to be nothing – or worse than nothing. Then 'the consensus values of society' are, quite simply, meaningless.

\*

There can be no neat-and-tidy ending to a book of this sort. (In fact there may be *no* ending, for the author. After writing *A Place Apart* I became more involved in the problems of Northern Ireland than I ever was while collecting my material.) At the end of a travel book you pick up the atlas and think about the next journey. At the end of a book about people's unhappiness, the feeling is very different. You cannot put down your pen and walk away from it all. There is nothing much to be done. But you still want to hang in there, with the friends you've made.

## *Cameroon with Egbert* (1989)
## Cameroon

Dreadful things can happen to rucksacks on aeroplanes and at Heathrow we had packed ours in a tough orange survival-bag, together with bit and bridle, riding-hat and picket. The picket had been specially designed and made for this trek by a young welder friend who knows a lot about horses – but not enough, as we were to discover, about Africa. It was a formidable object: two feet long, heavy and thick, with a wide loop on top, a four-inch half-bar and foot-long swivel-chain two-thirds of the way down and a very sharp point. To anyone unfamiliar with pickets (99 per cent of most modern populations) it must have looked like a weapon bought in some kinky Martial Arts shop.

Our sack was the last item to be disgorged. As we marched out to the customs area – Murphy Junior wearing a hard hat and a bridle round her neck, Murphy Senior grasping the picket – a frisson of alarm went through the assembled bureaucrats and jostling porters. We might have been arrested then and there – instead of much later – but for Rose's friend. Bernard had taken the precaution of bringing with him a senior police officer who quickly surmounted, on our behalf, the numerous hurdles of a Third World airport. Yet even a police escort did not deter one customs officer – while our protector was coping with 'health' [dealing with health-related airport bureaucrats] – from attempting to appropriate a tin of mini-cigars.

'For me!' he exclaimed gleefully, delving into my hand luggage and grabbing a tin.

'*Not* for you!' I contradicted, with a wave of the picket.

'I am joking!' he gasped, dropping the tin and backing away. I began to see that this picket might have secondary uses.

*

Now it was my turn to display some expertise. Danieli tested our sacks and conveyed approval of the weight distribution. Egbert continued to stand statue-still while the sacks were held up and I roped them to the saddle's central hoop – with real rope, brought from London. Our five-litre water-bottle was tied to one of the smaller front hoops and our two-litre bottle plus the heavy picket to the other. Two multicoloured raffia shoulder-bags, bought nine years previously in Morelia market in Mexico, were draped over the pommel to hold maps, camera, salt, rain-capes and food for the road. When Egbert's bright blue bucket, the smoke-blackened kettle and pot and our purple mugs had been tied on at various strategic places, with strong boot-laces, the ensemble looked decidedly tinkerish (sic). But it seemed secure enough and Egbert showed no signs of disapproval.

*

Certain interludes seem quite separate from the rest of one's life. They have the simple perfection of a Tang lyric, a Chopin *étude*, an Inuit carving. And they do not drift away, becoming blurred by time; mysteriously they continue to give sustenance. For me that first day of our trek was one such interlude. I experienced pure happiness – something quite different from the everyday underlying contentment which is my fortunate lot.

Following Rachel and Egbert down the red earth track from Doi's compound, life seemed wondrously simple. The sun shone warm, the breeze blew cool, Mount Ocu beckoned. My daughter had become a congenial adult, our horse was charming and amenable, the Big Bad World (including my latest troublesome typescript) could be forgotten. Time was meaningless; it didn't matter when we reached where – or, indeed, if we ever reached it. Should there be no habitation in sight, our tent would go up at sunset. Should we feel like lingering for a few days here or there, or turning east instead of west, why not? Uncomplicated months stretched ahead, or so I then imagined. Hundreds of miles of glorious unknown territory also stretched ahead, populated by warm-hearted people not condemned to hopeless poverty. With difficulty I overcame an impulse to skip, instead of walking.

\*

The first two hours, through flat, dull farmland, were cloudy and just tolerable. In the hamlet of Ngu we enjoyed an eccentric breakfast of avocadoes, salt and beer; to my secret relief, neither Top nor Coke was available. But beer for breakfast, when it's 95°F in the shade and there isn't any shade, must be condemned as irresponsible and probably contributed to our sorry noon state. However, at 8 a.m. Ngu's off-licence was already quite crowded with jolly male drinkers who didn't have to exert themselves during the heat of the day.

The usual juvenile swarm gathered to watch us but soon grew bored and resumed their play. As so often, this consisted of impromptu dancing to the music (surprisingly sweet) of instruments ingeniously contrived from old tins, scraps of wood, lengths of string, bits of wire. From the day Cameroonians can toddle, making music and dancing comes as naturally as breathing. Why do some British Blacks, and White anti-racists, scream 'Stereotyping!' if one refers to the Africans' inborn sense of rhythm? Pretending that Africans are not exceptionally gifted in this respect is like pretending they have straight hair.

\*

Now I always recall Mr Eyobo, when Whites assert that Christianity is unsuited to Africa. Perhaps what Whites have made of it doesn't transplant well. Christianity didn't start in Europe. We adopted it and fashioned it into a many-branched religion to suit our own cultural/intellectual/national inheritances, shedding much blood in the process. And then, characteristically, we pronounced that ours was the *real* Christianity. Africans have for a few generations been in the process of refashioning it to suit *their* inheritance. And what right have we to judge that Black Christianity is less 'real' than the White version?

I often wondered about the beliefs of people we passed in the bush. We noticed many charms in the fields: bones and palm-fronds hanging over junctions on the pathways, little archways of saplings erected between fields, bundles of feathers and leaves secured to rocks with lengths of vine, plaits of straw tied to bamboo poles. Undoubtedly, despite much mosque- and church-going, many villagers remain close to their 'traditional religion', known in my youth as 'paganism'. Recently, 'paganism' and 'heathenism' have been excluded from civilised vocabularies not only because they offend Westernised Africans but because their heavy connotations of 'irreligious', 'immoral' and 'unenlightened' are grossly misleading. By instinct Africans are profoundly religious, in the sense of not believing that feeble and fallible mankind can fend for itself. They believe in a Creator, one remote all-powerful God, who may best be worshipped through intermediaries – various spirits (*not* thought of as gods) and the living-dead. Those last are family members so recently dead that they can be remembered by someone still alive. Their importance in the traditional scheme of things is incalculable and they are thought to be very much amongst those present – helping, or if necessary punishing, their descendants.

\*

The next few hours had a magical, almost eerie quality: we seemed to be in a fantasy world. Nothing was familiar – fruits, berries, nuts, ferns, fungi, vines, mosses – even the leaves were strangely shaped and hued. The sounds and smells were also new; muted bird calls, though we saw no birds, and an amorphous rustle peculiar to this place as thousands of palm-fronds imperceptibly swayed all around and far above us.

This area gets more than its fair share of rain. The air was pungent with the odours of permanent damp, piquant fungi and who knows what mysterious, powerful herbs – the raw material of medicine-men. Sometimes the path was an almost sheer slope of skiddy mud and we had to help each other up. Sometimes streams racing to the Metchum formed miniature waterfalls, leaping from ledge to ledge. Occasionally the path wound level around outcrops of rock, from which massive webs of roots and vines hung like man-traps; on these stretches the black liquid mud was inches deep. Once this path must have been a main route, hence the bridge. Now it seemed little used; on the southern side of the range a circuitous motor-track links Mukuru with the ring-road. We met only one man – not in a sociable mood – carrying a spear and followed by four hunting-dogs wearing belled collars.

\*

One morning was spent sitting on the verandah of a congenial senior officer named Basil. ... Basil's two-and-a-half-year-old daughter sat on my lap reading aloud, unaided, from her Ladybird book – one young Cameroonian who is unlikely to have academic problems.

Remarkably, that Ladybird Reader and the We gendarme's eccentric Nigerian dictionary were the *only* two books we saw in Cameroon, outside of the cities – and this despite our having stayed in several teachers' homes. Nor did we once see, in the possession of a Cameroonian any newspaper however rudimentary (most Cameroonian newspapers are very rudimentary), or any pamphlet, magazine or even comic. For all practical purposes rural Cameroon remains a pre-literate society, though a percentage of the younger generation is able, after a fashion, to read and write. This must partly explain the frequency with which Mungo Park's comments could be applied to our own experiences and observations, almost two hundred years later. On one level those two centuries have utterly transformed Africa, on another level they have made astonishingly little difference. The continent's veneer of modernity – national airlines and universities, architecturally pretentious capital cities, armed forces equipped with the latest weaponry and jet-fighters – can cause people to forget that many Africans are no better informed, and have no wider a world-view, than their pre-colonial ancestors. Certainly we over-estimate the educational potential of the ubiquitous transistor radio. Our young friend under the tree by Lake Wum cherished his trannie but it had manifestly failed to enhance his knowledge of the outside world. For the illiterate (or semi-literate), it is not educational to listen to good news reports on China's changing political scene, or astute analyses of conflicts in Central America or the Middle East, or panel discussions on the expansion of Japanese industry. Many Cameroonians have not the faintest notion where these places are. They cannot visualise or comprehend things or concepts outside their own experience. They cannot distinguish between a republic and a monarchy, democracy and dictatorship, capitalism and communism, an Arab desert and an American wheat prairie. For us it is hard to grasp the intellectual inflexibility and isolation of a society indifferent to the printed word.

*

For decades Whites have avoided openly discussing the 'mindset' aspects of some African problems. The post-colonial mood was of guilt and repentance and 'taking the blame', but now that taboo is weakening. After a quarter of a century of increasingly shambolic Independence it no longer makes sense to pretend that *all* Africa's problems are 'our fault'. And it helps that the emotionally crucial matter of the slave-trade is beginning to be viewed more dispassionately. Britain's 'greatness' was firmly based on its revolting cruelties and enduring miseries, which are associated with still-familiar names.

Barclays Bank was founded by David and Alexander Barclay on their profits as 'slavers'; Lloyd's first flourished as slave-traders and soon needed bigger premises than a coffee-house; the development of James Watt's steam engine was financed by West Indian slave-owners and traders. Yet Black slave-merchants also benefited ...

Given the viciousness of the slave-trade, good race relations need an admission that both races rode on that gravy-train. Although fuelled by White demand, it could not possibly have rolled without the enthusiastic co-operation of Blacks. From the sixteenth to the nineteenth century, Europeans lacked the military resources and preventative medicines to invade Africa's interior and enslave the estimated eleven million young men and women who were shipped off to plantations. Nor did African merchants have to be bullied or coerced; they knew a profitable line in trades goods when they saw it. They were of course corrupted – dazzled by goodies – but they never had any scruples about selling fellow Africans into slavery. Moreover, if those awaiting shipment on the coast, and costing quite a lot to feed, were not bought because of some unexpected drop in demand, they might be used instead as human sacrifices. Human rights were not a big deal, on any continent, during the centuries under consideration.

*

All along our route we tried to discuss the AIDS threat with our drinking-companions, male and female, and found many touchy on the subject. Some of the worldly-wise (police and army officers, government officials, secondary school teachers) dismissed the 'AIDS from Africa scare' as an invention of decadent, scapegoat-hunting Whites. The virus, they insisted, had been brought to Africa by American perverts and was not a serious threat because among Africans homosexuality is almost unknown. They refused to believe that African blood banked in Kinshasa in 1959 held HIV antibodies and were sceptical about the role of heterosexual promiscuity. Sometimes I quoted stark statistics: 'A few months ago in one trucking town in eastern Zaire 76 per cent of barmaids were found to be HIV positive and 33 per cent of long-distance drivers passing through. And some of those were on their way to and from *Cameroon.*' But statistics, however ominous, made no impression. As Rachel remarked, 'They won't take it seriously until they *see* their friends and family dying!'

Even if Cameroon's government had the will, money, equipment and trained personnel to confront this crisis, there are formidable 'mindset' problems. Westerners now see a new disease as a challenge, but to most Africans disease remains something that must be accepted unless the medicine-man can intervene. So they react fatalistically to warnings about a new lethal virus. Also they tend to live in the present and to become bored or impatient if advised to take precautions *now* to avert disaster several years hence.

\*

Just beyond the town, as I was bringing up the rear, a handsome, well-built, sad-faced young man emerged from a side path and quietly returned my greeting. He was carrying an axe and was oddly dressed in a shirt and shorts of grey and black striped material. When I asked if he was going to Bafmeng – hoping we might have a guide all the way – he replied in excellent English. He wished he could go to Bafmeng, but he was a good-conduct prisoner who, having served seven years of his sentence, was now allowed out once a week to collect firewood for the prison kitchen. This frankness encouraged me to ask 'Why were you imprisoned?' And his reply shook me because one couldn't not believe him; he was that sort of young man. His father, a prosperous We farmer, had set him up as a butcher in Wum market at the age of eighteen. A few months later he bought twenty cattle from a Fulani who had rustled them. In court he claimed not to have known they were stolen and proved that he had paid the full market price. Yet he was sentenced to twenty-five years' imprisonment. And the Fulani was executed by firing-squad.

Despite the brevity of that encounter it remains one of my most indelible – and saddest – Cameroonian memories. There was something extraordinarily moving about the dignity with which this young man accepted a gross injustice. We shook hands where he turned off to climb a jungly hillside and I stood for a moment watching him walk away alone through the bush. I felt our short conversation had helped him; that meeting had a curious flavour – almost as though it were designed.

\*

Early next morning, after a third sleepless night, I was back in the dentist's queue. He appeared at 9.20 a.m. and looked very taken aback on seeing me; he had forgotten my x-ray. When he had at once returned to his home, in some distant salubrious suburb, my fellow-sufferers might have been expected to complain but didn't. ...

That x-ray was not a pretty picture. It showed a triple abscess, afflicting three molar roots, and it had to be cured before its cause could be investigated. All now depended on the antibiotics, which were as yet having no effect.

For four days neither of us wrote up our diaries and my recollection of events is somewhat confused; by that Tuesday I was almost delirious with pain. Yet the Egbert news [their horse, who had run away, had been relocated] had induced a euphoria that on one level transcended the abscess – so strangely does mind dominate matter.

Rachel's ulcers were not responding to the tetracycline and seemed to be worsening hourly. I found them much more worrying than my own condition and was reprimanded for this – 'I'm grown up! You must control your maternal instinct!' Yet the reverse syndrome was also operating. That evening Joy put Rachel in a separate bedroom, since I, plainly, was not going to be a soothing companion during the stilly watches. But within an hour she came limping back: 'I'd prefer to be here to keep an eye on you.'

By then I did look alarming – rather as though I had had a stroke. My face was twisted, with one eye half-closed, and even had I wished to eat I could not have swallowed. The new pain-killers were no more effective than the old. All night I sat up in bed, rocking to and fro non-stop and reading P.D. James's *Death of an Expert Witness*. Few authors could have delivered me from madness that night; P.D. James did. I have ever since felt grateful to her for writing that book. Meanwhile Rachel was sleeping – but restlessly. Could our Wum SSP friend have seen her legs, he would certainly have diagnosed leprosy.

That night was the abscess's climax. At about 7 a.m. the pain began to ease slightly; my antibiotics were winning. But Rachel's were not. There remained only one thing to do: take a bush-taxi to Yaoundé on the morrow (Thursday). …

In Cameroon it is not possible to telephone your friends in the next city to tell them that two diseased Irish vagrants are on the way. But the Farmers gallantly made us feel that diseased vagrants are their favourite sort of overnighters. And in their opulent guestroom history was made at 5.50 p.m. when my abscess burst – the physiological equivalent of a hurricane. Suddenly, wondrously, I was free of pain. (Not of course free of soreness but soreness and pain are two quite different sensations.)

# 1990s

# OLDER AND BOLDER

*Dervla had been entranced as a child by Walter Starkie's book* Raggle
Taggle *on the Gypsies of Transylvania. She decided to go to Rumania
as soon as she possibly could, mere days after the public execution
of the Ceausescus on Christmas Day, 1989. She therefore began the
nineties on a bus heading eastwards. Having been curious for decades
as to what it was really like there behind the 'Iron Curtain', she could
finally see for herself:* Transylvania and Beyond *is the result.*

*In January 1992, having bought herself a Dawes Ascent mountain
bike for her sixtieth birthday, she embarked upon 'a four-month
mystery tour' on a circuitous route from Kenya to Zimbabwe. It was
only in retrospect that she discovered what was to be the theme of* The
Ukimwi Road, *the next book: Ukimwi, which is AIDS in Swahili. She
shied away from no detail on this huge African trip.*

*Dervla had wanted to go to South Africa first in 1983, when
apartheid was being challenged. She could only get a 60-day visa,
which she thought too short a time, so she applied for a 12-month work
visa to write a travel book but was refused by the South African state
– as she said, 'rightly distrusting my motives'. She went to Madagascar
instead that year. She ended up taking three trips to South Africa to
gather material for the epic* South from the Limpopo, *in '93, '94
and '95, after the end of the apartheid regime. The book was highly
praised in reviews by Kadar Asmal and Donald Woods. It is probably
my own favourite of them all.*

In April 1996, she visited Rachel and her husband Andrew who were living near Lake Kivu in Zaire at the time. It was to serve as a holiday after the enormous work she had done on her South African book. She had been researching this in April/May 1994, when the Rwandan genocide had occurred. She intended to go to Rwanda to trek through the mountains in January/February 1997 until she found out that it was impossible. Her trip turned out to be more controlled and monitored than she would have liked because of 'tiresome security problems' but she covered a lot of ground in her book Visiting Rwanda.

In 1997, Laos was suggested to her by a friend, Catherine, and she shelved her plan to go to Sri Lanka. She heard what she called her 'inner click', 'suddenly determined to visit a country previously unconsidered'. She trekked in places that no doubt no longer exist, as the country was subjected to such a feeding frenzy by loggers, hunters, road developers, miners and energy companies, who saw this pristine countryside as a cookie jar to be plundered. Among the people she interviewed for One Foot in Laos were those who were unable to farm land because of unexploded ordnance (UXO) and therefore starving – directly affected by the aftermath of the Vietnam War, so many years afterwards.

## *Transylvania and Beyond* (1992)
Rumania

Part of Rumania's present demoralisation must be rooted in its pre-Communist history, though various 'revised versions' glorify some of Rumania's least savoury leaders as national heroes. However, a people's social history does not have to be learned from books, in each generation, to influence their gut-reactions. And one comparatively recent chapter – foreign profiteering – must surely be contributing to the post-revolution reluctance to see Rumania's economic doors again thrown open to Free Marketeers. Rumanians have never had a democratically elected government with responsible public representatives concerned about their constituents' welfare. Why should they believe that in the 1990s a coalition of fundamentally right-wing parties, however prettily tinted with 'liberalism', will not yet again betray them for its own profit?

\*

An embarrassing feature of many Rumanian discussions is the inability of intelligent people to think a problem through – or analyse an event – logically and consistently. Healthy saplings, planted in the wrong place, must adapt to constriction, and many good brains seem to have been alarmingly stunted. Every day I was becoming more aware of the gravity of Rumania's long-term problems. Decades must pass before the country can be expected to recover from an educational system designed to paralyse independent thinking, an artistic and intellectual life warped by censorship, a legal system (if one can call it that) based on terrorism, an economic system based on the ambitions of a megalomaniac, a social life overshadowed by fear of informers, a domestic life dominated by the quest for food and medicines, a sex-life inhibited by bizarre restrictions. A few of my friends defined their country, in 1990, as a lunatic asylum, a land in which no one, including themselves, was quite sane.

*

Even immediately post-revolution, a glance at any crowd revealed a minority of comparatively prosperous 'survivors'. These were not necessarily, I soon realised, Securitate or Party activists, but ordinary folk who knew how to operate the system. Typically, university lecturers or school teachers conserved energy during official working hours and later earned their 'supplement' as private tutors. Their pupils desperately needed extra tuition because the schools' standards had fallen so low – and anyway most teachers were conserving energy … Rural pupils paid in *tuica* [liquor], wine, meat, dairy produce. Others paid in goods or cash acquired by parents who, in their own jobs, knew how best to glean personal benefits from the system. A furniture factory official might sell to a teacher whose tuition fees enabled him to afford a chair (For Export Only) that would not fall apart in months. Then that factory official could engage an eminent professor to coach his son or daughter for university entrance examinations. (In practice, a variant of private education had long since evolved.) Again, supplementary income might go to buy foreign luxuries – soap, coffee, chocolate, contraceptives, cigarettes, alcohol – with which to barter for the scarcest everyday goods: razor blades, new tyres, electric light bulbs, a piece for the broken cooker. Workers who stole these essentials from their factories could always sell the luxuries for many lei, often to a wealthy doctor, and thus afford under-the-counter food.

To me this merry-go-round seemed inordinately complicated. Why couldn't a worker who had stolen – for instance – a tyre, sell it for lei to a doctor instead of bartering for whisky with a teacher and then selling the whisky to the doctor? But of course it all depended on who knew what about an individual's needs at a certain time, and who could trust whom, and who had access to what. As a way of life, this keeps certain areas of the brain agile but shreds the nervous system.

*

Of the Ceausescus' multiple cruelties, none repelled outsiders – and tormented insiders – more than their demographic decrees. In October 1966 abortion and contraception were outlawed, taxes on childless couples increased and a minimum of five children decreed. Hence the now-famous 'decree babies', born in 1967–9 and reputedly the most recklessly brave of the revolutionaries in Timisoara and Bucharest. Their growing-up coincided with the collapse of the economy and there were always far too many of them for the facilities available in state crèches, primary and secondary schools, holiday camps, universities. ...

When it became apparent that the Ceausescus' ambition – thirty million Rumanians by the year 2000 – was not going to be fulfilled, taxes on recalcitrant non-breeders were raised again, even harsher penalties were imposed for trafficking in contraceptives, or having or performing an abortion – and the Baby Police were established. These officers regularly visited workplaces (in some areas monthly, in others quarterly) to do abortion-blocking pregnancy tests and ensure that all miscarriages were reported to them for checking. Also they saw to it that every woman under the age of forty-five had a monthly gynaecological test. ...

Meanwhile living conditions were deteriorating fast. Dried milk had been rationed (wet milk was unobtainable) and the monthly allowance could feed a baby for less than a week. Power shortages had prompted a ban, enforced through frequent spot-checks, on the use of all household electrical appliances. Even the most adroit wheelers and dealers found it too dangerous to buy contraceptives and the abortion rate soared despite the risks – medical and legal. … When 'amateur' abortions went wrong, as they frequently did, and haemorrhaging women were rushed to hospital, they could receive no attention until they had told the police the name of their 'accomplice', usually a friend or friend of a friend. Over the years, thousands died because they refused to inform; the penalty was a heavy fine or a long term of imprisonment. In 1989, in Bucharest alone, over 20,000 women were treated in hospital for complications resulting from botched abortions. Also, during the 1980s – as the world now knows – countless babies were abandoned.

*

Liliana added to my anthology of gruesome gynaecological tales. On becoming pregnant in 1980 (aged twenty-one), she was found to have an ovarian tumour but her gynaecologist decided against an operation. A week before B-day he took off for a holiday in Spain, leaving as locum a kindly but ineffectual old man who reckoned the tumour must in fact have been a cyst because it had 'dissipated'.

At 10 p.m., when no gynaecologist could be expected to function, Liliana's time came. The hospital porter refused admission to her mother and boy-husband, the latter a severe case of pre-natal nervous prostration. She and a Gypsy woman had to share a single bed with filthy linen. Finding this intolerable, Liliana spent the night in a corner by the radiator (it was midwinter and far below freezing), crying with pain and fear, believing both herself and the baby to be doomed. It was 'lights out' at 11 p.m., when the eight women sharing four beds (all in labour) were scolded for being so noisy and told to settle down to sleep. Then the door was locked; the ward had a lavatory *en suite*. All night the Gypsy shouted obscene abuse at men in general and her husband in particular, which for Liliana added yet another dimension of horror to the experience. Before the staff reappeared at 7 a.m. three babies had arrived.

Hours later the geriatric gynaecologist bumbled in and during very difficult labour Liliana was repeatedly threatened with the loss of her baby if she didn't push harder. She marvels at the survival of both; many young women, less well-nourished and with fewer inner resources, left maternity wards in a box – and no doubt still do. On going home that evening she was told not to expect to feel well for a month and to return in six weeks – not before – *if* she had a problem. She did indeed have one, but dread of that hospital prevented her from admitting to it.

Three months later the acute pain in Liliana's lower abdomen was diagnosed as a kidney infection and treated accordingly. It was of course the tumour, by then wrapped around one of her Fallopian tubes and needing emergency surgery. Had her father not confronted the hospital Director (whom few would have dared approach) and demanded immediate attention, she might well have died.

*

The dawn showed a world all white and still. ... Descending the mock-marble staircase in semi-darkness, I slipped on a pile of vomit and landed five steps down with my right ankle twisted under me. It had taken all my body weight, plus a heavy rucksack, and I at once knew it was broken. Apart from the pain, there is an odd audible thing: the brain, if not the ears, 'hears' bones crunching. Picking myself up – some moments later, after the first pain-wave had ebbed – I accepted that now was the time to do some involuntary research into Rumania's medical service. But alas! now was *not* the time...

I could only find the *cabana* [cabin] manager's disagreeable wife, who informed me in French that the nearest town, Cimpulung, was currently inaccessible to motor vehicles. The prospect of languishing for days in a *cabana* bedroom, awaiting the thaw, with an injury in need of immediate attention, did nothing to cheer me. Being then unknowledgeable about broken ankles, I resolved to try to totter down to Cimpulung, but tottering proved impracticable; at my rate of progress it would have taken days to reach the town. And the pain was all the time increasing, naturally enough; as the doctor later pointed out, broken feet are not for use. I gave in when my leg began visibly to swell, even above boot-level.

An hour later, I was back in the *cabana* where – *mirabile dictu!* – an English-speaking final-year medical student approached me as I very slowly crossed the foyer, with no thought in my mind but to *sit down*. 'You have a problem!' exclaimed Virgil. Being by then speechless with pain I merely nodded and was helped up steps to a 'café area', with metal tables and chairs, where I gingerly took off my boot and displayed the damage. Firmly Virgil diagnosed 'Nothing broken!' – because I could wiggle my toes. I didn't argue but inwardly pitied his patients-to-be. …The Ceausescu era wonderfully revived folk medicine – perhaps its only beneficial side-effect – and while Teodor soaked my foot in icy water, Virgil requisitioned onions from the kitchen, applied layers of raw sliced onion under a very tight bandage and presented me with a bottle of cognac. …

At sunset my door was slowly pushed open and Bogdan timidly entered – a gnarled little gnome of a man, with tears in his bloodshot brown eyes. He it was who had vomited on the stairs and now, guilt-ravaged, he had come to crave my forgiveness, bearing a large bottle of *tuica*. I was quite overwhelmed; where else in the world, in similar circumstances, would the culprit have confessed and been so genuinely upset? By the end of the bottle (we were assisted by my nurse-attendants) Bogdan looked much more cheerful, having been assured that I quite understood his aberration – that occasionally I, too, had over-indulged to the point of throwing up.

*

Passing through the once-beautiful but now hideously industrialised town of Turda, *en route* for Tirgu Mures, I observed the essence of contemporary Rumania neatly concentrated in one incident. On a long narrow bridge over the Mures, a few hundred brown and white sheep, with half as many lambs again – the majority new-born – were causing a traffic jam of interesting proportions and attitudes.

This flock was in direct confrontation with one of those colossal truck-trailers that carry cranes from one high-rise site to another. The truck, having been brought to a standstill half-way across the bridge, was almost completely blocking it: but the sheep had to pass over on their way to the path to the river bank. From my roadside vantage-point, in front of the truck, I could see behind it a queue of seven long Gypsy wagons and a dozen vans and cars. On my side, too, the traffic was building up. And we were all accumulating unwholesome deposits as nine very tall nearby chimneys, belonging to three factories, poured clouds of stifling smoke (grey-black: orange-brown: purplish) over everything.

The three shepherds, wearing ankle-length fleece cloaks, carried intricately carved six-foot crooks. The two white sheepdogs wore spiked anti-wolf collars and their terror of motor traffic rendered them useless. The drivers' reactions interested me; all engines were switched off and, instead of showing their breed's usual ill-temper when there is a hold-up, they peered out anxiously and sympathetically as the shepherds coped with the chaos – which was considerable, as panicky lambs tottered off in all wrong directions, looking like bits of fluff beside the ginormous wheels of the trailer.

Finally one shepherd caught the flock leader, who was unhelpfully trying to retreat up the mountainside whence they had come, and dragged him through the narrow space between trailer and bridge: whereupon the rest began hesitantly to follow, apart from the numerous frantic mums of missing and vociferous lambs, who pursued them under various trucks, carts and vans. This blockage lasted more than twenty minutes; only when the shepherds signalled that every last lamb was safely down on the river bank did any vehicle move. Most Rumanians remain close to their rural background and shepherds hold an honoured place in traditional society. They are also among the richest people in modern Rumania; as Communism never impinged upon them, for obvious reasons, capitalism flourished in the mountains while elsewhere falling into ruin.

\*

Not far beyond the village of Sant, where I had become enmeshed in a riotous Moldavian wedding the day before, my walk started on a benign spring morning of warm sunshine, loud birdsong and dazzling wild flowers. At first however I was in shadow; for miles the track followed the young Somes river, here just another turbulently flooded stream between steep forested mountains. In this narrow valley all was as it has been forever, *sans* dwellings, pastures, logging scars. And the Somes, never more than a few yards away, became even whiter and louder as we ascended.

Then, rounding a sharp bend under an overhang, I saw a major snag immediately ahead. The terrain required a crossing of the Somes, but if this was a fording point it didn't look like one to me. Yet it was; beyond the seething waters the track continued, now at last leaving the river to climb high around the shoulder of the opposite mountain. Obviously people did cross here, though perhaps not often with bicycles.

The torrent was no more than ten yards wide. I removed the panniers, found a stout staff nearby, stripped naked and took the panniers over one at a time. The power of the waist-deep, icy water was formidable and the river-bed unstable, as is the way of mountain streams. I dreaded taking Luke across without the staff, but both hands would be needed to retain him. Then, as I stood holding him, summoning my courage, a wagon appeared around the nearby corner – its passengers three elderly men. They jerked their horse to a stop and for a surreal moment the naked Irishwoman and the Moldavian peasants were paralysed by shock of different kinds. Theirs was shock/horror, mine shock/ relief. Mercifully, I had planned to transport my clothes on my head when fording with Luke. Swiftly I bent and pulled on my long shirt. Then, cautiously, the wagon advanced. Not much sign language was needed. Averting their eyes from my lower limbs and adjacent areas, the men hauled Luke aboard while I hauled on my trousers before joining him. The horse shared my reservations about the fractious infant Somes and plunged in only after considerable coaxing. On the far side my rescuers tentatively intimated that I might continue upwards with them but looked hugely relieved when I declined their invitation.

Before continuing, I stoked up on bread and *slanina* [pork fat] and wondered as I munched – *could* I have got Luke across? Or would the Somes [river] have stolen him? We'll never know … I still think of the appearance of that wagon at that moment as *magical*, part of a Carpathian fairy-tale. Until I reached the motor road, four hours later, there was no other trace of humanity.

*

By 5 o'clock it was cold and I donned my padded jacket. Soon after, to my astonishment, the surface improved enough for slow cycling across a wide level saddle. Happily bumping along, I wondered if this reprieve would last beyond the saddle. Then ferocious barking alerted me. I tried to speed up but the four powerful converging dogs – two coming from each side – were racing like greyhounds. They attacked without hesitation, tearing my jacket sleeve, wrenching two spokes from Luke's back wheel and causing me to fall into the ditch on my right elbow – which still occasionally reminds me of this episode. An agitated young shepherd called them off just in time. Apart from the very real risk of being savaged to death, rabies is quite common in Rumania and had I not been wearing a jacket – had one of them even slightly broken my skin – I would have felt obliged to go home at once.

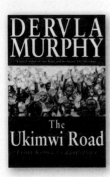

*The Ukimwi Road* (1993)
Kenya, Uganda, Tanzania,
Zambia, Zimbabwe

[Uganda] Apart from petrol tankers, the local traffic was mainly two-wheeled. Most cyclists carried improbable loads: a passenger or two, huge jerry-cans of water or home-brewed alcohol, long sacks of charcoal, formidably heavy bunches of matoke (green bananas) reaching almost to the ground on both sides, pyramids of firewood, unidentifiable cloth-wrapped bundles, hens in wicker coops and, on one carrier a sleek chestnut kid curled up in a shallow wooden box and apparently enjoying his excursion. As the land became more fertile, untidily thatched square or round mud huts huddled in unfenced compounds amidst unkempt shambas [smallholdings]. In the few drab, destitute townships rusty tin roofs were balanced, often precariously, on disintegrating grey shacks. Busoga's almost bare shelves made Kenya's rural dukas seem like Harrods. Only the women brightened this landscape, all wearing spotless ankle-length dresses with exaggeratedly puffed-up shoulders and wide sashes tied in a big bow above their conspicuous buttocks, or, occasionally tied diagonally across their equally conspicuous bosoms. As they walked gracefully by the roadside this shimmering flow of contrasting colours – rose-pink, deep yellow, pale green, crimson, royal blue – made a glorious mobile pattern in the dappled shade of mango, fig, and blue-gum trees. By comparison, Kenyan women seemed dowdy and shapeless in their shoddy mass-produced Western garments. I later learned that this Ugandan fashion was instigated by missionaries in the 1890s and designed by a Goan tailor.

*

Switching off the light, I was resigned to the inevitable; one learns to live – even to sleep – with mosquitoes. Moments later the fleas became apparent; several fleas, simultaneously settling down to their evening meal. I resigned myself to those, too. Given their way, fleas soon become replete and desist; to interrupt them merely wastes energy and prolongs the agony. And anyway the mosquitoes were going to give me an itchy night. Then something else made itself felt, something unfamiliar and dreadfully numerous. Switching on the light, I found the bed swarming with mites – creatures much too small to be lice, so minuscule that one could see them only because they were moving. I looked at my naked body; they were swarming on it too. Then another movement caught my eye: truly this room was an insect game-park. Down the wall from the wooden ceiling scores of red-brown bed-bugs, the size and shape of a little fingernail, had been marching – until the light went on. Bedbugs are allergic to light and now they were in disarray, scuttling to and fro instead of proceeding in an orderly fashion to their destination. Experienced travellers maintain that bedbugs and fleas cannot co-exist; this fallacy I am now in a position to disprove. Having rid myself of the mites (that took time) I slept in the bath with the light on. Only the mosquitoes followed me.

*

As the sun rose, a rough footpath led me straight down a grassy mountainside to the shore. Half a dozen boats were moored in the reeds beside a long jetty, built of stones and earth, and in a nearby hamlet of grass huts fish-bones littered the sandy ground. Beyond, a faint path wandered through waist-high golden grass, stretching for a mile or so to the edge of the semi-encircling forest. In a secluded corner, before the trees met the water, it was possible to swim unobserved. The clear lukewarm lake was disappointingly shallow near the shore and I dared not swim too far from my money-belt. Yet those were the best hours of each Bugala day – floating beneath the pastel morning sky, listening to the bird-calls in the forest, watching the fish-eagles gliding, gliding, gliding, then suddenly diving, splashing, swooping back to their young with a shiny catch.

The weather dictated my daily routine. Despite nocturnal downpours the midday heat remained enervating. Those hours were best spent strolling in the coastal forest, where only chips of blue were visible through the tropical canopy high above, or just sitting very still in the green-tinted shade, eventually being ignored by the many birds and few surviving monkeys.

*

On my last evening I followed a wide path between shambas where children were weeding the maize, or driving cattle home, while their fathers relaxed – as they had been doing all day – and their mothers squatted over small fires, cooking matoke. Then a boy of about 12 came running after me – not begging, or cheerfully calling 'How are *you*? How are *you*?', but taut-faced. Seizing my arm, he whispered urgently, 'Come, my mother to see you!'

We passed between tall glossy plantains, lanky papayas, spreading mango trees, an Irish potato patch. In an oblong hut his two older brothers, in their early twenties, were lying side by side on straw mats, both close to death. One was in a coma, the other conscious but speechless. Their bodies were skeletal, their feet hideously swollen. The anguished mother, seeing an elderly *mzungu*, had assumed me to be an 'expert' from some powerful Western organisation and in her despair was convinced I could help. She spoke no English and the boy's was minimal. 'Medicine!' he pleaded. 'You give medicine!'

I could only state bleakly that no one has medicine for the slim disease. To see the momentary hope extinguished in that mother's eyes was unforgettably harrowing. I knelt beside the young men and held their hands, then looked up at their mother, trying to convey that I would have helped if I could. She seemed to understand. As I left the fetid hut she embraced me, then darted sideways into a corner and returned to present me with a hand of bananas.

*

Those ninety miles took two days; on Day One I had to walk twenty miles, on Day Two, twenty-five. The manufacturers of mountain-bikes would have us believe that these can be pedalled across any sort of surface. Not so. Even an aristocratic Dawes Ascent is quite often defeated by African roads. Normally I enjoy walking as much as cycling but 'walking' hardly describes the pushing of a laden Lear up near-vertical hills through slithery mud or skiddy deep gravel, or dragging him over rocky outcrops and four-foot-deep erosion channels. (Luckily the local mud was not adhesive, as in Kenya.) These gradients were incomparable; on mountains that in more effete countries would be furnished with several hairpin bends the track went straight up and down. Freewheeling on such slopes and surfaces was impossible and on arrival in Kyenjojo the brake-muscles in my thighs were throbbing. Traffic, however, was not a problem. On Day One I met two vehicles, on Day Two three. All were overladen truck-buses travelling at about twelve miles an hour. Astonished excitement caused the passengers around the edges almost to fall off when they saw me.

*

[Tanzania] While struggling through liquid mud I fretted about the new 'development' behind me. Sisal and tobacco … export crops on all those fertile acres, Africa still providing what the West needs at prices decided in the West – a generation after Independence. It would be absurd to suggest that sub-Saharan Africa could now be flourishing had true independence been granted. Not one of the leaders allowed to take over had a coherent policy about where their country should go, and by what route, once the national flag had been raised. All were sitting ducks for the World Bank and IMF – even Nyerere [Tanzanian President], behind the scenes, for all his posturing about 'self-reliance'. However, the present shambles would certainly be less shambolic had genuine self-reliance been encouraged by the retreating colonial powers. It is inconceivable that new cash-crop plantations can help to alleviate Tanzania's poverty. Some employment is of course provided, thus slightly alleviating the poverty of a few hundred families at the cost of all the ills traditionally caused by migrant labour – plus, now, the spread of AIDS. But such projects only happen *because* the bulk of the profits flow West. Africans should be employed producing food for Africans; not until enough has been produced (including a stored surplus for drought years, as was the habit in pre-Communist Tibet), should any labour be deflected to cash crops grown by Western consortia. That is a truism. Yet African governments seem too befuddled to see it – befuddled by the miasma rising from the swamp of IMF and World Bank calculations and arguments. (Or can it be that the majority of Black politicians are happy with the opportunities for personal gain inherent in neo-colonialism?) Certainly economists are among the most dangerous animals on earth, skilled at making situations look so complicated that only their own solutions can solve the problems they themselves have created. And by combining insidious bribery, blackmailing bluff and intellectual hypnosis they can pressurise even well-meaning leaders into consistently betraying their own people by collaborating with the West.

\*

Familiarity was blunting the exasperation provoked by an agglomeration of malfunctioning Western imports – tarmac streets as eroded as cattle tracks, factories closed or operating at 25 percent capacity, telephones that don't work, banks that have no currency left, moody electricity, officials who are never in their offices, schools without textbooks, post offices without stamps, hospitals without medicines, courts without justice. Parallel to this world of pretence the ordinary folk survive – somehow. By setting up a bathroom weighing-scales on the pavement outside the bank and charging passers-by a penny a go; by pressing people's clothes while they wait with a charcoal-filled iron; by squatting in the wayside dust selling a few combs, mirrors, razorblades, soap bars (probably stolen) spread on a plastic sack; by turning a bicycle upside-down and sharpening knives and axes on a whetstone attached to the whizzing rear wheel – by 101 stratagems bred of desperation. The phrase 'subsistence economy' is cold and hard, an idea in an academic mind unrelated to everyday life. The reality, when one pauses to observe the individuals engaged in it at the lowest level, is harrowing and haunting.

*

Mafinga's motel – crudely smart, advertising a nightly disco – was newly built and evidently designed to pull in the best-paid international truckers. The restaurant boasted clean tablecloths and for £1.80 provided an ample meal of soup, bread, butter(!), steak, chips and tomato salad. The dual-purpose waitresses wore tight satin frocks with much cheap jewellery; their lips and nails were dark purple. Mine was a tall slender girl from Bukoba, her darkness accentuated by a sleek shimmering crimson gown, her diamante and gold watch not acquired in the bush. I invited her to have a coffee with me. Three years previously her parents had died of AIDS, aged 42 and 40. She had five younger siblings dependent on her earnings and nothing to sell but her body. AIDS naturally worried her; intelligent and forceful, she claimed to have converted many men to condom use. 'I argue,' she said. 'I tell them how my father and mother died slowly and it was like hell. Men are surprised when I tell them about my parents but they like me and want me. I show my report, I'm tested and clean. I say I want to stay clean and – OK, they want me, they use condoms! And carefully, not like a joke. Men are not so bad, if women are strong they listen. Many are scared now and like to find a clean girl. I make good money – they come and ask for Margaret because their friends tell them I'm clean. It's not true men won't use condoms but women must be strong – *very* strong!'

\*

[Zambia] Those 500 miles were covered in six days. I was by then in top condition, despite intervals of malnourishment, and between Lundazi and Chipata I set my personal record for the journey: 115 miles in eight hours on a smooth, level, almost traffic-free road – much of it within Kasungu National Park, which is in Malawi, on my left. My lodgings were varied: in Chipata – by mistake – a tough brothel (that was quite a tense night); in Katete a convent of young Zambian nuns; in Nyimba village a stable-like doss-house; in Rafunsa hamlet a one-roomed police station; in Chungwe trading centre the home of a teacher met in a bar.

\*

Having pedalled almost 3,000 miles along 'the *ukimwi* road', I was now sharing fully in the Africans' anger at the shameless development of the AIDS industry. At Entebbe, there is a White-run Virus Research Institute, one of three in the world, where all enquiries about the ethical standards applied to its work in Uganda are sidestepped. Other Western academics briefly visit Africa to pick up information painstakingly gathered and collated by African colleagues. Then they fly off to present these findings – apparently the result of their own research – at one of the AIDS industry's numerous and extravagantly run international conferences. These jamborees encourage AIDS 'experts' to mouth earnest platitudes and relay dramatic statistics for the benefit of the media, and to read papers written in impenetrable jargon for the benefit of each other, all by way of competing for funding for the next unconstructive project. Unconstructive, that is, for AIDS victims in Africa or anywhere else but lucrative for the experts. Meanwhile, out in the bush, the genuinely caring and knowledgeable Whites – always too busy to attend conferences – cannot afford basic medicines to relieve the agonies of the dying.

*

A few hours later, near the base of the escarpment, the fever flared. Dismounting, I put a hand to my forehead and belatedly diagnosed 'malaria'. Dizzy, trembling and wanting to vomit, I dragged Lear into the bush and collapsed, laying my pulsating head on a convenient pile of dry elephant dung – the size and shape of one of those round fat sofa cushions beloved by our great-grandmothers. But the ground beneath felt unlike a sofa; flinty stones, swarming ants and long thorns, shed by the leafless tree above, suggested a move. But to where? For forty miles in every direction stones and thorns prevailed. Anyway I felt incapable of moving. This was my first experience of malaria: why had no-one ever told me that when the collapse comes, an irrational lethargy takes over?

I thought, 'Thomson [Joseph Thomson, British explorer] didn't react like this, he just bashed on regardless up to the next escarpment.' I remembered Ali in Kyenjojo asking, 'You get a fever alone in the bush, who helps?' I recalled Mary Livingstone, lying dying of fever on a mattress spread on three tea-chests – that was at Shupanga, not far from here, during the ill-fated Zambezi Expedition. Then I thought, 'Must move, must take Halfan.' Halfan is the very latest malaria cure; not a prophylactic, only for the stricken. I looked at Lear, leaning against a baobab tree eight yards away. He seemed virtually inaccessible. Four baboons loped past, then paused to survey me. In game reserves they don't feel threatened by humans. Feverishly I resented their insolent staring. A big male sat scratching his private parts – a misnomer in the case of baboons. The curious baby laid both hands on a pedal and when it revolved took fright. Her family followed; she was too small to be left unprotected.

\*

Is it not time we quit Africa – cutting off the corrupting flow of billions of dollars, withdrawing the thousands of parasitical 'experts' and leaving the Africans free to sort out their own future? What is our continued meddling achieving *for the Africans*? Aren't we merely prolonging the process begun a century ago, of undermining their self-respect and self-confidence? The argument about global interdependence at the end of the twentieth century doesn't convince me that Blacks must be forever locked into our manipulative Rich Man's economy. Africa is after all a continent and not long ago was self-supporting. The notion that if given enough 'aid' – financial and technical – the Africans can soon acquire a Western lifestyle is simply absurd. ... The graftings onto Africa of Western systems of education, administration, justice, worship, agriculture, industry and commerce have demonstrably been a failure. None has taken. All are systems so profoundly alien to Africa that they have provoked every sort of collapse – moral, political, economic. Nor is there any reason to hope that in time those graftings will take. Why should they? Why should a complex civilisation slowly built up by one race be assumed suitable for instant adoption by another – by peoples who a century ago or less were without written languages, wheeled vehicles or a cash economy? Western civilisation being more advanced gives us no right to assume it can solve other peoples' problems – an inherently racialist assumption. Yet we still treat Africa as our forebears did in the 1890s, operating behind a different screen with the same (or worse) greed. Now it is our 'duty' to deliver irrigation schemes, factories, grain silos, motorways, agrochemicals, multi-storey hotels and conference centres, multi-party democracies and human rights (our own code of human rights, which some Western countries find easier to preach than to practise). All this denies African civilisation its own dignity and integrity.

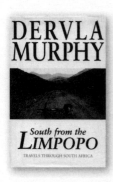

*South from the Limpopo* (1997)
South Africa

Between pre-colonial Africa and Ireland's ancient Gaelic society there are certain mysterious links, baffling to historians, concerning land tenure and cattle ownership. A contemporary link is the funeral – as a public display of solidarity with the bereaved, a social occasion far removed from the furtiveness with which the British bury (or cremate) their dead. In modern Ireland, long after wakes have been abandoned, hundreds of mourners may be observed thronging to small rural graveyards, some from other counties, other countries, even – in the jet-age – other continents. As a development of this Northern Ireland's 'political' funerals draw thousands of marchers, the mourning occasion transmuted into funeral-as-demo. In a parallel evolution here, township funeral rallies in the local stadium may be attended by fifty or sixty thousand. ANC [African National Congress] marshals control crowds waving ANC and SACP [South African Communist Party] banners, proclaiming loyalty to Nelson Mandela and singing the praises of the MK [Umkhonto we Sizwe, pre-election armed wing of the ANC]. Even when these rallies were illegal, the security forces couldn't arrest so many 'subversives' simultaneously breaking the law. However, they could intervene and during the last phase of the Struggle much of the violence was provoked by police attacks on funerals – leading to more deaths, more funerals, more attacks, more deaths ... A bloody spiral, the blacks now unconquerably defiant, the security forces increasingly ruthless.

*

For abstruse geological reasons, the Karoo's colours and contours are also unique. As is the silence. It is a rich, alive silence. It feels like a blessing. It is awesome, a religious experience – somehow utterly different from the equally flawless silence of never-inhabited mountain regions. Here is an underlying melancholy; the Karoo stirs emotions more opaque than the joyous liberation felt amidst the high Andes or Karakoram. Although so desolate, this silent place is companionable. Mysteriously, one never feels alone. Is it too fanciful to think back to the San, whose ghostly paintings smudge many rocks? The Karoo was not always so underpopulated and San stone tools still litter the ground; yesterday I collected several, to adorn my desk. ...

It bothers me that the importance of silence now goes generally unrecognised. Surely this must be one of humanity's not-so-minor problems at the end of the twentieth century. Why, during our endless inconclusive debates about juvenile delinquency, does no one ever mention the loss of silence? It seems so obvious that not to know silence – never to have known it – is to be dangerously deprived at that deep inner level where human beings, as they mature, get themselves sorted out. Yet most contemporary youngsters rarely encounter true silence and are frightened of it if they do.

*

Over coffee and brandies, my companions recalled their childhood days in the 1920s. Both grew up as poor whites in the Eastern Cape, their families bywoners [tenant farmers]. They walked barefooted to school, in winter carrying heated stones to thaw their feet on arrival. When the mealie [maize] crop failed – the 1920s were drought-stricken – they went hungry for months on end. New clothes were unknown, they bathed in tin tubs in the kitchen and used an outside earth-closet.

Potent memories of the Anglo-Boer War were passed on. Mr de Necker's father had been a *bittereinder* [Boer commando] who fought all the way; his maternal grandmother and two of her children died of typhoid in the Blomfontein concentration camp.

Viewing the Nats' [National Party's] 1948 victory through de Necker eyes, it can be seen as the long-delayed, hard-earned liberation of a downtrodden white tribe. At last Afrikaners were free to elevate their own hitherto scorned language above English, to compete academically and economically with the imperialists and, most important of all, to govern 'their' country for their own benefit. Only then, said Mr de Necker, were they given 'a fair chance' to climb the prosperity ladder – in his case some considerable way up, through a civil-service sinecure.

'Our only mistake,' said Mrs de Necker, 'was to give apartheid a name. Every country has segregation, nobody would have noticed ours if we'd kept quiet.'

\*

Khayelitsha covers I don't know how many acres of the sandy Cape Flats – enough acres to make square miles. You see its edges from the N2 motorway: a classic shanty city, pullulating with people, the frail dwellings cobbled together out of bits of this and that, litter strewn beyond one's worst nightmare, apparently an instant monument to desperation, destitution and despair. The population is said to be at least half a million – perhaps closer to a million? No one knows and not that many care. All the time the numbers increase. The unemployment rate is around 80 per cent … Most white and Coloured Capetonians speak of Khayelitsha with fear and disdain, as do many blacks from the older townships. It is supposed to be, and probably is, a dangerous place for whites. …

I had done some forward planning. In such places it is best not to seem a curious sightseer, gawping at local miseries, but to have a purpose. So I was carrying my jungle-trousers – after more than 5,000 miles of saddle-friction, between Nairobi and Cape Town, major repairs were needed. Ostensibly I was visiting Khayelitsha in search of a seamstress.

*

It seemed my arrival had been eagerly awaited and soon Blossom's shack was packed. Little welcoming gifts were brought: a strangely shaped stone from the Transkei – a model bicycle made of wire, perfect in every detail – a model Xhosa stool, carved from driftwood. Comrades set about teaching me essential Xhosa phrases and how to toyi-toyi [traditional dance]. The latter lesson I found easier than the former though it does test one's stamina. These Comrades take their toyi-toying very seriously; there must be no cheating with only one hop and that double hop is what wears out the novice. Then it was decided I should be given a Xhosa name. After some debate (in Xhosa) I became Comrade Noxolo, meaning 'Peace', which touched me deeply. As did the conferring of the Comrade title, marking my acceptance as a reliable friend, a person with the right attitude. But there were admonitions, too. I must be disciplined, stay close to my minders, obey them. Regrettable things happen in Khayelitsha. Only two months ago a young Englishman, a volunteer social worker, had been shot in the back and head while playing soccer in the Community Church Centre. No one knew by whom or why. 'Except we can guess,' said Blossom. 'By the PAC [Pan-Africanist Congress], because he was white.'

*

Day after day – almost hour after hour – people begged me to find them a job. They pleaded with the sort of urgency that makes one feel guilty about one's inability to help. Don't I know someone in

Cape Town who needs a maid, a gardener? Or someone who could employ an electrician, a hairdresser, a plumber, a tailor, a bricklayer, a tinsmith, a weaver, a shoemaker, a carpenter, a baker, a seamstress? In Khayelitsha live many who are skilled yet hungry; where little cash circulates, local jobs are few. A favoured white theme – 'most blacks only pretend to look for work, they wouldn't stick with a job if they found it' – has been infuriating me for months past. Now it makes me gibber with rage.

*

I felt sad, going from shack to shack, saying goodbye. As usual Sisi was busy outside her door, having that morning loaded a supermarket trolley (the commonest township vehicle) with sheep's hoofs and shanks discarded by a Mitchells Plain butcher. … Ndima was shoe-mending outside his one-roomed shack, a handmade shoe hanging over the door to advertise his craft. Blossom was boiling water for a client on her new oil stove; she expected to have an exceptionally busy week because of an approaching wedding. Mrs Mgidlana and her fellow-seamstresses were busy making attractive children's garments from offcuts. Mrs Sekgonyane was washing bullocks' guts in a baby bath and hanging them out to dry on the clothes line; they brightened the scene, glistening pink and ivory and purple. When dry, these too are grilled, in strips, and bought for a few cents each as a special treat. In the ANC Women's League-run crèche, donated food was being cooked for twenty-six toddlers whose parents are too ill to cope with them. The crèche is an unfurnished and seriously leaky shack, its floor always damp. Outside, Women's Leaguers sat in the sun teaching a few small girls how to weave village-style. Spaza shops [small local shops] were selling minute quantities of essentials. A carpenter was converting three broken tables, retrieved from a dump, into one sound table. A tinsmith was converting dog-food tins, also retrieved from a dump, into trays for domestic use – price: fifty cents. When you look closely at a corner of Khayelitsha, many people are hard at work.

Unemployment statistics belie the industry and inventiveness of the 'informal sector'.

*

The fourth of August 1993 is a date I shall never forget. Early that morning I heard deeply distressing news from home and for the first time – being in a state of shock – neglected adequately to guard Lear. Two hours later he was stolen from my friends' back garden.

Two black workmen in an adjacent garden witnessed the theft. When they questioned the intruder he claimed Steve owed him money but had refused to pay so he was taking Lear instead. The workmen must have known this was nonsense but they said no more. Were they afraid lest the thief might pull a gun? Or did they feel some sympathy for his enterprise?

Everything possible has been done to retrieve Lear but I never had any hope. At Steve's insistence, a dim-witted Coloured police officer came this evening to take a statement. However it would at present be unreasonable to expect the SAP [South African Police] to exert themselves in pursuit of a cycle thief. I offered a R500 reward – NO QUESTIONS ASKED – on the front page of the *Natal Witness*, this being the local price of a new mountain bike. To publicise my loss, the *Witness* also ran a half-page interview complete with a pathetic photograph; I didn't have to feign looking stricken. ... It is ironical that after months of dodging the sort of publicity likely to attend a female sexagenarian's bicycle tour of South Africa in 1993, that journey has had to end under the spotlight. ...

I am absurdly upset. On the practical level a bicycle is just a machine, an inanimate object easily replaced. But not so on the emotional level. To me Lear was a friend, my only companion on quite a long journey that started in Nairobi. I feel utterly desolate without him. (What would a shrink make of this admission?) One could argue – I have to try to make excuses – that a bicycle is not after all, 'just a machine' as is a motor-car. The cyclist and the bicycle form a team; they work together as the motorist and motor-car do not. Perhaps other cyclists exist, somewhere out there, who can understand this. Or perhaps not. Maybe I'm uniquely dotty.

Now I must count my blessings. In fact only one is visible at the moment: that this journal was not stolen. It might have been, as it lives in a pannier-bag. But having rummaged through both panniers and found nothing of value to him, the thief ripped them off, no doubt fearing they might arouse suspicion (obvious 'tourist property') as he sped away. The only balm on my wound is the certainty that he needs Lear, in material terms, more than I do. A similar theft at home would have enraged me: you can't feel enraged in South Africa when a black steals from a white.

… Buying a bicycle is a momentous event, akin to marriage: you are acquiring a partner. Now I have acquired Chris (in memory of Chris Hani [assassinated leader of the SACP]) and it remains to be seen how our relationship will develop. Lear was a thoroughbred, Chris is a mongrel – bits and pieces from Singapore, Taiwan and Korea, assembled in South Africa. Riding him feels like riding a carthorse after a Derby winner. But I daresay shared experiences will eventually make that invidious comparison seem irrelevant.

*

However little they may deserve it, the whites do at present arouse sympathy – emotional earthquake victims, their whole world collapsing, fear of bloody chaos a dark shadow, incomprehension of blacks distorting their view of the future. An incomprehension nonetheless heartbreaking for being inevitable, in South Africa – and of course vehemently denied. How often I've had to listen to both Afrikaners and English-speakers explaining why they understand blacks so very well – because as children they had no other playmates and went off to boarding school speaking better Sotho/Xhosa/Zulu than Afrikaans or English. The implied insult to African culture is breathtaking. Imagine a Chinese child growing up to the age of 10 on some remote nineteenth-century European farm, playing only with the children of illiterate, impoverished labourers and on the basis of that experience claiming as an adult that he understood Europeans very well. People would laugh at his stupid arrogance.

*

27 April. A still grey morning, clouds low, a hush over the city as I cycled to the nearest polling station at 6 a.m. Already the queue was in place and lengthening by the minute. Hundreds of Coloured, blacks, whites: not talking, looking rather solemn. As yet there were no Monitors or Observers on duty and only one of those 100,000 police officers. Strangely, unchecked cars were allowed to park within easy bomb-reach of the queue.

Sitting on a bollard I thought, tritely but accurately, 'This is the day – the hour – for which so many have suffered so much.' And then my mind roved over all those places I know, between Cape Town and Messina – everywhere everyone queuing together, in a ritual discarding of the past.

Many steps lead up to the entrance to Woodstock's polling station. At the head of the queue, on the top step, stood an elderly black couple. Precisely at 7 a.m. the door opened and they entered to cast their vote. That was the trigger. A wave of emotion rippled through the crowd. Still no one spoke but people turned to look at one another, whites and blacks and Coloureds communicating without words. Tears flowed, including mine. Ostensibly this was a political event, the election of a government. In reality it was – what was it? It felt then, and all day, like a sacrament of healing. …

Today only the weather was unkind. As I cycled to Retreat and Grassy Park, stopping at various polling stations en route, a strong wind drove sheets of cold rain along the Peninsula. But this did nothing to shorten queues or dampen spirits. Instead, it emphasised the prevailing harmony as umbrellas or plastic sacks were shared, and whites who lived near the queues made thermos flasks of tea for shivering blacks and Coloureds.

At Newlands I heard about this morning's 7.15 car-bomb at Jan Smuts airport – a mega-bomb, its timing significant. Inexplicably no one was killed though three were seriously injured and much structural damage done. ...

Soon the first convoy arrived from Khayelitsha and parked on the main road. Again tears came to my eyes as I watched those Xhosas toyi-toying and dancing down a side-street to the polling-station, cheering and singing and laughing and clapping, waving South Africa's new flag and radiating joy. Many habitually wear ANC T-shirts or baseball caps or badges; today, all respected the rule forbidding 'party favours or colours'. On reaching the end of the queue – more than half a mile long, stretching around two blocks – they joined it in as orderly a fashion as any citizens from Constantia or Green Point. And for hours they stood there, patiently, happily, singing and laughing and being drenched at intervals when another squall of rain came riding on the wind. Many young women carried babies and did a brisk trade of renting them to those who could afford to expedite their exercise of the franchise. (Baby-laden mothers were given special treatment and infants were not invisibly inked.)

But where were all the thugs, the tsotsies, the hooligans, the extremists of every colour? Nowhere to be seen today in any region of South Africa. Yet this influx of township voters was the very stuff of pre-election white nightmares – the invasion of 'our' areas by thousands of hyped-up young blacks who would certainly run amok. Those fears proved how little whites understood the significance for blacks of 27 April 1994. Why should they, on today of all days, run destructively out of control? Now the new flag of liberated South Africa – *their* flag! – is to be seen flying high, outstretched in the wind, above every police station, army post and public building. Moreover, all SAPS officers have a tiny patch of sticky tape at the end of their name badges obliterating the old flag. To people who have suffered so much at their hands (and their batons, guns and dogs) this is the most potent symbol of all.

\*

Nelson Mandela's dedication to reconciliation – that supremely civilised concept – is often seen as the keystone of the new South Africa. His reconciliation campaign began years before his release and by the mid-1980s was having an effect within Afrikanerdom. Since 1990 he has been tirelessly preaching: 'Let everybody start from the premise that we are one country, one nation, whether we are white, Coloured, Indian or black.' From most politicians this might sound like an expedient exhortation, from Madiba it sounds like the expression of a passionate, personal longing for harmony. His sincerity seems to have touched all but the most fanatical right-wingers; even those who continue to revile him verbally have been reassured, within themselves. They know they are not going to be victimised in the new South Africa. But – is Madiba attempting the impossible? It takes two to reconcile. If only one is dancing to that tune, does 'reconciliation' become a euphemism for 'appeasement'?

Yesterday President Mandela spoke of the need to 'heal the wounds of the past' and construct 'a new order based on justice for all'. Those wounds were inflicted by whites in pursuit of wealth. And in 1994 the fragile national 'prosperity' remains dependent on the exploitation of black labour. An increasing number of blacks will now have access to wealth but rich blacks are no more (sometimes less) sensitive to the needs of the poor than rich whites. Constructing a new order must involve wealth-sharing and that would sink the reconciliation boat. In the real world, 'justice for all' and Madiba's noble ideal of reconciliation are incompatible. And because this incompatibility is built into the foundations of the new South Africa no political construction engineer would certify it as a sound edifice.

Here and now, these may seem inappropriate – even heretical – reflections. But South Africa is like that. It spawns inappropriate reflections and irrational mood-swings and intellectual culs-de-sac. It is the most confusing country I have ever travelled through – not surprisingly, given its past, present and future.

*

**INTERLUDE:**

Serious injuries should happen in appropriate settings: during a war in Central America, an election in Angola, an earthquake in Armenia or on some daring journey through trackless wastes. Merely to have tripped over the cat outside the kitchen door adds indignity to injury and I could hear my friends involuntarily giggling at the other end of the telephone. Huffily I protested that this was no giggling matter, that for the first three of my five days in hospital I had been on a morphine drip, that numerous shattered bones (originally my left elbow and forearm) were now being held together by eight pins and a strip of metal. Penitently, the friends sympathised. Too late! To punish them I pressed on, explaining that now, back home, the vibrations of a door banging in the distance – never mind *any* movement of the body – caused exquisite pain. That lowered my friends' telephone bills: they couldn't ring again because they wouldn't want to occasion bodily movements...

It happened at 9.15 p.m. on 2 June when Sebastian – a frail elderly feline gentleman – was mugged by the neighbours' ginger tom, a notorious hooligan. Hearing an agonised wail I raced from my study, rounded a corner of the cobbled courtyard at speed and tripped over the fleeing victim. Luckily, I fell to the left. Had I fallen to the right, my head would have struck the sharp edge of a stone step and I might well have been moved not to a casualty department but to a mortuary. ... The exact sequence of events is a blur but I vividly recall the radiologist's expression when she looked at the X-rays, then at me. 'You've done a thorough job!' said she, almost admiringly. The plates seemed to show a pile of kindling thrown in a grate; here was a thrilling challenge for an orthopaedic surgeon.

*

One young giant had shoulders like a bulldozer, curly yellow hair and a coppery tan. He offered me a lift to Nongoma tomorrow. 'If you go on your bike you'll be hacked to death – slowly. There's big trouble these days around the King's palace.' My declining to be protected upset his companions. One said, 'We've trouble enough here without more bad publicity. We're trying to put Pongola on the tourist map, we don't need foreigners getting killed. It was in all the papers last year when a Swiss woman on a bike got murdered.' I promised to work hard at not being killed and said goodnight. ...

After a gradual fifteen-mile climb, through sugar-cane and rough pasture, the end of the tarred road marked my re-entry into KwaZulu. From here a bone-shaking track ran level across unpopulated acacia savannah, then climbed into bare mountains. Soon I dismounted; on a surface so ravaged, walking is faster than pedalling. I met only three vehicles over today's fifty miles.

\*

My last day in Khayelitsha was spent with the 'Gang of Four': Aki, Muriel, Pius and Sam, my middle-aged ANC community leader friends. They are uneasy about the future. Not only the younger generation in Khayelitsha feel alienated from – almost rejected by – their new government. This has nothing to do, emphasised Pius, with 'unreasonable expectations'. It is much more complicated, a hurtful awareness of a gulf having opened up between the ruling elite and the millions whose courageous opposition to the old regime enabled black politicians to gain power and suddenly become conspicuously rich. The Struggle, as Sam pointed out, was unifying. From world-famous Nelson Mandela to the anonymous 12-year-old revolutionaries in every township, all were in it together. At that time the foot-soldiers never foresaw – how could they? – that liberation would split the ranks, leaving them still hungry though equal before the law. While blacks and whites got together to form a new controlling class, apparently for their own mutual benefit...

But the bitterest humiliation/disillusion, at the end of the generation-long Struggle, has to do with being suddenly uninvolved, unimportant, without a role. This is a cruel paradox, as Aki noted. In theory the vote gets every citizen politically involved. Yet it was the Struggle, rather than the exercising of the franchise, that gave the blacks a feeling of shared responsibility for their country's future. ...

To cheer everyone up (including myself) I pointed out that *uhuru* [freedom] has brought about one hugely significant change: future wrongdoers will lead much less comfortable lives with the sword of exposure hanging over their heads. This country is healthily thirsty for freedom of information and freedom of speech, liberties abhorred and outlawed by the old regime. Nowadays bureaucratic inefficiency is exposed. Educational chaos is exposed. Racial discrimination is exposed. Diplomatic ineptitude is exposed. Political stupidity is exposed. Regularly dirty linen is washed openly on the riverside of public opinion. It is even possible for new South Africans to sniff the dirtiest linen of all, still hidden in the laundry basket awaiting the attention of the Truth and Reconciliation Commission. ...

Will it work? Despite my well-founded doubts about this unique experiment, I do have hope (hope rather than faith) that eventually justice will prevail – though the mechanism whereby it could do so at present remains invisible. It would be good to return in, say, five years' time and discover that my doubts were not, after all, well founded. Sometimes it is exhilarating to be proved wrong.

## *Visiting Rwanda* (1998)
Rwanda

By 6.45 I had secured a front seat in a minibus about to depart for Kabale – according to its driver. Two hours later it was full and we took off, or seemed to. But that was an illusion. Beyond Mbarara several individuals and groups appeared by the wayside, desperate to get aboard, and a vehicle licensed to carry fourteen passengers ended up carrying twenty-two. Delay-wise, the extra passengers themselves are no problem. But it does take time to load their chairs, poultry, matoke, planks, sacks, cartons, baskets, bundles, blankets and rolled-up mats. Then it turned out that not all passengers were going to Kabale. At intervals we stopped and much hectic unloading took more time – much more, if the disembarking person's sack was under other passengers' possessions. And always, before anyone's belongings could be retrieved, it was necessary to remove the two chairs roped to the open back door. Happily, I readjusted to the rhythms of African life. But the Kampala businessman beside me registered extreme impatience. 'Time is money!' he fumed, repeatedly unzipping and rezipping his briefcase in a near-paroxysm of frustration. ...

From the pass above Kabale I glimpsed the Virunga chain of volcanoes far away to the west, their rugged austerity seeming extra dramatic in contrast to Kigeza's lushness. I longed to disembark here and walk the last few miles. But the disinterring of my rucksack would have caused such a time-consuming upheaval that the Kampala businessman might have succumbed to hypertension.

From the pass, the road plunges into a narrow valley, then rises again, gently, to enter Uganda's highest town (about 6,000 feet), where a cool breeze tempers even the noon heat. During the afternoon blue-black clouds suddenly filled the sky and soon delivered an hour's torrential rain to lay the dust and fill the water barrels. In this congenial little town the local traffic consists mainly of bicycles; scores are registered cycle-taxis with cushioned carriers and number-plates. Kabale is the 'base-camp' for backpackers and overlanders en route to the mountain-gorilla reservation near Kisoro, most of whom stay in the Visitour hotel (£2 per night).

*

It took me five hours to cover the fourteen miles to the border. At 11, in the straggling, down-at-heel village of Kamuganguzi, I walked past a queue of twenty-seven oil-tankers and trucks, their drivers evidently taking Sunday off in Uganda where prices are much lower than in Rwanda. The ramshackle frontier barrier-gate stood open and a predatory Ugandan policeman, masquerading as a customs officer, beckoned me into his small round tin hut and ordered me to unpack my rucksack. Pouncing on 200 mini-cigars he accused me of 'smuggling and illegal import' and demanded a US$25 bribe. Then he was distracted – fascinated – by those books I had hoped to give Marie. He checked my passport, to confirm the name, then exclaimed that he had never before met a writer of books. We negotiated. He settled for *In Ethiopia with a Mule*, autographed and personally inscribed. As I remember noticing on a previous visit many Ugandans are gratifyingly addicted to books.

In the customs building across the track a genuine customs officer was uninterested in my rucksack. The immigration officer, while stamping my passport, warned, 'Be careful over there, be very careful – they don't like *muzungus*.'

*

We took the main, ladder-steep path to the town – not yet visible, hidden by two lower intervening hills. From the edge of the hamlet, I was baffled to see a line of about thirty men ascending with hoes over their shoulders, uniformly clad in apparently brand-new pale pink shorts and bush-shirts (without pockets). Only when I noticed their four guards, wearing scruffy civvies but carrying rifles, did I realise that these must be prisoners from Gisenyi's enormous jail. Most looked cheerful and reasonably well fed – of course by their families. Then suddenly one powerfully built young man leaped off the path and vanished amidst the banana plants crowding the steep slope. His fellow prisoners stopped, stood still, stared after him. Glimpses of pink could be seen for moments through the drab green of the foliage. Evidently the guards' rifles were not loaded because two flung their weapons towards the escapee. Then I came as near to death as ever I have. From close behind me my escort fired, shouting angrily. I felt his bullet passing my left cheek and stumbled sideways as the soldier led the guards in pursuit – all the guards, leaving the rest of the work-gang to their own devices. They were grinning from ear to ear, leaning on their hoes, peering into the bananas. The shot had brought a score of youths to the scene and now the atmosphere was all excited violence. Rather shaken, I hastened on my way, then realised that my left ear was aching and my head buzzing. I sat under a tree to recover.

*

Hitchhiking out of Gisenyi was easy. An aged Belgian nun, driving a minibus-load of handicapped children to Kigali, gladly picked me up and was disappointed to hear I didn't want to go all the way. She told me she belonged to the Sisters of the Assumption. On 26 April 1994 six Tutsi nuns from her convent were raped and murdered at nearby Birambo. In Gisenyi town fifteen nuns belonging to other orders were massacred. Within this prefecture scores of Tutsi priests were killed on the hilltops, usually by their own parishioners. A Belgian priest was also killed while trying to escape into Zaire with two Tutsi friends who died beside him at the border post. Yet the leaders of the Catholic Church in Rwanda refused to condemn the genocide and oppose its organisers – recalling the Vatican's attitude to another genocide.

*

Nothing more clearly defines the particularity of genocide than the deliberate seeking out and killing of children – especially male children – not only *en famille* but in hospitals, schools, orphanages, homes for the handicapped. Millions of children, worldwide, are bereaved and traumatised by wars and natural disasters. After an earthquake or a bomb attack they may find themselves lying beside or under their parents' corpses … In such circumstances, however, they are incidental victims. In Rwanda, once the killing started, all Tutsi children of an age to understand language knew they were targets. And countless Hutu children witnessed their own fathers – sometimes their mothers, too, and their older siblings – killing their friends and playmates. Such experiences, as Nganga noted, do not merely leave scars. A scar marks the place where a wound has healed. In many cases the wounds inflicted on Rwanda's child survivors are unlikely ever to heal.

Is the West's indifference to this genocide partly racist? Images of children seeing and hearing their parents being hacked to death, of spears being thrust through babies on their mothers' backs, of babies being flung into rivers by their mothers to save them from the other sort of death, of toddlers being beheaded or disembowelled, of seven-year-olds having their arms chopped off, of eleven-year-olds smashing five-year-olds' skulls – such images are of course dreadful but perhaps insufficiently shocking because this is what Europeans have been conditioned, over generations, to expect of Africans. Yet we know there is nothing specifically 'African' or primitive about genocide; the country that produced Dürer, Beethoven and Goethe also produced the gas-ovens that eliminated six million Jews and other 'undesirables'. Nganga dryly remarked that very likely the impersonal high-tech Nazi method strikes some Westerners as less barbaric that the chopping up of one individual by another with a machete. Although the end result is the same, the European way might somehow seem tidier, more discreet … He could have a point there. Many journalists became oddly obsessed by the killers' using agricultural implements – and, later, by the refugees' bare feet. They seem not to realise that both phenomena are simply a measure of where this country is at, economically. Most Rwandan peasants habitually go barefooted, and if they want to kill a goat, or a bullock – or a person – they use bare steel, just as our own ancestors did before the invention of gunpowder.

Thinking on from there, is it fair to see a difference in degrees of culpability between the credulous, illiterate Hutu peasants – cunningly brainwashed and by tradition submissive to authority – and the thousands of educated Germans (and others) who collaborated to make possible the Holocaust? Not to mention all those Germans who for years knew what was going on but pretended not to notice. Or am I now, as Nganga hinted, being racist in a convoluted way, tending to blame Africans less because I expect Europeans to be more capable of defying a criminal régime?

We asked ourselves then, can there be such a thing as an understanding of genocide? Does anyone understand the Holocaust? Knowing why and how it happened doesn't really enable 'normal' human beings to comprehend the level of depravity involved. Or perhaps, as Nganga suggested, we don't want to understand, are afraid to understand – because genocide exposes what we prefer not to know about ourselves as human beings. It is reassuring to imagine a clear line separating 'normal' people from genocidal Turks, Germans, Rwandans. But given the combined pressures applied by the organisers of Rwanda's genocide, how would each of us react? Can we be certain we would continue to behave like 'normal' human beings?

*

Elsewhere, I visited a housing project specifically for parentless children – a modest project, run by a small NGO.

Over-emotionalism is not one of my flaws yet among those children I more than once came close to tears. For a young family to be orphaned is under any circumstances tragic – but normally, in Africa, a supporting network of relatives and friends remains. For many of these Tutsi orphans there is nobody left. Everyone they or their parents were close to is dead. The combination of their utter destitution and their joyless, haunted faces shattered me. And their terrible aura of hopeless loneliness was accentuated by their physical isolation as they struggled to build new homes on remote plots.

The first family on Angeline's list (five children, the eldest a girl of fifteen) lives thirty minutes' walk from the motor-track. Their present home is a leaking round thatched hut no bigger than many African poultry-huts – barely high enough for me to stand up in. Their possessions are: one battered *dechi*-type saucepan, one ladle, one blanket (donated) spread on banana fronds. Nothing else. Not even one spare garment between them. They use pieces of wood as hoe-substitutes. Theirs is a Catch-22 situation. They are too small and frail to cultivate the three family plots and must remain too frail while they are so malnourished. Neighbours sometimes help but themselves have little surplus time or energy. The building of their new three-roomed shack has been delayed because the young man hired by the NGO to do the job – he comes from the nearest *ruga* [settlement] – fell ill two weeks ago. Now he is back on the job, helped by several small boys enlisted as voluntary labour. An unexpectedly urban note was struck by a cocky young man wearing new blue jeans, a striped anorak, a green baseball cap and trainers. He sat on a camp stool cradling on his lap a giant ghetto-blaster with its aerial fully extended. Happily this machine was not working. When we arrived he remained seated and ignored us. In turn Angeline and Eugene – her team-mate, also Hutu – ignored him. He is this cellule's *responsable* and takes it upon himself to 'supervise' NGO-funded building in the hope of being able to extract a 'fee' from some naive foreign aid worker. 'He should be in prison,' Angeline said afterwards. 'He was a killer.' ...

En route to the next commune we passed two large level plots conspicuously uncultivated amidst miles of flourishing bananas, sweet potatoes, manioc, beans, tomatoes. Obtusely I asked why so much fertile land has been left to the weeds. I should have realised that these are mass graves, as yet unmarked. Some communes have by now erected massive headstones recording the date(s) of the massacres and the approximate number buried together – 6,000, 7,000, 8,000 ... In Kigali, on the first anniversary of the start of the genocide, 100,000 bodies – collected from temporary graves in the city and surrounding communes – were ceremoniously re-buried.

\*

A student accompanied me back to the town; he had spent hours taking notes in the geology room. Corneille is a survivor, one of those Tutsi saved by Hutu neighbours who knew they were thus putting their own lives at risk. All three generations of his family were killed, either on their hill or in Kigali. His Hutu friends hid him in a shallow grave in the soft earth of a banana grove, scattering loose withered fronds over a small ventilation hole. For six days he lay there, being given just enough water, at irregular intervals, to sustain life. Urination had to happen *in situ* and that was, he said, the worst of it – even worse than the immobility. When disinterred, by night, rashes and sores covered his thighs and lower body. By then there were, apparently, no Tutsi left alive in that commune – only heaps of putrefying corpses – and the death squads had moved on. Yet Corneille remained in danger; some local Hutu, their cunningly aroused hatred still glowing white-hot, would have needed no further urging to kill him. His friends concealed him in their *ruga* for two months, a time of extreme tension. The possibility of being detected and 'pointed out' often felt like a probability.

\*

All my life I have passionately opposed capital punishment yet now I see the execution by the state of the organisers of the genocide as necessary – though the notion of 'healing through execution' so offends our recently acquired Western European sensibilities. I am convinced that the creation of an atmosphere in which reconciliation would be possible requires the judicial killing of the organisers. If the government cannot, or will not formally, ceremonially, execute those criminals, then ordinary Rwandans will kill (are killing) the people within reach – most of whom are other ordinary Rwandans. After genocide, there has to be retribution. To me it is not immoral or uncivilised for the state, on behalf of the survivors, to seek vengeance, whereas a world that allowed the organisers to evade punishment is frighteningly uncivilised. And it signals to others that if any minority becomes too much of a nuisance there are ways of dealing with the problem while the international community averts its eyes. Most of my friends won't be able to understand why one particular set of circumstances, 'Genocide in Rwanda', should have compelled me to abandon such an important principle – 'Killing is Wrong'. I'll find it impossible to argue coherently about this, to justify making an exception for criminals who may never, personally, have murdered anyone. No doubt some will accuse me of a sort of blood-lust, an impulse coming more from the heart than the head. Yet there is one practical argument in favour of execution as catharsis. Even if the organisers were sentenced to life imprisonment, the public would believe that their power, wealth and influential friends would soon bring about their release – or 'escape'. Thus the culture of impunity would be seen, by all, to continue to flourish.

*

Only on stepping out of Rwanda, back into the easy-going friendliness of Uganda, did I realise how unrelaxed I had become among those Thousand Hills. Rwanda has been a scary experience. Not because of the tiresome security problems but because it forces one to confront the evil inherent in us all, as human beings – however humane and compassionate we may seem as untested individuals. The deeds done there I have described as 'inhuman'. But that's escapist talk. Nothing done by humans is inhuman.

## *One Foot in Laos* (2000)
## Laos

This attractive *ban* (village) – fifteen minutes' walk from the Mekong, centred on a large, poorish wat – had few other expat residents and was never visited by tourists. Its tall trees crowded greenly around colonial bungalows or overhung laneways lined with traditional homes on high stilts, their walls of woven split bamboo. Soon I was familiar with the neighbours' routines and was recognised and smiled upon by food vendors, shop owners, tuk-tuk drivers, grannies sitting on their balconies, children going to school – and was greeted with thumping tails by dogs lying on thresholds. Sometimes, at 4 a.m., I could hear the wat drums, a muffled, ghostly booming that marks the moon's phases. At dawn a procession of orange-robed monks – barefooted, shaven-headed, some novices as young as eight – collected their daily rice from a few elderly women and even fewer elderly men who knelt and stood, respectively, outside their homes, praying as they awaited the monks' arrival. After each donation the monks chanted a brief blessing in unison – automaton-like, in the style of routine prayers everywhere.

The term 'wat' describes all the monastery buildings found behind low walls in a large compound, often guarded by a sacred bodhi tree. The central building is the *sim* (temple) – always rectangular, with very beautiful tiered sloping roofs. The tiles may be orange, black, red or green but never a mixture of colours.

Triangular gable boards depict the Lord Buddha, the Wheel of Life, Indra riding Erawan the three-headed elephant (my favourite) and/ or various Hindu gods which arrived in Laos via Cambodia.

*

Mountain walls were close on two sides, west and north. I sat on the platform's edge enjoying the silence and the beauty of this place while Mr Tang knelt by the log, blowing until it flamed. Then two loud shots sent echoes reverberating weirdly around those rock walls – double, triple echoes. Sadly I thought, 'Two less of some endangered species!' Mr Tang pointed to the knife-crested summit of the highest mountain in sight and boasted that he and the older man, an experienced climber, had recently reached the top and shot for the pot two big birds – he didn't know the name in English – and a gibbon. I made no comment. If one wishes peasant cultures to survive, hunting for meat must be accepted. It is a much less off-putting activity than game-bird shooting and fox or stag hunting for fun – not to mention big game hunting. Mr Tang asked what animals people hunt in my country and looked puzzled on hearing that Ireland has no hunters who risk life and limb to feed the family.

In Laos the main threat to endangered species comes from commercial hunters, using modern weapons and sometimes helicopters; these merchants supply the insatiable Chinese demand for aphrodisiacs. (Perhaps the Worldwide Fund for Nature should distribute free Viagra throughout China?) Also, the border regions where ill-paid soldiers are posted amidst dense primary forests have been devastated. Hungry men sweep patches of forest with machine-gun fire, killing everything – including butterflies – then gather what is accessible and edible from amidst the general carnage. Unhappily there are many such army posts; Laotian border areas tend to be both politically and ecologically sensitive.

*

Beyond one bamboo forest, the path became a little wider, and rocky, before suddenly plunging down to river level – then at once climbing again. Here I was walking through a curious green-tinged twilight, so close to one another were the mighty trees. On this mountain several deep gullies presented minor problems. Their sides of soap-slippy red-brown earth were ladder-steep and I had to accomplish these descents on my bottom, clutching at vegetation as a brake regardless of snakes. There is something peculiarly undignified – with cowardly undertones – about proceeding on one's bottom; this is not the image people have of intrepid travellers confronting the unknown. However, it has to be admitted that sexagenarians who over the decades have broken many bones do lack the physical self-confidence, and therefore the agility, of the young. What I most dreaded was having to cross a gully by a single tree-trunk bridge, a device to which all mountain folk are inexplicably partial. Even when young, I balked at those. Within the next hour two such horrors challenged me. Mercifully both were avoidable by clambering down, sloshing through shallow water and mud, then pushing my way up through the low, dense vegetation that always grows near water. By this stage I had become fatalistic about snakes.

*

Half an hour later we rounded a hairpin bend and the driver braked so violently that my right foot, caught between the seat and that iron bar, was severely wrenched. Also, my left shin was cut… But at the time I scarcely registered my injuries as we all tried to see what had caused our abrupt stop. …

When we disembarked I did register the damage to my foot. Then I saw that our driver was bleeding from the teeth – not surprisingly, as his seat consisted of two upended beer-crates. …

I was asleep as 1997 became 1998; I can never keep awake for New Year's Eve jollifications. Next morning, when it seemed that Time was not going to be the Great Healer, I limped to the provincial hospital at 7.15. This run-down colonial complex of one-storey units has many beds, a few nurses, a score of servants, and several doctors most of whom tend to concentrate on their private practices. ...

A young woman doctor – elegant, sympathetic – spoke scraps of English and listened to me attentively. Having examined the swollen and inflamed ankle she wrote a prescription for two kinds of pills and a half-litre bottle of pale pink liquid made in Thailand. All that, and a bandage, cost 5,850 kip – about US$ 2.25 – in the hospital pharmacy. Then, inexplicably, I was led across the compound to the radiography department. Why an X-ray after treatment had been prescribed? In a dingy outbuilding the radiographer was still asleep on a mat, his blanket over his head. However, the equipment worked better than the Rumanian machine which in 1990 X-rayed the same foot and found three broken bones. In another unit a teenage trainee nurse, advised by two older colleagues, clumsily bandaged the Foot. Eventually an older, male doctor arrived bearing two X-ray plates (no charge). All was 'normal', he confirmed – but then advised me not to walk for three days and to keep the Foot 'elevated'.

Back in the guesthouse, I read the tiny print on the bottle's label; this liquid was guaranteed to cure heartburn and flatulence, afflictions with which I am happily unacquainted. The pills may well have been for a kidney infection or some thyroid dysfunction so I discarded them. ...

The Foot caused me to spend a fortnight in Luang Prabang, a week longer than planned. After its three non-curative days of rest and elevation, and one painful day of limping around the town, I realised that trekking was *out* for the foreseeable future – though not, oddly enough, cycling. New plan: back to Vientiane by boat – renew visa – buy bicycle – make for Xam Nua and adjacent tourist-free zones.

*

During my six days in and around Xam Nua I saw no other *falang* (foreigners), apart from the German leader of a bomb-disposal team and a Filipino road engineer – a fellow guest.

In winter a strong cool wind tempers the noon sun and a two-hour limp revealed that there is much more to Xam Nua than its main street. Between the street and the Nam Xam lies a bustling area of laneways lined with traders' stalls. Downstream is a pleasant semi-rural residential area of small two-storey Western-style homes interspersed with the traditional dwellings of tribal groups – unstilted. There are no opulent villas or mansions such as one sees around Vientiane and Luang Prabang; Houaphanh is far from the source of NEM [New Economic Mechanism]-generated wealth. As usual the riverbank was the scene of much activity; people bathing and hair-washing, women washing clothes, dishes and vegetables, boys fishing, little girls swimming or just happily splashing around. ...

My limp-about ended in a friendly little restaurant near the bridge where a Beerlao cost double Vientiane's price, for the obvious reason. Here a ground-shaking explosion, close enough to be deafening, interrupted my diary-writing. I looked around in wild surmise. No one else seemed to have noticed the noise, which made me wonder if I had suddenly become prey to hallucinations. But when two more explosions followed, at ten-minute intervals, realisation dawned: a bomb-disposal team at work.

*

Beyond the archway junction an earth track, quite well maintained, ran through a narrow valley – paddy on the left, maize on the right – with an enticing mountain wall at the valley's end. Here I saw another UXO [Unexploded Ordnance] disposal team, waving their magic wands over sloping paddy fields where five days previously a 'bombi' had killed two young women and a toddler – none of them born when those cluster bombs were dropped. The black scar of that tragedy stood out on the golden-brown stubble. Then one of the team noticed the *falang* and shouted and came running towards me. I could not continue: this area was temporarily forbidden to *falangs*. To prove his point he bent down and picked up a fallen

231

wayside sign – trilingual: Lao, German, English. To me it said
STOP! DANGER WIT EXPLOZONS!

Every day in Laos, as in many other countries, people are
being killed or maimed by the leftovers of wars which had to be
fought (we were told) to defend democracy and human rights and
protect the world from the horrors of Communist domination. Yet
now, when the Soviet threat to US global hegemony is no more,
the Americans are ingratiating themselves with the Chinese – still
in theory Communist and continuing relentlessly to repress the
Tibetans, among others. But with a market like China's opening up
none of that matters. Democracy and human rights – forget them!

*

Here I could appreciate the grandeur of the Annamite Chain –
range after range of almost sheer mountains, untouched by man,
their tropical montane forest extending into long narrow valleys
1,000 feet below me. For hours the road wound upwards through
deciduous monsoon forest – not to be confused with rainforest,
unknown in Laos. Here the tallest trees attain 100 feet or more,
their bark whitish, their single trunks quite slender. Many other
hardwoods form the middle canopy – I could identify only Asian
rosewood and teak – and beneath them flourish a wondrous variety
of shrubs and multicoloured grasses. During my next descent the
slopes were bright with blossoming wild plum trees – the first sign
of spring, their delicate luminescence seeming quite magical under
that grey sky amidst the sombre evergreens.

Only the road-builders marred this paradise. Occasionally
an ex-Soviet truck, loaded with gravel and exhaling asphyxiating
fumes, slowly overtook me. Or an empty truck came towards
me. On a mile-long stretch, recently widened, earth-movers had
savaged the landscape, casting magnificent wayside trees into the
abyss below. Indisputably, Route 6 needed attention – but if only it
could have been of a more appropriate kind, a skilled modifying of
the terrain rather than the brutal use of giant machines.

Passing through this desecrated zone, I brooded resentfully, as is my Luddite way, on the many negative aspects of modern technology. Those incongruously aggressive machines were another example of the Rich World's insistence on exporting to the Poor World its own over-dependence on technology. ... We have become the planet's dominant creature because we can think creatively, communicate lucidly, and take responsibility for our personal well-being. If technology reduces most people to a state where such responsible thinking is no longer perceived as necessary – or even possible – what is the prognosis for *Homo sapiens*?

\*

Five minutes later both brakes failed completely and I discovered that a runaway bicycle is much more frightening than a runaway horse – an animate creature with its own sense of self-preservation. Obeying a law of nature, the unrestrained Hare soon gained the sort of speed (30 m.p.h.? – maybe more) that is fun on a tarred road but here was potentially lethal. On one side lay a sheer drop of hundreds of feet, on the other rose a rock cliff. The surface presented multiple hazards: large stones embedded in the earth or loose – mega-potholes – wide patches of fine dust six inches deep – erosion channels between corrugations. ... I was aware of operating on two separate levels, being emotionally sickened by fear while remaining mentally in control, totally focused on judging in fractions of seconds how to negotiate the hazards. Sometimes using the gravelly verge above the drop was the only way to avoid erosion channels which would certainly have unseated me. As Hare's speed increased, I would have been shaken off had I not kept my feet forced down on the pedals with all my strength. No doubt a half-century of cycling experience helped; a bicycle – even an out-of-control bicycle – feels like an extension of my body. ... As we came to the last bend – mercifully not the trickiest – Hare's rattling chain-guard prevented my hearing the approach of a truck. Here the road had been reduced to a single lane by high piles of gravel and the truck had to be on its wrong side – not that the concept of right or wrong sides means anything in outer Houaphanh. Rounding the bend I saw its grey bulk only yards away, apparently blocking the entire track. 'This is it!' flashed through my mind before I saw a narrow space between truck and cliff. Swerving into deep dust, I glimpsed the driver's alarmed face. With only inches to spare on either side, I wobbled wildly – then was beyond that hazard and continuing to hurtle downwards, bounding over ridges and stones. (Not until later did I register a bleeding cut on my left hand where I must have touched the truck.) Now my ordeal's end was visible, the beginning of the next ascent. How long did this ordeal last? The distance covered was about three miles so assuming an average speed of 30 m.p.h. – because in places the gradient eased slightly – it lasted mere minutes. Some minutes!

\*

Tentatively, Mr Phyvan offered rice-beer. My appreciation of this, and my skill at imbibing through the bamboo tube, delighted the family – which included Mrs Phyvan's thirteen-year-old sister and Mr Phyvan's mother, her teeth and mouth hideously disfigured and discoloured by decades of betel-chewing. Mrs Phyvan remained slim, supple and serene-looking after bearing five children, aged nine years to six months. Her husband looked eighteen but was thirty-one; he used his fingers to convey people's ages and everyone watched, giggling incredulously, when I similarly conveyed 'sixty-six'. By then the juvenile neighbours had arrived *en masse*; I counted twenty-five adolescents and children, many with babies on backs, as they sat on the floor, wide-eyed, speculating about me in half-whispers. Photographs of my family, including cats, enthralled them. These, accompanied by the oil-wick lamp, were passed from hand to hand almost reverently, the little ones not being allowed to touch them. For some reason my cats – especially in conjunction with my granddaughters – aroused most excitement.

At the conclusion of this soirée, Mr Phyvan cooked supper while his wife fed the pigs and the eldest daughter fetched firewood from under the house. First my host concentrated on the soup, already simmering gently over glowing logs. Repeatedly he tasted it while adding bits of this and that – dried leaves, crushed nuts, pinches of powder – from the overhead basket. ... Next Mr Phyvan plucked the four birds, having singed their feathers, before grilling them on a bamboo spit: one for each child. The seven-year-old girl then grilled five baby rats; her eldest brother, assisted by the family bitch, had found the rat's nest in the forest. Small fingers dexterously wrapped the tails around a skewer and when half cooked the fur was neatly scraped off with an incongruously enormous knife. These too were for the children; both birds and rats were eaten whole, guts and all – beaks, legs and tails being crunched with relish.

*

All afternoon we sat on the balcony with Grandad, who moved stiffly and breathed with a whistling wheeze. In 1988 a man working two fields away from him struck a bombi (cluster bomb) with his hoe and died instantly: bombis inflict damage over an area of 5,000 square yards and Mr Bounthanh will never fully recover. He lifted his shirt and pointed to his ribcage; numerous steel pellets were visible under the skin. Others are invisible – the cause of his difficult breathing. In 1996 his niece was killed with her four small children while weeding in her field between Muang Kham and Nông Hèt. In the same field, her husband had been killed five months previously. But this was their only field; if they didn't cultivate it they would have no food. ...

This was the poorest *ban* I had stayed in – UXO poor. Cultivable land was nearby; I had been overlooking it, far below on the banks of the Nam Ghouan, as I sat by the roadside. But everyone feared its contents. ...

We dined by oil-wick light, my host and Mr Bounkhoun sitting with me on a mat near the door – all these houses were windowless. The others ate at the shadowy far end of the room, beyond a large *phi* shrine decorated with fresh flowers. This was the only piece of furniture, if it may be so described. Our noodle soup, faintly onion-flavoured, contained none of the interesting ingredients to which I had become accustomed. There was nothing else; Mrs Bounthanh apologised for the lack of rice. The children looked – were – underfed. To the outside world, the Second Indochina War is away in the past – history. To many thousands of Lao, it continues to determine their present and future.

# 2000s

# ENDURANCE TESTS

*Dervla travelled to the Balkan region a few times, but the main trip was in spring 2000, four and a half years after the Bosnian war. She very strongly opposed NATO's military intervention in 1995 and its continued 'peace-keeping' role in the region. Tensions persisted until 1999, shortly before Dervla spent time in the area. Her doggedly cheerful disposition saw her through hard times, as usual.*

*In 2002, she decided to go to Siberia based on a random mention on the World Service that Vladivostok and its hinterland of Ussuriland were 'at present without facilities for tourists' – the prospect of a tourist-free zone was catnip to her. She hurt her knee very badly on her first trip and returned in early 2004, as she had fallen in love with Lake Baikal and felt she had to see it again. She really loved the cold.*

*Dervla first visited Cuba with Rachel and her three granddaughters in late 2005, then immediately returned alone, in early 2006 and again in autumn 2007. She loved Havana, despite her customary allergy to cities, because, she surmised, habaneros behaved more like villagers than city dwellers. Her trip didn't manage to dampen her admiration for Castroism, despite the everyday hardships endured by Cubans, as it always endeavoured to provide for basic needs and to achieve excellence in many fields.*

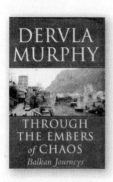

*Through The Embers of Chaos:*
*Balkan Journeys* (2002)
Serbia, Croatia, Bosnia-
Herzegovina [BiH], Albania,
Montenegro, Kosovo

[Serbia] Mika, a maths graduate who could find no appropriate job, spoke almost perfect English and recalled that during the air war Serbian TV had shown Europe's anti-NATO demos again and again and again. Here my tale becomes improbable but is true. After only a brief conversation Mika glanced sideways at me and exclaimed, 'I think I know your voice! You talked against NATO in some Irish city where that Clinton woman was being given publicity – am I right?'

I affirmed his memory; I had indeed spoken at a protest meeting in May 1999 when Mrs Clinton was being given the Freedom of the City of Galway.

Said Mika, 'Here ordinary Serbs are suffering so much – for what? Who gains by our suffering? What aim does it achieve? Why are we being punished? And what will happen next? Many fear a terrorist campaign run by NATO and the CIA – so they can have Serbia as well as Kosovo!' ...

\*

As we enjoyed our *chorba* (soup) and fresh bread rolls, Jasminka continued predictably: 'NATO is the world's biggest bully!'

'Anyway the biggest since Ghengis Khan,' interposed Janko.

239

'Why did they attack a country that couldn't defend itself from high-altitude bombers? How could they forget we fought with them against Hitler?'

Everywhere in Serbia I found this last point giving rise to an acrid disappointment, a genuinely baffled sense of betrayal. By way of uniting the new socialist federation, Titoism presented Yugoslavs with a selective history of the Second World War, concentrating on the Partizans' heroic deeds (which were truly heroic) and scarcely mentioning those other Yugoslav fighters, including thousands of Serbs, who sided with the Nazis.

Janko then announced that he would borrow a friend's car next day and show me many more 'war crimes' in and around Niš. When offered similar tours in Belgrade I had pleaded 'lack of time' but Niš provided insufficient diversions for that excuse to be plausible.

On my way to the Deligrad Motel, I brooded on the 'international community's' 'new idealism'. To the Serbs, whether or not they condoned or condemned their government's brutal counter-insurgency methods in Kosovo, that campaign was their own business – a domestic matter, not an excuse for NATO to violate their sovereignty, without declaring war, and shatter their economy. The air war apologists' attitude they would have found incomprehensible, had they been aware of it. When your own human rights are being literally hammered into the ground, you are unimpressed by the argument that our world has moved into a new era and henceforth the 'defence of human rights' must take precedence over respect for national sovereignty. Who can imagine NATO disregarding, on behalf of their afflicted minorities, the sovereign rights of China or Russia, or Turkey or India?

\*

[Croatia] In the village's main cafe – a tawdry 1980s structure – the floor had been cleared for dancing by stacking most tables and chairs along one wall. Younger people were in a minority though what passed for music was geared to their taste. Truly dreadful cacophonies were exacerbated by shrieking men and women who, if heard in another context, would immediately be identified as torture victims. ...

The hours passed, the cigarette-smoky fug became eye-stinging, the pile of empty beer-crates outside the entrance to the loo rose rapidly. By midnight I was wearing a pair of outsize shiny plastic boobs with ostentatiously erect nipples and was balancing a chair on my head while a man sporting waist-length golden ringlets stood on a stool trying to thrust his plastic mega-penis into my left ear. This is known as 'entering into the spirit of things'. Mrs Veselica was running around with a plastic axe pretending to castrate young men who feigned terror at her approach. And Melita, wearing a bearded mask, was attempting to 'rape' a teenage girl clad in a transparent pink nightgown augmented by a knee-length, shawl-like black wig. It could all be described as good dirty fun, peasant-style – hilariously vulgar but not even slightly salacious. This is a community, I was later informed, where even in the year 2000 pre-marital sex is OUT; so perhaps these carnival capers serve as a safety valve of sorts.

A long time after midnight we wavered home, all drunk – Mrs Veselica, Aunty, Melita and I linking arms and giggling and stumbling. Then we ate vast amounts of blotting-paper bread and cold sausage, followed by mugs of an excellent chicken broth prepared by the children while their elders were misbehaving. And so to bed after goodnight kisses all round.

\*

[Bosnia-Herzegovina] I found a row of concrete-filled tar barrels blocking the BiH border, which explained the blissful lack of motor traffic all the way from Glina. Ruairi [her bicycle] could have been wheeled between the barrels but a surly young man, emerging from a nearby shrapnel-scarred house (the only building in sight) wordlessly discouraged this illegality. He pointed to an earth track leading to the main Vojnić to Velika Kladuša road and the official crossing. Thus I came by chance upon Batnoga, the infamous Agrokomerc chicken-farm refugee camp described by Tim Judah as 'the epitome of the Bosnian nightmare'. Here my imagination didn't merely boggle, it cravenly swerved away from the image of 20,000 frightened human beings enduring confinement for four months in a few battery-henhouses within sight of their own hilltop homes in Velika Kladuša, less than two miles away. Not until the end of 1994 were those thousands released from their torment. ...

Most 'Abdić refugees' eventually returned to Velika Kladuša (what choice had they?) where it did not surprise me to find the atmosphere uncheerful. It takes more than four and a half years for people to recover from such a sequence of severe communal traumas.

*

Typically, in the course of this well-planned terrorist campaign, Chetnik [Serbian forces] paramilitaries overran a town, murdered many Bosniak [Muslim] and/or Croat civilians and expelled the rest. Surviving Bosniaks of military age were either used as slave labourers or held in concentration camps under unimaginably cruel conditions. Next the JNA [Yugoslav National Army]-protected local Serbs were put in charge, with orders to demolish their town's mosques, madrasas, hammams and other centuries-old relics of Ottoman civilisation. Many of the Chetniks were criminals who had been released early on condition they 'fought well'. Milošević's secret police controlled their military activities and colluded in their black-marketeering.

In mid-April 1992 the Bosniak Mayor of Cazin and his Chief of Police pleaded pathetically for the UN to take over the administration of the whole Bihać Pocket and eject the JNA. By then Bosanka Krupa's Bosniaks knew an attack was imminent; the town's Serbian women and children had been temporarily evacuated. At about 5 p.m. on 21 April the first shell was fired and the Chetnik gangs went into action with assault rifles and machine guns. For three days the shelling continued, until all the Bosniak buildings on the right bank of the Una had been reduced to irreparable ruins. Then the 'cleansing' began. Prisoners from the town jail were used to collect corpses and clear rubble. No one will ever know how many men of military age were murdered. More than 3,000 women and children, from Bosanka Krupa and surrounding villages, were dispatched to concentration camps.

At first, in BiH's mixed villages (and most were mixed), the Chetniks could not rely on local Serbs to kill or evict their Bosniak friends, neighbours, work-mates – sometimes in-laws. The solution for this problem was also used by the Interhamwe leaders of Rwanda's genocide. A gang would arrive in a village, approach a Serbian home and compel the head of the household (or his grown-up son) to accompany them to a Bosniak home where any available male was bidden to join the party. Those neighbours were then taken to a public place where the Serb was ordered to kill the Bosniak and provided with an AK-47 or – more usually – a knife. The many Serbs who refused to co-operate when this campaign opened were instantly shot dead. Soon all Serbs could be relied upon to obey Chetnik orders to 'cleanse' their villages.

*

Battered, shattered, devastated, demolished, ravaged, razed, levelled – I'm running out of adjectives. Even in combination, those words hardly describe what was done to Kožarac. They relate only to structures (none was spared) and don't begin to convey the immense melancholy of the place eight years afterwards – the terror and suffering and grief held in the atmosphere, suspended above the scene like a cloud of emotional dust.

Only a few elderly Serb peasants had drifted back to the ghost of their hometown because they had nowhere else to go. When I stopped to photograph a dynamited mosque one of them shouted at me angrily, waving a clenched fist. The madrasa was too big for its seventeenth-century magnificence to have been totally obliterated by JNA artillery. Some construction had been started by an EU-sponsored Austrian company but they seemed to have abandoned the project.

I spent half an hour in the enormous graveyard, covering acres. (All my life I've been addicted to graveyards.) The earliest legible headstone, exquisitely carved, was dated 1688; the latest was dated 2000 – not a headstone, just a simple wooden memorial to a Bosniak brought back (from where?) to lie in the earth to which he belonged. This was a mixed community of the departed, Bosniaks and Serbs lying together in death as they had lived together until their leaders divided them.

*

Then – tension. Three policemen arrived, demanding to see my passport. The oldest, balding and obese, could easily be imagined organising a massacre. The fortyish one obviously hated foreigners. The young one, their interpreter, seemed pleasant enough but was not allowed to converse with me.

Baldie angrily accused me of having an expired Serbian visa. I retorted that that was irrelevant: I was in BiH. Baldie insisted that tourists must have a Serbian visa for Republika Srpska. 'Rubbish!' I scoffed. 'This is not part of Serbia.' Baldie, red with rage, pocketed my passport and said the visa fee was DM50. I laughed at him and said 'No deal!' He shouted something which was not translated, buttoned the pocket holding my passport and lumbered away, followed by his subordinates – the junior giving me a furtive sideways glance that might have been of admiration.

'Bad men!' muttered the manager. 'Very rich, after the war, everyone running away to Croatia over the bridge must pay them. Anyone don't give them all their marks can't cross.'

An hour later Baldie and the youth returned. If I paid for my visa next morning in the police station my passport could be retrieved. Cheerfully I lied. 'In Sarajevo I can easily get a new passport – now I'm going to bed.' Standing up, I collected my journal, pens, photographs, maps, then said goodnight to the manager, ignored the police and departed the scene.

I was brushing my teeth when there came a knock on the door. The manager, beaming, handed me my passport. 'You're too smart for them!' he chuckled.

*

[Albania] On this high plateau the road rose and fell between the bare crags of mountain summits, with grassy valleys wide and shallow on my right. Soon after brunch I passed five children (two girls, three boys) sitting with a granny-figure on a long slab of rock overlooking their grazing flock. When greeted, they stared at me with a blend of incredulity and excitement. Moments later, coming to a severe gradient, I dismounted and only then noticed that the children were pursuing me – as friendly and curious children have done in a dozen countries. These, however, were neither friendly nor curious but predatory. Crowding around me, they grabbed at Ruairi, demanding DM, and were only briefly deflected by the contents of my purse – a few hundred leks, thrown downhill. Luckily that incline was short but as I remounted they caught up with me, pushed me to the ground, and one lad tugged at the rain-cape strapped to the carrier. Standing up, I seized the pump and laid about me, striking two boys on their heads – whereupon they all fled. But they didn't flee far. When I had to dismount for the next steep climb they were already in position up the mountain on my left, from where they pelted me with sharp stones. I know they were sharp because one of them cut my scalp.

That encounter shook me, despite the brigands' age – seven to twelve-year-olds, I estimated. They had after all knocked me to the ground, my right elbow was grazed and aching and my scalp was bleeding. Moreover, I sensed that the granny-figure would have condoned their robbing me. Then, stopping to pee, I realised that they *had* robbed me; both pannier side-pockets were empty. This astounded me, given the design of those pockets, with strong zips concealed under tight rain-proof flaps. Going on my uphill way, I mourned the loss of my indispensable Marco Polo map, a plastic wallet holding precious addresses of people already met and contacts yet to be made in Kosovo, a leather photograph wallet, James Pettifer's *Blue Guide to Albania*, Misha Glenny's *The Fall of Yugoslavia*, Serbo-Croat and Albanian mini-dictionaries and phrasebooks, my spongebag-cum-first-aid-kit, a blank notebook, four unused films and a large packet of 'emergency rations' peanuts. Few of those items would reward the children's remarkable dexterity. By far the most serious losses were the map and the addresses. I hope those to whom I should have written gratefully on my return home will one day read these lines. ...

Most of my journeys have been through countries where any Westerner, even me on a bike, seems rich – yet never before have I met children like these. And now what about my ardent support for non-violent methods of conflict resolution?! How does that fit with my physically attacking children? Very quickly, under pressure, our ideals go phut and brute force seems the obvious response. I also ask myself – if the local peasants produce criminal children, capable of such well-organised attacks, what must the adolescents and adults be like? I'm not going to stay around to find out. Next stop Kosovo – by vehicle.

*

If asked to put my impressions of 'Kosovo 2000' in a one-word nutshell I could only say 'unreal'. Pretence permeated the atmosphere. The pretence that all KLA [Kosovo Liberation Army] members could be either disarmed or converted to a socially responsible Civil Defence Force. The pretence that the ragbag UN police were willing and able to perform as a cohesive, disciplined unit. The pretence that the Trio (UNMIK, OSCE, K-For)* could persuade the Kosovars to roll out 'WELCOME' carpets for Serb

* UNMIK: United Nations Mission in Kosovo; OSCE: Organization for Security and Co-operation in Europe; K-For: Kosovo Protection Force (NATO led)

returnees, that both communities could be induced to 'co-exist and collaborate in an atmosphere of mutual tolerance'. The pretence that because the Security Council opposed an independent Kosovo it could be kept off the agenda forever. The pretence that *one man* was the problem and post-Milošević all would be well. And the central pretence that the Trio formed a resolute, caring, united team.

*

[Montenegro] In the village groups of women and girls, fetching water from standpipes, seemed startled to see me. This fertile valley's farmhouses were surrounded by fields of alfalfa, decorated with seeding dandelions looking like a powdering of silver fluff. A few cows and herds of goats grazed in securely fenced pastures.

I breakfasted not far beyond the village, sitting on a slab of rock. All around me grew minute unfamiliar flowers: orange and pink and yellow and every shade of blue. As I exercised my jaws on what passes for salami in Cetinje, the day's third car appeared, then stopped. The driver leant out to offer me a lift – an elderly man with kind eyes. He looked both worried and perplexed when, having expressed much gratitude, I declined his offer.

This reminded me of the Zagreb friend who had investigated me on the internet and discovered a derogatory review of *South from the Limpopo*. The reviewer wondered, 'Why does the author travel by bicycle? What is she trying to prove?' Sadly, there now exists a generation too motor-dependent to be capable of understanding a cyclist's motivation. *I* often wonder, 'Why do people travel by car/bus? What's the point?' Had some misfortune compelled me to cross the Lovćen Pass by motor transport, a few stops to 'admire the view' would not have consoled me. Cyclists know the joy of being *with* a place, rather than glimpsing it from inside a speedy machine. ...

Before beginning the descent I counted eight hairpin bends, precisely aligned, directly below me like the steps of a stairs; and there were twenty-four more. ...

Lovćen's precipices – emphatically not slopes – are quite densely forested: mostly pines on the higher ground, then oak, hazel, beech, juniper, cypress. Some trees have grown *through* vast smooth slabs of rock, split by the 'power of plants'; others protrude from the precipices at grotesque angles, between massive outcrops that make them seem like weeds. This was my most dramatic ever descent with a bicycle. (Trekking descents, amongst serious mountain ranges, are in another league.) I write 'with a bicycle' because I chose to walk down; in certain places, even bicycles are too speedy.

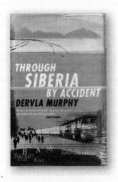

## *Through Siberia by Accident* (2005)
## Siberia

We were still chugging through the heavily industrialised Urals – their low sprawl extends for hundreds of miles – when misfortune struck. In the minuscule loo-cum-washroom passengers fixated on personal hygiene 'shower' themselves from the basin tap, leaving the metal floor soap-slippy. As I opened the door to leave, a young woman was approaching with babe in arms – a projectile-vomiting babe. Hastily I stepped backwards and simultaneously the train gave one of its not infrequent violent jerks. Losing my balance, I reached out to clutch the handbasin and didn't fall but twisted my right leg awkwardly. At the time I felt only a slight momentary pain in my knee, seemingly of no consequence. But in fact a fall might have been less damaging; I woke next morning to find myself maimed, the pain intolerable when I put weight on my right leg. Because the knee was unblemished – no bruise, scratch, swelling or inflammation – the diagnosis was easy: a damaged cartilage for which the only cure is rest.

Without visible evidence, explaining my plight to Mrs Baranskaya and Aline required much dictionary use, supplemented by a pantomime which seemed to irritate Mr Baranskaya and sent Dima into convulsions of laughter. Mrs Baranskaya spent a quarter of an hour excavating a tube of ointment from the depths of an enormous nylon sack, then expertly massaged the injury; she was a

249

nurse by profession. Physically this treatment achieved nothing but emotionally it gave comfort.

*

Dr Babenko had examined my knee thoroughly but gently, Dr Kutuzov was much rougher and to my fury undid some of the healing already achieved. However, no one could accuse him of not devoting time to his patients. He drew several diagrams to illustrate what had certainly happened and what might have happened. Possibly fat had oozed in between cartilage and bone and was impeding healing in which case an operation would be inevitable. Hence the need for an X-ray next morning and now my leg must be put in 'gyps'. That word made me flinch; in Rumania a ton-weight of nineteenth-century plaster of Paris, also described as 'gyps', had burdened my right leg for eight weeks. Nor was plaster the appropriate treatment: another waste of scarce resources. And anyway my knee had been healing slowly but surely until Dr Kutuzov jerked it. Forcefully I said 'No!' to the gyps – very likely with flashing eyes – but when the doctor showed signs of surrendering Igor threw a tantrum and attacked him for not being more resolute which provoked me to snap, 'I'm off to the Yunost!' (Momentarily I had forgotten that without assistance I couldn't go anywhere.)

*

For thirty-six sweaty hours I had been looking forward to a cold shower, or at least a cold wash. But this was not to be. As her home lacked a bathroom, Yulia had arranged for me to 'enjoy' a friend's *banya*, ten minutes' walk away. It was nearly midnight and very dark as we stumbled through a cabbage patch to a wooden hut on stilts, its stove pipe sticking through the shingle roof. Normally *banya*-dependent families light the furnace only on a Friday or Saturday, for their weekly cleansing of the pores, so Yulia's friends had gone to a lot of trouble on my behalf. Soon I wished they hadn't, as I stood naked enduring 36°C and not knowing what to do next. Jugs stood beside a big tin bath of hot water and a big enamel basin of cold water. The stove consisted of three tar barrels welded together and half-full of red-hot stones. A slatted bench ran the length of one wall and above it hung big sheaves of leafy birch twigs. Sweat cascaded off me as I washed in the lukewarm 'cold' water. When Yulia came to collect me she was both amused and disgusted to find her guest throwing dirty water onto the cabbages. Had I used the *banya* correctly, the water poured over my body would have flowed away along the sloping floor to its appointed exit. Later I learned that one is meant to lie on the bench while an appropriate family member, or a friend of the same sex, beats one with the twigs, a process widely believed to cure most diseases.

*

Suddenly I was out of the taiga [forest], approaching a steep cliff, overlooking a still expanse of blueness. On a calm day, under a clear sky, Baikal's blueness is intense, peculiar, indescribable, heart-stopping. I hastened down to the sandy shore and moments later Lake Baikal had received me. As one plunges into these blessed depths all the famous statistics seem irrelevant. Centuries before scientists had recorded its physical uniqueness, the few who lived around Baikal's shores – and many others who lived far away, in the mountains of Mongolia or on the northern tundra – recognised and revered this lake's magic, knew it as 'the Hallowed Sea'.

It boosted my morale to be able to use my body vigorously without pain. The water's temperature was much the same as an Irish river's in early summer, exhilarating but not chilling. Sometimes I relaxed and floated and gazed at the surrounding mountains – ranges aloof and austere, known only to a few local hunters. (And allegedly, in their more formidable recesses, as yet known to nobody.) Half a dozen other swimmers were visible in the distance and smugly I pitied those millions who in August pullulate on the beaches of tourist destinations.

As I dressed, two fishermen were standing in the shallows, teaching small sons how to cast. And on my way back through the taiga mothers were teaching even smaller children how to identify edible mushrooms – picking inedibles, prodding and sniffing them, then decisively discarding them while grimacing. I would have liked to lie on the mossy cliff edge, in the shade of pines and larches, revelling in the Baikal blueness far below, but a coalition of vicious midges and tiny biting ants deterred me.

*

Although Severobaikalsk's port looks shambolic – an unhealed developer's wound along the shore – Lake Baikal is what counts. My grass-surrounded hut was only thirty seconds' walk from the depths (I timed it) and on my balcony I could hear wavelets whispering over the sand. This didn't seem at all the sort of place where disaster would strike.

During the small hours on that first night I went out to pee by starlight. Had I been sensible and used a torch I would automatically have avoided those planks of rotten wood covering a four-foot-deep hole. (The hole's provenance is obscure and irrelevant; possibly someone at some stage had wanted to bury a body, it was of grave dimensions.) This, unlike the BAM [train] accident, was serious; all my weight came down on my right leg and for long moments the pain was extreme. Having pulled myself out of the hole – I can't remember exactly how – I sordidly peed in my pants, crawled back to base on all fours and collapsed on the bed. I was too shaken to assess the damage but able luridly to curse my stupidity; this was a tormenting 'if only …' situation. Then I slept: on such occasions the body's chemistry rapidly provides an analgesic.

At sunrise I woke, stood up, walked a few steps, rejoiced that no bones were broken. My diagnosis, based on previous experiences, were: a torn calf muscle, a twisted ankle (very swollen) and further damage to my knee, perhaps something displaced because when bent it made a funny-peculiar clicking noise and the pain was sharp. Oddly, the original problem hadn't been exacerbated; walking, though agonising, remained possible, as it had not been on the BAM. Initially the torn muscle caused the most pain, yet it was the first injury to heal completely.

Swimming, miraculously, was almost painfree and I took physical and emotional comfort from Baikal's magic while adjusting to the fact that I was not destined to visit Ussuriland in 2002.

*

Before returning to Raisa's flat – a no-smoking area – I relaxed with a *pivo* [beer] at my favourite open-air café. The sun was still hot and cheerfully chatting 'after-workers' in summery attire strolled up and down a long plaza, overlooked by dour 1970s office blocks and lined with improvised bars, food stalls and kiosks. A canal-like concrete 'water feature' stretched the length of this plaza with variegated litter floating on its surface and fountains feebly playing. Pigeons and sparrows competed for crumbs beneath café tables. Here were several of those Irkutsk citizens who most disturbed me: my contemporaries, old women at the end of respectable, hardworking lives whose pensions had evaporated in the heat of capitalism. They never begged but scavenged desperately with downcast eyes. Empty beer bottles were especially coveted and watchfully they lingered around the tables, then seized each empty bottle to add to a little collection which, when sold, would enable them to buy a loaf of bread. One babushka paused at the just vacated table beside mine to gather a few crisps left in a saucer and dusted with cigarette ash which she blew off before relishing this treat.

*

At 7 a.m. a thick chilly mist hovered above the [river] Lena. Its embankments were deserted, all important cargo having been taken on the previous evening, and as I explored I seemed to have the steamer to myself. Down at steerage level, I peered into the malodorous dusk where raucous snoring startled me: two young men, evidently adenoidal, lay asleep on the floor wrapped in nylon sacking. They were, I later discovered, working their way to Yakutsk as porters. ...

Ornithologically the Lena is more rewarding than the BAM line or Lake Baikal. Within a few hours I had seen black and white duck, herring gulls, kestrels and even a few lordly eagles circling high and slow above the taiga. I also listed the day's traffic: five oil-tankers, four vehicle ferries, two small hydrofoils serving Kirensk, two coal barges returning empty to Ust'-Kut and another colossal barge packed with scores of BAM freight wagons.

At 8.10 the sun set, leaving a sky tinted peach to the meridian and the Lena suffused with rosy ripples in our wake. And then, suddenly, the air was cold. Some time during the night we would arrive at Kirensk, our first port of call, founded by Vasili Bugor and his posse of Cossacks in 1530.

That evening I got very drunk very quickly on only two litres of *pivo* [beer]. Conveniently I was already settled on my bunk, writing, so I could gracefully keel over where I sat; a footless babushka would not have amused Katarina. Next morning the label told me that Ludmilla had provided top quality 'alc. 8 per cent' instead of the standard 'alc. 4 per cent' – and one shouldn't drink 'alc. 8 per cent' quickly. I'm still puzzling over the last barely legible and totally irrelevant lines of my diary for 12 September. 'Being an o.a.p. does have lots of advantages, to compensate for certain disadvantages.' What can those advantages be?

\*

When I mentioned going by bus to Neryungri people frowned, or drew in their breath sharply, or looked sympathetic, or bluntly advised me to fly. Ksenya said, 'Most of us fly, even if we have to borrow the fare.' Feodor gave me a bottle of vodka 'for emergencies'. ... This was my farewell to the Lena. ... When I looked at my watch on the far side, it astonished me that we had spent an hour crossing that six-mile expanse. The Lena is hypnotically soothing. Much has been written about 'the spirit of place', some of it tiresomely fanciful, but truly the Lena spirit does take one over. ...

The rain had stopped when I registered a new sound, a mysterious, erratic thudding or bumping, as though someone were hitting the rear of the bus with a mallet. Was this another defect being made manifest, or merely the bus's reasonable reaction to a neglected gravel surface? Then our pace slowed, and slowed – to cycling speed – to walking speed – and at 4.20 we stopped in the miserable little settlement of Uluu. Everyone silently disembarked, accepting that this was a major mechanical crisis. ...

By five o'clock I was so cold, despite ceaseless walking, that prudence dictated a retreat to the bus. As the heating system didn't work when the engine was off its temperature had dropped far below freezing and some sleepers were awakening and rummaging frantically through their luggage for warmer garments. I unrolled my flea-bag, snuggled into it – only my nose left exposed – and within moments was again asleep. ...

For a mile or so, on the road's uncarpeted side, we descended yard by yard, our movement scarcely perceptible. Then Mitya [driver] had to contend only with the humdrum hazards of the M56: craterous pot-holes, permafrost molehill-like eruptions, eroded verges and so on. I unclenched my fists and took another, celebratory, swig of vodka. ...

A few passengers disembarked at Neryungri's AYaM station, some two miles from the city centre. Then, evidently as a 'thank you' for our cheerful acceptance of multiple misfortunes, Mitya – despite his own exhaustion – took everyone to their widely scattered individual destinations, instead of leaving us all at the bus terminus. I was put down near the PNILZ hotel at 2.20 p.m., exactly thirty hours after leaving Yakutsk. A slow cyclist, doing an average of 8 m.p.h., could cover those 456 miles in only twice that time.

\*

I found Pavel in rather low spirits; a few recent incidents involving his university friends in various cities were troubling him, incidents to do with 'destructive bribery in the groves of academe'. Plaintively he continued, 'Soviet corruption was widespread, but rare in the academic world. Russians had intellectual integrity and were proud of it and respected for it internationally.' The cynical and ruthless precision of the bribery pay-scale struck me as peculiarly morally repulsive: 200 roubles for a 'satisfactory' mark, 300 for a 'good' mark, 500 for 'excellent'. A lecturer/professor with scores of students does very nicely, thank you. Some degrees can be bought for $50, paid in dollar bills.

*

I was alone on the shore for my sunrise reunion with Lake Baikal. Rounded banks of deep pink cloud were touching the sharp crags, now snow-blunted, of its guardian mountains. Waves pulsed loudly on the gravel and sand, curling whitely before a strong wind. As I walked the wind dropped, the clouds faded to shades of grey – were broken – and through them streamed rays from the hidden sun, tinting the distant summits until they matched the autumn taiga on the cliffs above me. Then Lake Baikal, responding gloriously to the subdued light, became a trembling expanse of bronze.

*

In Olga's view, the retention of internal passports and residence permit regulations was not the result of inertia or ignorance about other systems. 'It shows Putin wants to keep democracy *out*! Under Yeltsin, even under Gorbachev, we relaxed and felt more free to criticise openly. Since 1 January 2000 that's been changing, at first slowly, now faster and faster. Putin cuts back on support for most state institutions but gives extra power and funding to law-enforcement agencies. The police beat up opposition political meetings. The Kremlin again controls most of the media, taken over from the big-business gangs who'd got control by the end of Yeltsin's time. Putin loves the Americans' "War Against Terrorism", all groups he doesn't like can be called "terrorists", given no media chance to make their arguments, imprisoned without trial forever. When the US is doing that to groups they don't like, the West can't criticise Putin for doing the same!'

Everyone listened in silence, no one commented. Most of my friends among Siberia's younger generation seemed cynically indifferent to everything connected with politics, not unlike their contemporaries throughout the superficially 'democratic' West.

\*

West of the Urals we suddenly entered a rainy zone where light snow was thawing on wide fields, exposing short green grass – vividly green, almost home-like. Here the embankment shrubs and birches had not yet shed their leaves; the Urals, puny as they seem, do make a difference.

An hour short of Moscow my respect for our pristine coach was negated by a large jar of red caviar, a farewell gift which I had been assured would survive the journey. When I began to pack and moved it, it literally blew its top, spurting a singularly sticky substance all over the lower bunks. (Happily Viktor had already packed and moved to the buffet car.) There was nothing I could do to repair the damage; a major operation, involving some anti-fermented-caviar detergent, was called for. Guiltily I slunk down the corridor to our *provodnitsa's* [conductor's] office and confessed, using vigorous sign-language. I hadn't seen this buxom blonde smiling once in four and a half days but now she laughed aloud.

*Silverland: A Winter Journey beyond the Urals* (2007)
Russia & Siberia

Siberia's rulers, rather than its climate, were to blame for those extremities of suffering long associated with the land beyond the Urals. In fact, given enough food and clothing, inhabited Siberia's winters are fun and so regarded by the average citizen. Only when the wind blows do they complain of the cold. Sunshine all day almost every day fosters cheerfulness, while snow and ice generate enjoyable activities as rain and mud do not. People can skate, cross-country ski, roll around naked after a *banya* [sauna], then cook multi-course picnics over bonfires. However, in mid-winter the fine, dry snow resembles caster sugar and children must wait until the thaw is imminent to make snowballs and snowmen. Then every public space becomes a battlefield and snowpersons breed fast.

This atmospheric dryness also has drawbacks. Within days my maps and paperbacks had become wrinkled and brittle and my Rymans notebook was shedding its leaves – an inconvenience to this day, as I work with it on my desk. Then the leather jacket of a hip flask disintegrated, which rather upset me; it was a cherished mascot, presented to me in November 1974 by my publisher, Jock Murray, on the eve of my departure for the snowy Karakoram.

From Severobaikalsk's taiga-fringed clifftop a wide, steep track leads to Baikal's narrow shore, sandy in summertime and blissfully free of notices, advertisements, seats, kiosks or any other 'amenities'. Here the autumn blizzards pile up broken ice, then smother it in snow. Before that fall has time to freeze solid, youngsters dig caves and mould embrasures, creating a winter-long play area – also enjoyed by grown-ups who may be seen posing for photographs as they peer out of caves, holding aloft gigantic slabs of ice.

*

In 2005 a reviewer, Damian Thompson, diagnosed me as 'a typical old Irish Leftie [who] cannot disguise her sneaking regard for the Soviet Union'. Not quite a bull's-eye but Mr Thompson didn't entirely miss the target. However, there is nothing specifically Irish about recognising that beyond its borders 'the evil empire' caused much less suffering than Western developers cause. Third World citizens who attempt to oppose First World commercial interests are repressed as ruthlessly as ever the Soviets repressed their dissidents. Democracy, so loudly lauded, is undermined whenever a democratically elected Third World government seeks to control its national economy for the electors' benefit. In the Soviet Union many 'human rights', as futilely defined in the UN Charter, were routinely trampled on; yet most citizens enjoyed certain fundamental rights denied to victims of the capitalist alliance (trans-national corporations, corrupt post-colonial governments, international financial institutions). In their fatally muddled way Soviet economists did put people before profits and, given the opportunity, millions on three continents would have opted for a local adaptation of Communism, such as the Kerala model. A full belly (however monotonous the diet), a weatherproof home (however cramped), adequate clothing (however drab), free education and medication – those 'rights' come first for most people. But while corporate capitalism Rules OK, billions throughout the Third World ain't gonna get 'em.

*

Beyond the small town of Khani something odd appeared above the stillness of the distant frozen river – a serpentine swathe of mobile mist, perhaps 300 yards long, curling upwards like steam. Which is what it was: not really odd in this region of extinct volcanoes, daily earth tremors and numerous hot springs. As BAM [Baikal–Amur Mainline] ran closer to those springs, and slanting sun rays touched the scene, we were in a magic silverland. For brilliant miles, every hoar-frosted tree, bush and reed glittered and shimmered, their embellishment – never normally seen in Siberia's extremity of dryness – seeming the creation of some tutelary spirit. Twice during the next few hours this phenomenon was repeated.

*

That afternoon Olesja's friend Andrei dropped in, his visit coinciding with Anna's. Anna was Eva's twenty-five-year-old English teacher, keen to practise with a native speaker, so I heard something about Andrei's exploits as a junior army officer in Chechnya in the mid-1990s. He himself had killed twenty-seven 'terrorists' – or so he claimed – and his unit had lost only two men. He had had 'a good war'. Now he wished he could be back on the scene of action but his mother had bribed both himself and his senior officer to keep him safe in Tynda. Thousands of terrorists, he assured me, had come to Chechnya from all over the Middle East, from Afghanistan and Turkish Kurdistan 'and other Mussulman places' – all armed with 'the best weapons', all carrying 'sacks of dollars', all intent on destabilising Russia and 'fighting the Orthodox Church'. Observing Andrei's expression as he recalled his personal bag of twenty-seven, it was too easy to imagine him gleefully participating in violence – as it seems the majority of young males will do, almost anywhere, if misinformed and roused to anger.

*

In a small café near the museum I met my first outgoing Komsomolskian – Angelica … As I paid for a *pivo* no words were exchanged but her friendly smile lifted my spirits. While diary-writing I was conscious of being observed. Then Angelica was replaced by a younger woman, obviously her daughter, and she came to my table to offer me a *pivo* 'on the house'. Twenty minutes later, after an arduous dictionary-led conversation, we were on a trolleybus together, going to a distant suburb. Angelica's youngest daughter, Nina, dreamed of talking to English-speakers…

By current Western standards, Nina's ambition was almost banal: jobs in 'glamorous' cities, saving enough to backpack around the world – to her capitalist contemporaries, a human right. But this Komsomolsk eighteen-year-old was in a position not unlike my own in 1950, trapped in a little Irish town, longing to be free. I was constrained by family responsibilities, she by her economic circumstances and other peoples' immigration laws. Roubles and a Russian passport don't take you far. As we considered her career prospects I recognised a true kindred spirit; Nina didn't want to migrate to get rich, her wanderlust was genuine. And she wished to travel alone, off the beaten track – not that the twenty-first century offers many unbeaten tracks to solitary travellers. It can be destructive to rouse false hopes but given Nina's doggedness, and the propellant power of her motives, it seemed reasonable to predict that she would soon be out of Komsomolsk, though perhaps not in London or New York. …

Nina accompanied me to the centre where she was meeting her Korean boyfriend of whom Angelica disapproved because he drank too much. As we parted she said, 'Thank you! I feel now not crazy, you show my dreams can be real life!' …

In the station waiting-room at 5.45 p.m. two figures rose to greet me – Angelica and Nina. Guiding me to my *platskartny* [carriage], they requested a steely-eyed, square-jawed *provodnitsa* [conductor] to cherish the Irish babushka, presented me with a plastic bag of sustenance (bread, salami, chocolate, *pivo*), then vigorously hugged me before withdrawing to make way for a throng of heavily laden passengers. Nina and I are still corresponding.

*

Over breakfast, Zoya became red with rage and torrentially voluble when I mentioned 'conscripts'. She was, Leo explained, a Mothers' Rights Fund organiser and currently engaged in helping to investigate a scandal.

In both Komsomolsk and Khabarovsk I had noticed groups of off-duty conscripts – undersized and wan, looking malnourished to the point of illness, markedly deficient in the joys of youth. Their appearance shockingly recalled photographs of labour camp inmates: the Old Russia intruding on the New. Annually, 400,000 youngsters are recruited for two years' training – a programme the army can no longer afford – and the latest scandal was the small tip of a very large iceberg.

On 3 December 2003, 194 conscripts had been flown to the Far East to act as Federal border guards, their families not knowing their destination when they left the Moscow region, dressed for European rather than Siberian temperatures. At Novosibirsk, where their plane broke down, they were ordered to sleep without bedding on a barracks floor and given no supper. That night the temperature was −18°C. Subsequently, during two refuelling stops, they had to stand on the tarmac, still inadequately clothed, for more than an hour in temperatures between −20° and −25°C – with a wind. On arrival at Kamchatka warm clothing was issued but by then all were ill – eighty-four suffering from acute respiratory diseases and in urgent need of hospital care. Nine days later they were flown to Magadan, one of Siberia's coldest inhabited regions, where another two weeks passed before the eighty-four were admitted to hospital. The doctors diagnosed malnutrition in addition to their multiple infections. One eighteen-year-old died after four days in intensive care. As we spoke, in mid-February, forty remained in hospital and were unlikely to be fit for 'training', said Zoya, without a prolonged convalescence on a good diet.

Had I not chanced to notice those forlorn conscripts Zoya's story might have seemed incredible. 'How could it be allowed to happen?' was my first reaction.

Another angry torrent from Zoya. Leo translated: 'My mother says it was always the same, under czars or Soviets conscripts never had value. If they collapsed or died it was cheap to get more. They're treated like serfs were by bad landowners. Now the Mothers' Rights Fund is collecting evidence, looking for punishment for officers. Putin says they will be punished but I don't believe him.'

\*

The hut track began not far from the Ski Lodge and I was on my way by dawn, at −21°C, under a clear sky. The first climb was steep – and suddenly the taiga seemed hung with golden lanterns as the rising sun burnished each pine's frozen burden. On the ridge-top I hesitated and without Fyodor's sketch-map would certainly have gone astray – straight ahead instead of sharp right. For a mile or so the lorry-wide track ran level on this long ridge: easy enough walking despite deepish snow. The stillness was absolute: not a bird fluttering, not a pine cone falling, no sound but my own squeaky-crunchy footsteps – until someone coughed hoarsely. I paused, slightly startled: no other prints marked the track's virgin snow. Looking towards the sound, I saw amidst the trees, scarcely twenty yards away, a large dark brown bear lumbering through snow almost up to his belly. Simultaneously the bear saw me and also paused, perhaps to consider this unexpected source of protein after his winter fast. Sensible Baikal bears hibernate until at least the end of March (I had checked with Fyodor) but perhaps the previous snowy day's warm noon hours – up to −13°C – had misled this one. Siberian bears like their meat and are six to seven feet tall when upright, a posture occasionally adopted to kill reindeer or people. As this fine specimen of *Ursus arctos* stood staring at me, most probably with no ill intent, I felt seriously frightened. Vividly I recalled advice given me forty years ago about the Himalayan black bear, also occasionally homicidal and sometimes encountered in those days (but probably not now) on mountain paths high above Dharamshala. 'Lie with your face to the ground, feigning dead.

Don't try to run away, you'll lose the race. Bears like to amble but can move fast when they choose.' Snow had drifted to the side of the track between the bear and me and when I dropped out of his sight and lay flat I could hear my heart thumping with terror. It sounded louder than a gradually receding rustling crunch as the 'Master of the Taiga' went on his way. He was coughing again – could a chest infection have roused him prematurely? Reassuringly, his way was not my way; an hour later I saw his prints crossing the track. I assume he was a 'he'; a 'she' would surely have looked in cub.

*

That afternoon Yaroslav gave me the bad news. A crack had been reported by radio from Davsha, seventy-five miles north of Ust-Barguzin, a lakeside settlement of two dozen scientists, of various disciplines, dedicated to studying Baikal literally in depth. 'Crack' suggests a minor flaw but Baikal's cracks are something else, explosions audible over a considerable distance and weakening the ice for unpredictable miles around the crack's epicentre. So a 1,700-mile train journey must replace 220 miles on the winter road.

*

Now, on election day [Presidential Election Day, 14 March 2004], our carriage was enlivened by three English-speaking Novosibirsk students bound for a Moscow seminar on IT, their university subject. Olga was a friendly, vivacious blonde, the two youths were at first more inhibited about conversing with a native English-speaker but a *pivo* session helped them to unwind. They, too, were indifferent to the election; of their fellow-students who voted, most would go for Putin so why bother voting against him? Yet they detested and distrusted their President. 'His *face* is old KGB,' said Olga. 'You can see it in his *face*!' One of the young men added, 'He's dangerous. He has most Russians blindfolded, not seeing where he's leading them.'

I remarked that democracy is partly about voting against detested candidates – though while speaking I could already hear the response. Olga said, 'Vote for who else? We see no better person with a chance of winning. We know Putin has the power to keep the power. It's not like in your countries where people don't know the winner before the votes are counted.'

A young man said, 'We don't have enough people interested in professional politics to give a choice of good candidates, though students everywhere have many political groups. Some like the free market – some are fascists, all nationalism and Orthodox religion – some want back to Communism. All together they're only a minority. The rest are the same as us, no energy for politics, thinking about studies and careers and personal and family problems.'

Tentatively I suggested that their personal problems and Russia's political problems might often be linked, but any such connection was dismissed with shrugs – a disquieting end to that phase of our conversation.

*

As the first village appeared in the distance a small dented Lada overtook me, then stopped to offer a lift. … A mile or so farther on the brothers again overtook me and stopped some thirty yards ahead. They were no longer smiling. The passenger stood in the middle of the road, arms outstretched. I beamed and waved and pedalled faster. The driver leant out, still in his seat, and silently pointed a revolver at me – the long sort, carried by Russian policemen. As I braked, almost falling off, the passenger demanded, 'Give dollars!' I took out my purse, holding a hundred or so roubles, and emptied it into his hand. He scowled, tossed the notes to his brother and said, 'Give *more* money!'

I shook my head. 'No more, until the bank in Voronezh.' Both brothers sniggered their disbelief and the passenger stepped close to feel under my jacket and sweater, his fingers cold on my skin, his touch professional; this was not the first time he had sought a money-belt. Deftly he unzipped the pouch and cleared it of $200 worth of small denomination rouble notes, suited to rural commerce. But this didn't satisfy him. Angrily he pointed to my shoes and repeated, 'Give dollars!' When I feigned incomprehension he bent down and undid my shoelaces; these were indeed experienced tourist-robbers, a common enough breed around Black Sea coastal resorts. The driver was still leaning through the window, his gun more a stage prop than a threat. I had no fear of being shot dead if I refused to co-operate; the Don delta isn't the Caucasus and small-time robbers (off-duty policemen?) would be unlikely to risk killing a foreigner twenty miles from Rostov. But as one man could easily overpower me I meekly handed over my shoe-stashed dollars. The gratified brothers smiled again, then went on their way – not interested, curiously, in my other possessions: Swiss knife, camera, a velocipede worth many hundreds of dollars.

Turning back towards Rostov, I felt quite shaken; being robbed is unpleasant, however mild the procedure – though in this case my having mentally prepared lessened the shock. That apart, disappointment and frustration devastated me – but not anger, an emotion rarely stimulated when the comparatively poor rob the comparatively rich. Anger is more appropriately directed towards the greedy, those who cloak their immorality in respectability.

\*

If you take your Hermitage seriously, and are limited to eight days, there isn't much time left over for St Petersburg's many other wonders – or, indeed, for more than one-third of the Hermitage itself. In general I'm an inefficient sightseer, wandering and drifting and leaving things to chance. But on the banks of the Neva I changed gear, planned my days, set off before sunrise for a three-hour exploration on foot or by bus, clocked into the Hermitage at 10.00 sharp, left at 5.30 and collapsed in the downmarket Dragon Luck bar, almost beside Vladimir Putin's boyhood home and primary school (now a technical college). 'Piter's' upmarket bars feel rather unwelcoming; peering through the doorways, it is obvious that everything will be overpriced and a shabby babushka scorned.

As the sheer beauty of this city overwhelmed me, my ambivalent attitude to the fulfilment of Peter the Great's dream went into abeyance. While walking along the Neva Embankment with the Winter Palace on one's left, the University Embankment across the river and the Senate and Synod ahead, I stopped thinking about those countless thousands of workers who were mercilessly sacrificed to create all this in an area previously uninhabited by anyone because of its swamps and diseases.

*

I met no one who could honestly express optimism about Russia's future. Free marketers are running amok while government support is withdrawn from the poorest. Putin's regime, ever more daringly dictatorial, allows the army to commit crimes in Chechnya of which Western leaders wish to know nothing. Ominously, the septuagenarian Professor Tamara Pechernikova is back in the courtrooms, she who as a young consultant psychiatrist made many KGB-inspired 'schizophrenia' diagnoses of dissidents. Under Putin she and other veterans of the 'compulsory psychiatric treatment' era are again giving evidence, this time in defence of military personnel charged with torturing, murdering and raping Chechen civilians. Meanwhile, in the background, Green groups concerned to avert even more environmental tragedy are having their offices and homes raided, their computers confiscated and their personal property vandalised or stolen by the FSB.

## The Island that Dared:
## *Journeys in Cuba* (2008)
## Cuba

Outside No. 403 [where Dervla was staying in Havana] the olfactory tapestry was complex: defective drains, sub-tropical vegetation, dog shit, cigar smoke, inferior petrol, seaweed, ripe garbage in overflowing skips. Each street corner had its skip to which householders on their way to work contributed bulging plastic bags and empty bottles. Cats crouched on skip rims, cleverly reaching down to extract fish spines and other delicacies. Two dead rats in gutters proved that some cats had been busy overnight. Dogs swarmed, having been set free at dawn to do what we all do once a day, so one had to watch one's step on the broken pavements. A jolly young woman was selling tiny cups of strong sweet coffee from her living-room window; later, she would do a brisk trade in takeaway homemade pizzas which became popular with the Trio [Dervla's granddaughters]. Further down the street, an older woman was selling ham rolls and over-sweet buns from a plank laid on two chairs in her doorway. She and a neighbour were talking money, the neighbour a grey-haired, ebony-skinned housewife hunkered beside her doorstep, cleaning piles of rice on sheets of *Granma* (Cuba's only national daily, also the Communist Party newspaper). ...

On every street stereotypes appeared with almost ridiculous frequency. Grandads were relishing the day's first cigar, settled in cane rocking-chairs behind wrought-iron balconies high above the pavement. Ebullient schoolchildren in immaculate uniforms – each white shirt or blouse meticulously ironed – converged on their schools before 8.00 a.m. Young men rode bicycles held together with strips of tin, many wearing musical instruments over their shoulders. Older men were already playing dominoes, sitting at card-tables – usually improvised – outside their homes. Neighbours sat on doorsteps or window ledges, arguing, laughing, discussing, complaining, gossiping. Fruit-sellers pushed their homemade handcarts from group to group; when the recycled pram wheels had lost their rubber the rims grated loudly on the cobbles.

Superficially I was back in the Third World, aka the Majority World. But only superficially: no one looked hungry, ragged, dirty or obviously diseased. No one was homeless or neglected in old age. The contemporary Cubans, urban and rural, immediately impress as a self-confident people. Although Castroism has stumbled from one economic disaster to another, for a tangle of reasons, the Revolutionary ideal of equality bred two generations who never felt inferior because they lacked the Minority World's goodies. They appreciated their own goodies, including first-class medical care for all and a range of educational, cultural and sporting opportunities not available to the majority in such free-market democracies as India, South Africa – or the US. As for the third generation, now coming to maturity – I was to find that question marks surround them.

\*

Returning to No. 403 by a different route we passed a few *puestos* (state-run groceries) which the Trio didn't recognise as shops despite their counters and scales. These dismal places – most shelves bare – come to life only when supplies arrive. Then orderly queues stretch away down the pavement, each citizen equipped with much-used plastic bags and a blue *libreta* (ration book, about the size of an EU passport). The basic rations of rice, beans and eggs may be augmented by pasta, cooking oil and margarine. But always there is a daily litre of milk for children – now up to the age of seven, pre-Special Period, up to fourteen. Those with spare national pesos may buy meat, fowl, vegetables and fruits at farmers' markets regulated by municipalities.

To Fidel's critics, permanent food-rationing proves how hopelessly Castroism has failed. In fact, feeding all Cubans adequately (except during the worst years of the Special Period) has been one of its most remarkable achievements. In 1950 a World Bank medical team estimated that sixty per cent of Cuba's rural dwellers and forty per cent of urban folk were malnourished. No dependent territory is encouraged to be self-sufficient and Cuba was then importing, mainly from the US, sixty per cent of grain needs, thirty-seven per cent of vegetables, eighty-four per cent of fats, eighty per cent of tinned fruit, sixty-nine per cent of tinned meat, eighty-three per cent of biscuits and sweets. Hunger greatly strengthened popular support for the Revolution. The US embargo, established in response to the revolution, caused dire food shortages until the rationing system, established on 12 March 1962, ensured that no family would go hungry.

*

In some quarters the CDR [Committees for the Defence of the Revolution] have a bad reputation as groups of spies and bullies, ever ready to punish those who fail to uphold Revolutionary standards. While this may not be a baseless slander, it is certainly a wild over-simplification. When Fidel invented the system in 1960 he meant it to affect everyone's daily life as an important instrument of civil defence and socialist reform. The president (unpaid) of each CDR is responsible for three hundred or so citizens (a barrio) and it is his or her duty to find out how people earn their money, what they spend it on, who does or does not march in demos, who is absent from home, where they have gone and why and for how long. We instantly recoil from such a system. Yet whether people are for or against Fidel it seems to be generally agreed that Castroism could not have been so quickly or firmly established, and made to work so well, without the CDRs' energetic observing, organising and persuading (or bullying) of their barrios.

*

Two sluggish ceiling fans tried to cool the Casa de la Trova, its slightly raised stage overlooked by a local artist's hectic depiction of the Steps of Padre Pico. In this house lived one of Cuba's most beloved composers, Rafael Salcedo (1844–1917) and until 1995 his home retained its eighteenth-century dignity. Then crass, cut-price renovations were (surprisingly) permitted and the many famous performers whose portraits crowd the walls would grieve to see it now.

Between the stage and the seating (plastic chairs) people danced – anyone in the audience who felt like it, but no more than four at a time. We always sat in front, within touching distance of the performers, and this sense of intimacy is important; one might be at a family party.

One middle-aged couple (white husband, mulatto wife) achieved extraordinary ballet-like gyrations and were 'regulars' – always in the second row, smiling affectionately at one another, then he standing, bowing, formally requesting her partnership while the crowd laughed and clapped. The performances of some young couples were even more overtly sexual but it was the solo dancing of a mulatto youth – small-boned, low in stature, apparently made of rubber – that most enthralled the Trio. Loudest of all was the applause for his performance with a tall big-breasted black girl, her ebony skin gleaming against a scarlet halter and tight green pants. As the band played faster and faster those two achieved an acrobatic-erotic *tour de force* that brought some of the audience to their feet (and perhaps to something else).

*

271

A ferry sometimes operates between the dam and Jibacoa, twelve miles down the lake on the Manicaragua–Trinidad road. But for lack of fuel this ten-person motor launch was currently inactive. Instead, a three-hour downhill walk took me to the main Cienfuegos–Manicaragua road. When I crossed the dam before sunrise a colourless mist veiled Lake Hanabanilla and as the road wriggled around hills too steep for cultivation the rising sun showed their bushiness flecked with red and yellow blossoms. Dwarf palms studded narrow valleys where horses grazed on nothing much. Then isolated *bohios* [huts] appeared and distant shouts seemed to emphasise the silence as men guided humped oxen to the scattered fields where their ploughs awaited them. A joyous content filled me in this hidden little corner of 'undeveloped' Cuba but too soon a sharp bend revealed the plain below. There old tobacco fields and new eucalyptus plantations surrounded the town of Ciro Redondo with its incongruously urban apartment blocks and obtrusive munitions factory.

*

Even in February Bayamo is *hot* hot and by noon I was flagging and dehydrated. Wearily I plodded along a dual-carriageway, longing for a *tienda* [shop]. … I was about to take a horse-bus towards the centre when, outside the Astro bus terminus, a delivery man appeared carrying two crates of Hatuey. Following him into a bare little yard, behind a high blank wall, I saw five rickety round tables shaded by torn umbrellas. There was no counter, no shelving: one fetched Hatuey only from a small window in the bus station's rear wall. The young barman hesitated to serve a tourist: I should have been elsewhere, drinking Buccanero or Kristal. But he was a kind – and honest – young man who broke the law for this exhausted *abuela* [granny] and declined my proffered convertible peso, insisting on the correct Hatuey price: NP18.

The only other customer, a stocky white man in his mid-thirties, had observed my arrival with interest. On his way to fetch another

Hatuey he paused to look down at my open notebook and asked, '*Pais* [Country]?'

'*Irlanda!* My lovely country for reading! And you my first *irlandesa* to meet! Wilde, Shaw, Joyce – all translated I read! I am artist, painter, many pictures – and then the inspiration by *Ulysses*! But *Finnegans Wake* makes too much problems for me...You have time to talk, we sit together?'

I was very happy to talk provided my companion did not expect me to solve his *Finnegans Wake* problems.

\*

An hour later – above the stairway, close to a ridgetop – the path ran level along a bare, red-brown cliff-face for some fifty yards. I was nearly over when the earth began to crumble beneath my feet – and here a falling body would hit boulders rather than bushes. That was a nightmare moment. I completely lost my nerve and when I put my hand on the cliff to steady myself it too crumbled. I should then have hastened forward (safe ground lay scarcely five yards ahead!) but in panic I froze, leaning on my umbrella which of course sent more of the cliff gently dribbling down. At that I regained my nerve and proceeded, the path continuing to crumble in my wake. Back on safe ground something unusual because manmade caught my eye: a sign (white paint on wood) hanging from a branch. It said: PELIGRO DE MUERTE, pointing to the cliff. Where the stairway ended I had taken the wrong path. ... An odd phenomenon, panic. Its paralysing illogic cancels out one's instinct of self-preservation, supposedly our strongest instinct though I've never believed that. The sane and normal reaction to a shifting cliff-face is to get off it, fast – not to stand around poking it with an umbrella.

\*

No doubt my subconscious organised the next few days during which I saw not one human being. ...

Retracing my steps, I found a little-used level pathlet winding through jungle; here two hands were needed to cope with the dangling creepers. That led to another world, an open golden-grassed plateau marked by an extraordinary phenomenon, a track some two yards wide, made of massive slabs and boulders of smooth brownish rock. Yet *not* 'made' but embedded in the earth, matching the low outcrops visible all around between bottle-brush pines and an abundance of flowering shrubs: pink, yellow, blue. Until sunset I followed this track wondering if just possibly, over many generations, the feet of indigenous tribes had defined it?

I then gathered a mattress of pine branches; even by the most spartan standards all this uneven rockiness threatened sleep deprivation. During 'supper' (sardines and bread buns) the temperature dropped pleasantly and before slipping into my thin flea-bag I donned all my garments: three T-shirts, two pairs of trousers.

An important part of the bonding-with-a-country process is sleeping out, feeling united with the totality of a place, sensing its nocturnal activities. Also, it helps to get our own planet's worries in perspective if the stars are allowed to do their hypnotic thing. Rationally regarded, that twinkling universe reduces all human concerns to insignificance. But at 4.10, when I awoke shivering, my discomfort became of immense significance. One thinks of dew as something gentle and rather poetical. Given time, it isn't – and now I was very damp. I considered walking on in the dark (no moon) but even by daylight that rock-track demanded caution. …

By mid-afternoon I could see, in the distance, my track ascending to the crest of a treeless, grassy ridge. Half an hour later it became a boulder stairway before ending – just like that. I stood on the brink of a deep inaccessible ravine, directly below me lay an almost sheer pine-covered mountainside. … Descending to the meeting of three paths, at a stream crossing, I erected a 'tent' of pine branches to ensure a dew-free sleep. But of course the mosquitoes came to dinner; most streams have adjacent pools of stagnant water. …

While eating my last tin of sardines I noticed dark clouds massing to the west – rain clouds? … Any Cuban could have told me that strong winds accompany blue-black clouds and unluckily this quasi-cave faced the wrong way. For an hour around midnight a gale drove heavy rain into my refuge. Then the clouds were swept away, the stars twinkled again and I deeply regretted not having an emergency flask of warming rum.

*

In a stuffy room almost filled by two single beds I stripped quickly to inspect my tortured body and colonised garments. The invaders were bigger than human fleas but smaller than bedbugs: dark brown, hard-shelled, shiny, fast-moving – though easier to catch than fleas. They had fed chiefly off my buttocks, crotch, thighs and armpits with a few experimental forays elsewhere. Their bites were spectacular: crimson welts ten times their own size, extremely painful – throbbing that evening – and of incomparable itchiness. The itch persisted for a week and as time passed the bites oozed a nasty goo; then the painfulness became soreness. A fortnight later, at home in Ireland, I was still suffering enough to crave sympathy from those of my intimates who could decently be invited to view my buttocks and adjacent areas. Presumably these insects normally reside in my quasi-cave, feeding off small mammals. Despite my long walk, I did not sleep well that night or for several nights to come.

*

Where paths from opposite mountainsides met the road I joined five men and three women sitting on massive tree-root 'stools'. Some had been waiting since morning and one couple were prepared to go either way; they could do their business equally easily in Bahía Honda or San Cristobal. When a huge ancient open truck approached – less than half full – everyone cheered except me. How to get safely on board? This Soviet monster lacked a moveable back, or steps, and its rusty, thin, wobbly metal sides were so high one could barely see the passengers' heads. My practised companions scrambled up, using the colossal wheels as ladders while grasping a length of wire rope. Those already in situ shouted encouragingly and helped to haul them aboard. Eventually warnings about no other vehicle appearing overcame my solicitude for old bones. Up I went and two strong men heaved me over the loose, sharp side. …

When we stopped in a previously prosperous suburb two strong knights picked me up and delivered me over the side, like a sack, into the truck-driver's muscular arms. As my rucksack was being handed down a youth who had registered my accommodation problem shyly offered to help me find a *casa particular*. Sergei was no *jinetero* [tout] (a species endemic to tourist zones) but a typically kind Cuban who lived in this suburb and hoped one of his neighbours might shelter me. A false hope: we knocked on three doors and three householders understandably declined to break the law by entertaining an inexplicable old woman wearing a battered and by now oil-stained rucksack.

\*

Where the truck dropped me off, near the National Aquarium in Miramar, I had a two-hour walk to No. 403. The pace of change along the Malecón upset me. Granted, restoration was urgently needed – but not demolition. A quirkily handsome building had given way to a Fiat car showroom, its façade plastic-tiled. Other buildings, under the arcade, were being converted to tourist-bait shops while makeshift cafeterias had sprouted on recently cleared sites. All this within one month, since my visa visit. The Malecón buildings are not as old as they seem (mere centenarians) and as demolition proceeds, and one compares them with Old Havana's semi-ruins, they look much less soundly constructed. According to a too-credible rumour, various US fast-food chains had already made 'informal arrangements' to acquire certain Malecón properties in an unblockaded Cuba.

\*

From the museum one enters the mausoleum, a shadowy cave-like chamber. Here Che [Guevara] and seventeen other guerrillas occupy ossuary niches in the cliff wall. An eternal flame, lit by Fidel on 17 October 1997, flickers amidst boulders and greenery suggesting the jungle in which these *compañeros* fought and died. The atmosphere is reverential – and powerful. Those rare places where emotions, positive or negative, are palpably concentrated have always intrigued me. I've come upon them in Nepal, Coorg, Eastern Turkey, Northern Ireland, Rwanda, the Russian Far East but in Santa Clara, a mere decade after the entombment, this concentration was wholly unexpected. We have wandered onto contentious territory, the way ahead obscured by a cloud of unknowing. Politics, propaganda, the packaging of Che as a 'celebrity' don't adequately explain the atmosphere, generated by an accumulation of individuals' responses to Che's message. I left with a lump in my throat.

*

Juan described Cuban Socialism as 'a more authentic popular movement' than the Soviet version ever was. Yet even friends of the Revolution, he complained, didn't recognise – or misinterpreted – its genuinely populist foundation while critics ascribed Fidel's mass support to authoritarian manipulation. 'It's the other way round,' asserted Juan. 'Fidel's mass support gave a permit for authoritarianism – or what looks like it.'

My negative reaction to the word 'populist' brought a quick assurance that Fidel was a populist leader in the best sense, the ordinary Cubans' spokesman and facilitator, someone so directly linked to the populace and who empathises so strongly with them that he can voice their deepest wishes and often unexpressed thoughts. ...

'So where,' I wondered, 'does all you've said leave Castroism post-Fidel?'

Juan didn't feign optimism. He had a sharp-edged (or simplistic?) vision of the Revolution as a noble project demeaned by Sovietisation. '*Communism* wasn't – isn't – our problem. *Sovietisation* is still holding us back.' This idiosyncratic *fidelista* went on to define Sovietisation as a worse handicap, during Cuba's present critical transition phase, than the US embargo which only has practical consequences. He diagnosed 'intellectual paralysis' within the Sovietised bureaucracy, just when new thinking is needed to protect the Revolution's gains and build on the unity Fidel's populism achieved. He condemned the habitual use of stale Soviet-speak – a considerable irritant to the younger generation, a signal that their leaders feared to 'think new'. Meanwhile they were 'acting new', compromising with capital, openly looking to China as their model. At that point Juan shuddered – visibly, physically shuddered. After a moment's pause he said, 'China mixes the worst of both worlds, capitalist greed with communist tyranny. Odd how we don't hear Washington demanding "free and fair elections" before trading with those tyrants.' ...

Repressing my own pessimism, I argued that the current compromise with capitalism didn't have to lead to the abandonment of Castroism, only its modification. Capitalism Rampant is not being exposed as inherently unstable, dependent for its survival on the use of high-tech military power – therefore doomed eventually to be defeated by the Majority World's low-tech resistance. And it could be that Cuba's experiment will serve, throughout the bloodiness, to hearten those who believe in people before profit.

*

By the late 1980s increasing public discontent with over-centralisation had prompted Fidel and his advisors to institute certain reforms. In 1992 a major constitutional change enhanced Poder Popular (people's power) by establishing a new electoral system allowing the direct election of all members of the provincial and national assemblies. (Municipal assembly members had always been directly elected.) This adjustment has been so successful that voter turnout is now high enough to provoke incredulous sneers among those to whom the Cubans' highly developed sense of community is incomprehensible.

Because voting is not compulsory in Cuba the 1993 election was widely regarded as a referendum on Castroism. … On 24 February 1993 over a hundred journalists from twenty-one countries, and numerous foreign visitors, were free to observe both the voting and the counting. No one, anywhere, accused anyone of fraud. Support for Castroism came from eighty-eight per cent of the electorate, ninety-nine per cent of whom had voted – and this despite multiple external misfortunes and internal misjudgements having reduced the island to near-starvation point. Beyond doubt, the government had a renewed mandate. This was recognised even by Elizardo Sanchez, then President of the Cuban Commission for Human Rights and National Reconciliation and one of the government's best-known resident opponents. Five years later, after the 1998 election, he again acknowledged 'the renovation of the mandates and the legitimacy of the government'. In 2003 he made no comment when a ninety-seven per cent voter turnout gave Castroism ninety-one per cent support.

\*

To say '*adios*' to good friends I spent three days criss-crossing humid Havana – prudently, by bicitaxi. (A melancholy mission: we were unlikely to meet again.) Those concentrated conversations – some starting at 8.00 a.m., some ending at 1.00 a.m. – made me acutely aware of witnessing history: Cuba on the cusp. My contacts, though numerically limited, represented various social layers, from the sporadically employed victims of industrial collapse to the tourism-connected resurgent bourgeoisie to the securely employed but impoverished intelligentsia. Predictable hopes and fears were expressed, varying with an individual's circumstances, but everyone was quietly proud of the smooth transfer of power in August 2006, seen as a reassuring measure of national stability.

# 2010s

# AN ADVOCATE FOR JUSTICE

The month in which Dervla celebrated her 77th birthday, she embarked upon travelling in Israel and Palestine. She attempted to understand the conflict-riven region by her usual methodology of reading a wide range of background literature, travelling slowly and speaking to whosoever would speak to her.

Between November 2008 and December 2010, she spent three months in Israel and five months in the West Bank. She was living in Balata refugee camp near Nablus during 'Operation Cast Lead', the murderous 22-day Israeli attack on the Gaza Strip.

In June 2011, at the age of 80, she spent a month in the Gaza Strip, overcoming enormous difficulty in entering and exiting the region, because she just had to see it for herself. The material gathered during that month was enough to fill a separate book, which in the event was written first.

The resulting duo of books provides a rare insight into this region of the Middle East. She is clear that this is not a war between equals. The might of the US-backed Israeli war machine has made daily life for ordinary Palestinians a living hell. She nevertheless became a passionate advocate for the One-State Solution, the creation of a single, shared democratic space. Her experiences in Northern Ireland and South Africa gave her a sliver of hope for the possibility of this dream.

## *A Month by the Sea: Encounters in Gaza* (2013)
## Gaza

Most Gazans are monolingual but keen to help a stranger. When I asked the way to the beach by miming swimming two amused men directed me down a long, slightly sloping passageway between two slummy tenements – the edge of Shatti camp. Then, from a low embankment, I could see Ashkelon's tall factory chimneys smoking a few miles away to the north, in Israel. It was two and a half years since I'd walked along that unwelcoming beach on a cold windy Sabbath morning – I remembered gazing gloomily at Gaza, not believing I could ever clear the bureaucratic barrier.

Here I gave thanks for the relief of a frisky breeze off the Mediterranean. Below me children played on a poisonously littered shore – untreated sewage flowing into the sea, domestic garbage heaped around chunks of people's bombed homes. The municipality tries hard with limited resources but in many districts overpopulation defeats it. Mopping my sweaty face I strolled towards a wannabe café: a bent tin sheet propped on unequal lengths of half-burned spars with three battered plastic tables under two torn beach umbrellas. Five men sat staring at a patrolling gunboat, looking jobless – a look difficult to describe but easy to recognise. Ersatz coffee was served with a glass of water. Stupidly I had neglected to acquire coins and while a youth was seeking change the oldest man insisted on paying my bill. In Gaza 'Where from?' is always the first question and, as in most countries, being Irish is an advantage. Three of those men had had their little boats confiscated and done time in detention for fishing beyond the Israeli-imposed limit.

*

It was a relief to be able to move around unchallenged by the IDF [Israel Defense Forces], yet their mechanised nearness soon came to seem far more threatening than those personal encounters unavoidable on the West Bank. Gunboats patrol Gaza's coast, unmanned drones and F-16s patrol Gaza's sky, tanks, jeeps and APCs [armoured personnel carriers] patrol Gaza's border fence. Nor is there anything 'symbolic' about all this weaponry. Gaza, as a 'hostile entity', may legitimately (in Israeli eyes) be attacked at any moment from sea, air or land. Attacks are frequent though rarely noted by the international media; each kills or injures no more than a few Gazans. Warplanes also regularly bombard open spaces likely to be used as training grounds by resistance groups. Those massive explosions greatly distress children not yet recovered from the traumas of Cast Lead. Discussing all this with Nita, a Khan Younis cousin of one of my Balata friends, she told me that her youngest sibling, a five-year-old boy, has been permanently deafened by a sonic boom – another IDF terrorist technique. Then Nita offered to be my advisor and, crucially, my interpreter if I wished to visit some of the families bereaved since 1 January 2011. More of that anon.

*

Strolling around the almost-deserted harbour, I noticed numerous small bullet-holed fishing vessels. One sun-blackened granddad wore a short ragged beard and a ravelling woollen cap on tousled grey curls. He spoke basic English and pointed to a dismantled engine belonging to his son – a father of nine, dependent on fishing. The engine had been badly damaged within the three-mile limit; repairs would cost 3,000 shekels – an unattainable sum, unless the hard-pressed al-Tawfiq Fishermen's Co-Op could help. Yet granddad assured me that not all Israeli sailors are bad, some treat you fairly ... I often marvelled at this willingness, on the part of older Palestinians, to give Israelis their due – if earned.

Gaza's 40,000 or so fishermen are not refugees, therefore don't qualify for UNRWA [United Nations Relief and Works Agency] support. Yet the blockade has reduced them to destitution. Their average annual catch used to be around 3,000 tons, now it is less than 500. Families who were earning about £350 a month, before the Second Intifada, now earn less than £80. The traditional deep-sea fishing in international waters has been illegally forbidden by Israel. Boats must keep within a six-mile limit – often diminished, in practice, to three miles. Israel's navy is even more blatantly aggressive than its army if it even suspects the limits have been crossed. Nets are ripped to bits and explosives often used to disperse a shoal as crews make to draw in their catch. Boats are regularly rammed – or all lights may be shattered, causing the craft to drift off course. This can provide a pretext for arresting the crew, destroying their equipment and impounding their vessel. Water-cannon are a favourite weapon, their load of foul liquid (sewage or some chemical brew?) causing nausea, headaches and rashes. Naval trigger-happiness is so common that by now gunshot wounds are almost taken for granted as an occupational hazard.

Over the past decade, the ISM [International Support Movement] has assembled a solid body of evidence, visual and aural, proving that in the persecution of Gazan fishermen Israel violates the Fourth Geneva Convention every day and night. Volunteers often sail with the crews; less often, their own tiny boat (costly to run) joins a fishing fleet. Twice I hoped to sail but on the first morning a mini-gale confined everyone to harbour and on the second morning the ISM boat's engine resolutely refused to start and was pronounced by an expert to be in terminal decline. This was a big worry; to maintain its independence, the ISM is funded only by its volunteers.

*

Adel, a handsome twenty-year-old, spoke a little English and with Nita's help voiced strong views on the IDF's use of psychological torture (considered by some to be clinically sadistic). At noon one day, in nearby Khoza'a village, sixty-year-old Mahmoud was ordered by phone, 'Evacuate your house now!' His was one of three small houses built some fifty yards apart; married sons occupied the others. He and his wife gathered their few cherished possessions and took refuge next door with Hussein, whose wife and three children were absent, queuing at an ISI [Islamic Social Institutions] vaccination clinic. At about 2.00 p.m. a drone shelled Hussein's house, penetrating the roof but causing only minor injuries because no one was upstairs. The three 'lucky' ones retreated, badly shaken, to Mahmoud's house. An hour later the IDF phoned again, this time ordering Mahmoud to leave his home *within five minutes*. Everyone hastened away from the three houses – but none was attacked. And that sort of thing, said Adel, happens frequently up and down the Strip, playing on nerves already stretched taut.

*

The Israelis' sustained imposition of all-out collective punishment is by any standards a very frightening phenomenon. For decades they have been attacking defenceless populations through curfews, closures, sieges, house demolitions, olive-grove bulldozing, well poisonings, shootings, bombings, torture and indefinite imprisonment without trial. One of my Gazan friends proposed that this Israeli obsession, this conviction that collective punishment is the way forward, may well be a hideous hangover from the Holocaust when Jews were collectively punished for being Jews. The logic behind this proposal escaped me. But then my friend argued, 'We're not talking about *logic*! We're talking about something very deep and dark and twisted. Something so sick the international community is afraid to go near it.'

Several years ago, the same comparison was drawn by Richard Falk, UN Special Rapporteur in the OPT [Occupied Palestinian

Territories], a Princeton international law authority and himself a Jew. He said, 'Is it an irresponsible overstatement to associate the treatment of Palestinians with this criminalised Nazi record of collective atrocity? I think not.'

Perhaps this grim analogy no longer shocks because Zionist criminality is becoming ever more strident and arrogant. Now a retiring head of Israel's security forces feels free to brag on TV that 'Our successful operations have made political assassinations internationally acceptable'.

\*

I spent memorable evenings in the home of Dr Nasser Abu Shabaan, surgeon in Gaza City's al-Shifa hospital. I had first heard his name during Cast Lead, in Beit Sahour, where Professor Mazin Qumsiyeh was my host. When the IDF began to fire white phosphorus shells into Gaza, Mazin's advice was sought. I remember wandering off to the Shepherd's Field, sick with horror, while he tried to fax al-Shifa. The IDF couldn't deny that war crime. About 200 155-millimetre shells were fired into the Strip, where people subsequently collected the canisters to present as evidence to Amnesty International investigators. ...

Not until the younger generations had left for home did Nasser talk about Cast Lead; during those three weeks he rarely got more than one hour's sleep at a stretch.

When a white phosphorus shell hit the Halima farmhouse, at Siyafa village, the father and four of his nine children were killed, his wife and the other children grievously burned. Their neighbours, terrified by this uncontrollable mass incineration of human bodies, fled across the fields. The survivors were brought to al-Shifa and Nasser described the bewildered frustration of his team, who at first didn't know what they were dealing with. 'We had never before seen anything like these burns. They reached down to bone and muscle and continued to smoke for hours and that smoke had a sickening stench.' Finally, Nasser and a colleague 'took out a piece of foreign matter' and the colleague identified it as white phosphorus. That was the first of dozens of similar cases.

The IDF routinely used these munitions. On contact with air, white phosphorus ignites and continues to burn at 816°C until completely starved of oxygen – hence the smoking wounds, before Nasser and his team learned how to cope. Each air-bursting artillery shell spreads 116 burning wedges over a radius of, on average, 125 metres from blast point. The IDF deliberately fired phosphorus into densely populated areas. Among its public targets were al-Quds hospital, the Red Crescent headquarters, UNRWA's main Gaza City compound and an UNRWA school in Beit Lahia where more than 1600 'displaced persons' (bombed out of their homes) were sheltering.

Khoza'a village was declared a 'closed military zone' before being attacked. Six people died at once, enveloped in flames; more than a score were deeply burned and permission to evacuate them was refused. A Red Crescent ambulance, defying this ban, attracted more white phosphorus. Gazan paramedics can have no masks effective against this smoke. Its victims may fall unconscious for three or four hours, then seem to recover and be sent home – only to return soon, in agony, their extensively burnt lungs not responsive to treatment. In many cases, as the body gradually absorbs the white phosphorus chemical, potentially fatal damage is caused to all the major organs. Perhaps Ehud Olmert, the then Israeli Prime Minster, had this in mind when he warned: 'Rockets from Gaza will bring a severe and disproportionate response.'

Nasser also treated scores of injuries inflicted by other 'innovative' weapons. Some patients, apparently merely in shock when admitted, with not a mark to be seen on their bodies, began to deteriorate within hours – and within a few more hours were dead. Post-mortems revealed internal injuries consistent with the use of thermobaric weapons which Nasser showed me, close up and in colour, on his computer. This 'portfolio' included melted brains, shredded lungs, cooked livers, exploded kidneys. Do arms manufacturers and their politician customers ever look at such pictures? Do they ever think about children or parents gazing at bodies unidentifiable as their children or parents – mangled beyond recognition as human beings... And why did the Quartet [Russia, US, EU & UN] not demand an end to war crimes during those hideous three weeks? Instead, the *Goldstone Report* has been 'managed' to Israel's satisfaction, proving yet again – to quote Richard Falk – that 'the United Nations shows neither the capacity nor the will to implement its own resolutions'.

*

Islam is relatively flexible about contraception though there's always a vocal minority protesting that condoms and the pill are invitations to promiscuity – 'just look at the West's filthiness!' However, leaving sexual morals aside, this is a politically hazardous area at the centre of a demographic battleground. Some discreetly promoted family planning is possible (four or five children instead of ten or twelve) but the ideal twenty-first-century two-child family is unmentionable. On the West Bank one notices considerable hostility towards any foreign NGO [Non Governmental Organisation] suspected of colluding with Israel to lower the Palestinian birth-rate. On the Strip those suspicions seem even stronger though the NGOs are fewer.

To me this issue looked not entirely political – 'let's outbreed the Zionists!' Palestinians love children. Of course there have always been dysfunctional families and their numbers are increasing under the multiple strains of Occupation, a problem I consider in my account of the West Bank. That said, even under the most trying conditions, in the grimly congested camps and the semi-destitute villages where farmers can't safely farm, one sees parents and siblings *enjoying* the largeness of their families. On my melancholy last visit to Anwar we discussed this. As my wise old friend saw it, in a society as disrupted, deprived and insecure as the post-Nakba Palestinians', children are the main source of comfort, pride, security and independence. He said, 'People denied all the normal freedoms feel their children protect them against disintegration and guarantee survival – family, clan and communal survival. Within a big household they have a sense of being safe – even though they know they're not, under the Occupation. Am I explaining well? Can you imagine what I'm saying?'

I assured Anwar that I could well imagine it, despite being myself an only child and the mother of an only child. His words expressed the emotions I had intuited while visiting families all over the Strip.

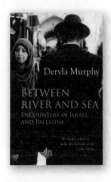

## *Between River and Sea: Encounters in Israel and Palestine* (2015)
## Israel and Palestine

Long before contemporary politics, Jerusalem's hallowed ground had been notorious for bringing out the worst in human nature. Today six Christian sects compete for control of their Holy Places – quite often coming to blows, needing to be separated by Israeli riot police. It's all peculiarly disedifying yet an expanding global tourist industry lures more and more ecstatic pilgrims to the Holy City – people who are swept along on a wave of religiosity that some observers find downright unhealthy. Usually I'm susceptible to ancient sacred places; their emanations can soothe and fortify, whatever the cultural background. But Zionism's physical and emotional violence has polluted Jerusalem, as once the Crusaders' rule must have done. To me the city now feels sick rather than sacred, its energies soured.

\*

Conversations on the roof could be harrowing, all the more so for people's sufferings being understated. It bothered me that most men weren't outwardly angry, but seemed resigned to being bullied for the foreseeable future. Sari had indicated that in general East Jerusalemites chose to distance themselves from the OPT's resistance fighters. Seemingly the second Intifada – the merciless suicide bombing and Israel's over-reaction to it – had engendered a below-the-surface despair. In 2008 things were comparatively quiet again; the bombers had realised their murdering of civilians were counter-productive, the tourists were back. Yet the average East Jerusalemite remained exposed to a police state routine of humiliating, relentless, low-key repression. Inevitably this erodes self-confidence, as it is meant to do. These harsh restrictions also affect OPT residents needing hospital treatment unavailable at home; they cannot visit Jerusalem without hard-to-get permits.

Palestinians born in East Jerusalem, of families rooted there for generations, are in an irrational category, one of many contrived by the Israelis. They are 'immigrants with permanent residence status'. (Immigrants from where?) Despite annexations, those persons are rendered stateless, denied the rights to citizenship, to a passport, to a vote in national elections. East Jerusalemites who need to work or study abroad lose their blue card if they cannot afford to return annually to renew it. Once lost, it's irretrievable and that individual can *never* return to his/her homeland. The government may then seize the 'absentee's' property, left unoccupied by the owner because he/she has not been allowed to return. Yet Zionism's 'Law of Return' gives all Jews from everywhere Israeli citizenship, with few questions asked about *how* Jewish they are. What percentage of the 1990s Russian influx was genuinely dedicated to either Judaism or Zionism? We do know that a high percentage were uncircumcised – to the vocal horror of various rabbis.

Zionists have nightmares about 'the demographics'; will Jews be in a minority in Israel by 2020? Hence the 2003 'Citizenship and Entry Act', preventing non-Jewish spouses from entering Israel – where one-fifth of the population is non-Jewish! If an 'immigrant' marries an OPT resident the couple must live apart, or the Jerusalemite must move and forfeit his/her blue card – or both must risk severe punishments.

*

Leah wore rose-tinted spectacles, a useful accessory helping her to feel less North African and more Israeli. There are many heart-wrenching accounts of how her parents' generation were received – sprayed with disinfectant as they embarked, loaded onto packed trucks without seats, transported by night to the chosen settlement sites. Always by night – then the truck hastened away and when sunrise revealed desolation all around, no other vehicle was available.

Leah's parents had arrived from Tunisia in 1952 when she and her brothers were toddlers. Brother worked for the municipality and was about to retire early because of rocket stress; two had landed on his street. Leah taught French and English and lived in half a small bungalow built (literally) by her father. ...

We didn't sit on the verandah amidst Leah's unusual collection of flowering cacti. Puzzled, I asked, 'Isn't inside more dangerous, if the roof's hit?'

Leah smiled and shook her head. 'They're usually not strong enough to come through a roof. Some do, but most victims get hurt outside.' ...

When Ellie told our hostess 'Dervla wants to learn about Israel' it seemed re-education time had come – then suddenly I was pitched into an abyss of prejudice and hatred. My companions, starting from very different backgrounds, had arrived, as Israelis, at a shared space: by the feet of Avigdor Lieberman.

Leah's being so obviously Mizrahi [Jewish from the Middle East and North Africa] gave an extra dimension of horror to my learning curve. She said, 'We want to finish with the Arabs, stop stupid talk about "peace" and "two states". Why do we bother with the scum in Ramallah? Why ask the PA to help our soldiers? Why pretend to trust Arabs?'

Jacob no longer looked like the kindly, cheery young man who had offered me a lift. His eyes narrowed as he said something vehement in Russian. Ellie translated. 'More settlements faster are our way forward. Forget Oslo, get back full control of Samaria and Judea.' She added, 'We've no room for Arabs, they've other places to go. Plenty places – Jordan, Egypt, Saudi Arabia. They're not so many and the Arab world is big.'

Leah said, 'They don't belong here, the British brought them in for cheap labour. Why do they want a separate state? They couldn't run it, they're illiterate! Best at thieving and corruption – how they run Ramallah.' And she went on to explain why voting for Yisrael Beiteinu offered the shortest route to 'a land free of Arabs'. ...

Although without thespian gifts, I do excel at concealing my feelings during Sderot-type conversations. Some critics deplore this, seeing it as tantamount to hypocrisy – or a sort of eavesdropping, my companions not knowing to whom, really, they are baring their souls. However, if one wants to find out what makes extremists tick, it's counter-productive to attempt a reasoned debate for which they, by definition, would have no time. Also, in particularly delicate situations, such as I was to encounter later on the West Bank, I carefully conceal my interlocutors' identities. And I sit steadily on the fence, eschewing leading questions. But sitting on the fence is not a restful posture; that evening I invented a headache and retired early.

*

Ten minutes later I stopped, transfixed. The way ahead was blocked by my destination. This natural grotto, some thirty feet high and narrow in proportion, was apparently supported by a semicircle of slender, soaring columns topped by symmetrical bulges – erosion's 'capitals'. Within lay a pool of spring water, now depleted and rather scummy; November had been alarmingly dry. On the surrounding mud, amidst many animal footprints, I fancied I saw a leopard's – not improbable. Nearby, proving the spring's subterranean vitality, stood a magnificent display of feathery reeds, twice my height, swaying slightly in a breeze I hadn't previously noticed.

For a long time I rested by the grotto, in a trance of delight. This [77th] birthday present felt very therapeutic.

The return journey might have been an anticlimax but wasn't. To climb out of the cleft – John had explained – one must find an iron ladder implanted half-way up a cliff where in times past the Nabateans, Romans and Byzantines had hewn steps in the rock and kept them free of vegetation. While seeking this 'facility' I slipped but fortunately (the lesser of two evils) fell into a retaining cactus – an amiable cactus, which didn't punish me too severely. Pulling myself onto level ground, I sat briefly, to recover from the fall and to say farewell to the grotto – its mysterious symmetry even more arresting, seen from above.

On the far side of this wide, level plateau, my faint path (too narrow for a pack-animal) rounded a bulky mountain with a sheer 300-foot drop on one side. I've never had a good head for heights and old age affects one's balance; that 20-minute ordeal made me sweat with terror. Then the Zin Valley was again visible, far below, and the path was replaced by a tangle of old goat tracks, wriggling between outcrops and into clefts and over mounds of loose shale. ...

To give myself a happy birthday I had been trying not to think about the Bedouin but in the middle of the Negev it's hard to filter them out. Without their homeland they are, as a people, doomed. Some individuals will thrive, given a chance, but such a distinctive culture cannot be transplanted. Desert nomads need their desert.

As I began the descent, two griffon vultures sailed into view just below me; they nest hereabouts on the highest ledges. My Negev souvenirs are six enormous snail shells and a fine selection of porcupine quills, now decorating the table on which I write this.

*

The name Balata Refugee Camp is inaccurate on two counts. The residents are not, strictly speaking, 'refugees' but displaced persons within their own country. And what began as a camp has become an urban slum. Yet they make a point of keeping 'camp' in their address – not that they need an address, there's no postal service. 'Camp' is important to signal they don't accept this urban slum as their permanent home. They cling to their 'Right of Return', granted in 1948 by UN Resolution 194. Some observers see that clinging as pathetic, to others it's gallant. At present it looks even less realistic than it did sixty years ago.

*

Since early childhood, graveyards have attracted me; where others might hasten towards the local beauty spot, I hasten towards the cemetery. (There must be a name – probably Greek – for this condition.) Balata's cemetery, two minutes' walk from my room, is by now as crowded and unlovely as the 'camp'. From its few raggedy palm trees hang colourful 'martyrs'' memorials', large wooden boards depicting one or more young men. Their expressions vary (determined, sad, scared, defiant, sulky); several bear arms, one wears academic robes – tragic role models for Balata's children.

The cemetery was rarely visited but one morning I met Nasr beside his maternal grandmother's grave. He had come for her funeral from his home village near Ramallah where he worked as a freelance journalist and stringer. At once he identified me as possible raw material and didn't share the Balatans' inhibition about visiting my room.

As I made tea, Nasr explained his fluent English, learned from an extraordinary great-uncle. This man, as a ten-year-old, had taken a bullet in the spine while his village was being 'cleansed'. His devastated parents, who had lost everything (house, land, animals) looked at their paralysed son and advised him to use his brains since he could no longer use his body. That advice would have been hard to follow but for the intervention of an orthopaedic surgeon, a 1930s immigrant from Germany. Anton Goldstein was so appalled by the Nakba that he unofficially adopted several of his Palestinian patients, subsidising their education. Eight years later Nasr's great-uncle was translating for a Jordanian businessman based in East Jerusalem; his mother pushed his wheelchair to and from the office. Then came '67... Again this family, like thousands of others, was displaced, driven out of the shack they had contrived to build in Silwan. Happily, great-uncle's employer stood by him and soon he and his younger brother

(Nasr's grandfather) were working in Ramallah, their wages minimal but their jobs secure. 'There are many good Jews,' said Nasr, 'but their government never hears them.'

*

In Balata I got to know six 'human shields', young men and boys abused by the IDF in a procedure outlawed by Article 28 of the Fourth Geneva Convention. Two seemed undamaged, or at least were able to conceal any damage by bragging about their ordeals. The others, according to their parents, had reacted variously. A fourteen-year-old, aged eleven when tied to the front of an armoured vehicle for three hours while it patrolled Balata's periphery, couldn't concentrate in school and was still having nightmares. Two others, said to be obsessively planning revenge, kept their mothers' anxiety levels at 'High'. The sixth, now aged twenty, had become 'always sad, never talking', as his father put it. Everyone was indignant because in 2007 a TV crew (Associated Press) filmed a human shield 'episode' in Nablus – why hadn't the cameras focused on Balata where the abuse was much more common? My suggestion that their insurance might not cover Balata caused some gratified amusement.

*

On the night of 17–18 February heavy rain delighted everyone – and undid me. Walking home next afternoon, via a short-cut through an olive grove on a steep slope, I heard shrill, terrified screams. Some way below the path two boys, aged nine or ten, were frenziedly beating a third with heavy sticks – an extreme case of a sadly usual Balata phenomenon. Shouting angrily, I rushed downhill – there was no one else around – then slipped on the red-brown mud. By grabbing an olive branch I avoided falling flat but my legs splayed awkwardly and my left hip went funny-peculiar. Stumbling on, I continued to shout 'Stop it!' (as though they could understand English!) yet they didn't register my presence until

I seized their sticks, one in each hand, and made as if to strike them. For a moment we stood in confrontation, both boys staring at me with an almost intimidating animosity. I played an old trick – crossing my eyes – which in disparate situations on three continents has served to cow potentially troublesome children. Here too it worked. Racing away, the pair shouted 'Fuck you!' over their shoulders: that much English they had learned from the IDF. Meanwhile their victim lay face down in the mud, his hands over his head, still sobbing in hoarse gasps and bleeding from a deep cut on his brow. As I helped him to his feet more blood could be seen oozing from his mouth. I tried to comfort him but he seemed terrified of me and went staggering away down the slope.

Slowly I limped home, each step more painful than the last. Later, getting to the loo involved an agonising journey and for three days I had to lie immobile on my bed, being fussed over by friends which made me feel ungratefully irritated. When ill or injured I much prefer to be left alone – like a cat. My own diagnosis was a pulled thigh muscle or groin tendon, for which time would provide the only cure. But my visitors became increasingly agitated, muttering about a fractured or displaced hip and other dismal possibilities. On the fourth day, two of them conspired to hire a taxi, kidnap me and present me at the Hamas clinic for an x-ray.

This impressive modern building, well equipped and efficiently staffed, is attached to a new mosque in the city centre, one of whose imams had just been imprisoned by the PA police. The Nablus government hospitals, run by the PA since 1995, are notably less impressive. I could see at a glance that my fellow patients were not the sort one expects to meet in a 'private clinic'. This enterprise is one of Hamas' non-profit-making contributions to the public welfare, probably funded by oily money but one doesn't refer to that.

In the x-ray cubicle an elderly male radiographer briefly left me alone while fetching plates. Automatically I removed my boots, jacket and trousers and lay ready on the couch. Returning, the poor man yelped like a trodden-on puppy, then retreated, slamming the door and shouting 'Get covered!'

In due course a tall doctor with a silver goatee beard studied the x-ray and made no diagnosis but prescribed ointment and ten capsules. He advised me that after a few days I could resume walking – slowly, over short distances – without hindering the healing process. My all-in bill came to €14. In the clinic pharmacy medications cost one-third the prices charged in Nablus's free market pharmacies.

Back on my bed, reluctantly relaxing, I reflected that this minor injury was a small price to pay for having possibly saved a child's life. To my visitors – bearing bowls of soup and plates of salad – I merely explained that I had slipped on the muddy slope. It would have been unkind to report that grim scene of juvenile violence. No doubt there was a back-story and the less said the better.

That evening, long after sunset, there was a brief gun-battle nearby. Twenty-seven men were arrested, six wounded – a commonplace incident, ignored by the media.

*

One morning near the souk entrance I saw four men unloading sacks of cement from a trailer for an adjacent project. As I peered through the relevant archway four conscripts approached and set about enjoying themselves. Two stood beside the van, demanding to see the municipality employees' IDs and their vehicle's various permits. The others stood at a little distance holding M-16s at the ready. When I moved closer to the van one undersized youth ordered me away. 'Go! Go!' he shouted. 'Get gone, fuck off!'

I beamed at him and said, 'I like standing here.' Angrily he jabbed his gun at my shoulder, repeating 'Go! Go!' I snapped 'Grow up!' and turned my back on him, the better to study his mates' hassling technique. One had taken out a jotter and biro and was insisting on writing down the three rows of numbers on each sack as it was being unloaded. If this infuriated the Palestinians their faces didn't show it. Military occupation teaches one how to keep emotions under wraps – until the next Intifada … Half-an-hour later, when the trailer was empty, the IDF sauntered away, giving me dirty looks, and the unloaders shook my hand and said 'thank you' in Arabic and English.

*

Of the IDF's 48 OPT bases, 14 are in the [Jordan] Valley which also holds eight 'Nahal' – mixed military/civilian settlements which never specify their quota of civilians. Road 90 shows a landscape defaced by militarism. On what should be pastureland, tank tracks compact the soil and unexploded mines menace pedestrians. IDF firearms practice targets and gross convolutions of razor-wire replace desert scrub. Since 2006 wide trenches have been dug deep to separate farmers from their nearest market. By the roadside wide red trilingual signs, twenty feet high, warn – 'DANGER! Firing range entrance forbidden!' Closed military zones occupy more than one-fifth of the West Bank and some 'Firing Ranges' soon become new settlements. Five Valley communities are now encircled by military zones and animals caught grazing on traditional pastures may be held to ransom while their owners' IDs are confiscated for indefinite periods. Alternatively, owners may be fined or imprisoned. 'Nature Reserves' are another dodge. Israel has set aside almost 50,000 hectares of Palestinian land as 'Nature Reserves' which cannot be cultivated; 30 percent of that area overlaps with firing zones. Halfway up the Valley, Salah pointed out a signpost to Ma'ale Efrayim, hidden away amidst one such reserve in very beautiful mountains.

Near Massu settlement we passed acres of greenhouses: commercial farming on an industrial scale. Behind that shiny expanse rose grey-brown rock-strewn slopes, deserted now, where Bedouin herds and flocks once grazed.

*

From No. 99 a short walk took me into this sad drab slum [Mea She'arim] where there was little motor traffic and everything needed repainting. Large locked buildings, with boarded-up windows, suggested a certain level of lost prosperity. The Haredi way of life is not conducive to commerce and most business premises seem ready to go into receivership. Along the main streets' pavements flowed a slow trickle of shoppers – all Haredi, mainly women with broods following. ...

Near the Kikar Shabbat junction I paused to transcribe a few of the numerous placards, banners and gable-end murals warning against 'clothing that would offend the people who live here' – against taking photographs or talking to children. I was wearing a long-sleeved, buttoned-up shirt, a borrowed headscarf and – despite the hot spring sunshine – ankle socks. So my attire can't have incensed the two boys who now raced past, kicking me so hard on the buttocks that I fell forward against a wall, dropping my notebook. They stopped at a little distance, to look back and jeer. Then a third lad darted from behind the wall, grabbed my notebook and joined them. (A tiny notebook, almost new, not a serious loss.) The boys were aged ten-ish with long, curly side-locks. In another ten years they'll have long bushy beards and (probably) wives. And ten years after that they are likely to have nine children, something which greatly concerns their secular, slow-breeding compatriots.

\*

During the bus ride from Mamilla I thought about terminology. In the Holy Land context, many words raise hackles. Claude Lanzmann, the Jewish-French film director, objects to 'Holocaust' because its literal meaning is 'a burnt offering to a god'. He prefers the Hebrew 'Shoah', meaning 'catastrophe'. However, the Arabic name for Zionism's 'War of Independence' – al-Nakba – also means catastrophe. And so I've been urged to retain 'Holocaust'; one must avoid any suggestion of an equivalence between the fates of Hitler's and Zionism's victims.

The Palestinian philosopher, Joseph Maddad, has strong feelings about 'conflict'. He sees his people engaged in a liberation struggle against European colonisers – hence 'conflict' is misleading and 'terrorism' scurrilous. Aida Touma-Sliman, General Director of the '48-ers' 'Women Against Violence', also rejects 'conflict' with its implication of equal forces. The mighty IDF, she points out, is deployed in an on-going *conquest* of the defenceless Palestinians. In like vein, Avi Shlaim had protested, 'Operation Cast Lead, to give the war its bizarre official title, was not really a war but a one-sided massacre.'

# JOURNALISM
## 1957–2011

*Dervla wrote hundreds, perhaps a few thousand, newspaper and magazine articles over her long writing career, especially in Ireland and the UK. Herein lies the tiniest of selections.*

*Irish Independent*, April 28 1957

**A Pyrenees Interlude: Irish Girl's Unusual Holiday Awheel:
Life Flows Here with a Smooth Rhythm – A Lesson for Ireland?**

**Article 7 of a series of 12**

Below my window a yard-wide irrigation channel ran along the base of the Fonda wall. The previous night it had been dry but now, the waters having been released from the reservoir, it was a swiftly flowing stream in which the kneeling older daughters of the *patrona* [owner] were laundering shirts and pillowslips. In the distance I saw a number of women carrying baskets of soiled clothes on their heads. I presumed they were going to the communal laundry-shed which exists in most Spanish towns. Clothes washing seems to form the chief occupation of the housewives, despite the chronic water shortage, and the poorest peasants in Spain, though they may wear rags will scarcely ever appear in dirty garments.

Several women were crossing the Plaza carrying home the day's supply of water. Most of them entered the bakery opposite to emerge a moment later with giant loaves a yard long and a foot wide – under each arm. One young woman was accompanied by her tiny daughter, who was endeavouring to balance a miniature water-jar on her head. '*Madre*' [mother] gave laughing advice and all the neighbours stood to watch the señorita's progress.

### Ageless Ritual
I felt no inclination to move from my balcony for I was pleasantly mesmerised by the ageless ritual before my eyes. A hundred years

ago, even a thousand years ago, the onlooker in Maella might have viewed an early morning scene identical with this in all essentials. It is in such places, rather than when sitting at a sidewalk café in Madrid's Puerta del Sol or viewing Valencia's flower market, that I have come closest to the Spain that I love so well.

Later, coming out of my trance I asked myself whether daily life in Maella might not be a mere round of monotonous drudgery, unnecessary in a well-run twentieth-century State. It was all very fine, I reasoned, for the visitor in search of escape from the standardised age to gloat sentimentally over the static way of life in remote Spanish towns. But how did conditions in Maella compare with those existing in a small Irish town? I live myself in an Irish Maella and I think I know the answer – they compare very favourably. We have the modern amenities but very few people left to enjoy them.

The Spaniards are a century behind us, but strange to say they are as contented with their lot as a rural community always is. In the past the ordinary Spaniard has suffered injustice and sinful oppression – as have the ordinary folk of most countries. If on a lesser scale – but the present regime has eased conditions. I saw little dire poverty in the rural districts of Spain: no-one is rich, but the peasants and their large families are healthy and apparently happy. Admittedly, it is otherwise in the cities, where I have seen such poverty as makes the observer illogically ashamed of his moderate affluence – poverty which brings children whimpering hungrily about one's feet and corrodes even the renowned Castilian dignity.

As I finally left my room, I came regretfully to the conclusion that if we Irish worked as the Spaniards work, and were content to enjoy such simple pleasures as they enjoy, and to follow a pattern of life befitting an agricultural country, then we too might have our towns and villages busily thronged and our houses swarming with young families.

### Narrow Streets

I should have started the day's cycling immediately in the comparative cool of the morning; but Maella so attracted me that I was reluctant to leave the town and spent the next hour wandering about the narrow streets, between rows of three- or four-storey houses. The majority of the buildings were whitewashed: many of the balconies had huge clusters of onions hanging from the railings and contained a variety of cacti in pots and from the top storeys came the incessant crowing of cockerels, for Spanish fowl are housed in the attics during the summer heat. Some of the doors were high and wide as a garage entrance, others were very low and nail-studded with massive iron rings as handles: a few had pictures of the Sacred Heart pasted on the outside.

In the poorer part of the town no streets existed as such, and the houses were so crowded together that I had the feeling of being continually trespassing in someone's back yard. Already many old women were sitting on low chairs in the doorways, knitting, sewing or merely superintending the frolics of their great-grandchildren who crawled about happily in the dust, often naked and usually attended by several pups and kittens. Seemingly, it never occurs to Spaniards to drown animals at birth: they are a race who prize vitality in every form and being generally untainted by materialism, they do not advert to the fact that it is more economical to destroy kittens and mongrel pups than to rear them with their own offspring. Incidentally, none of the infant population of Maella, whether human or animal, looked anything but well nourished.

The irrigation system was now working at full speed, with water crashing down the deep channels on either side of the steep streets. I followed one channel to the verge of the *huerta* [vegetable garden/field] and stood fascinated watching the precious liquid being automatically diverted into numerous smaller channels which carried it through the acres of fruit and vegetables. Little dams were built at the entrance to each section of the *huerta* to control the ration of water given to the various crops.

### Home Industry

On my way back to the Plaza Mayor I passed through the business centre of the town. Here the wide doors stood open and in the windowless interiors men worked beneath feeble electric lights – baking bread in yawning wall ovens, tailoring suits, weaving wicker pannier-bags for the mules, sewing leather harnesses, making cartwheels, hammering horse-shoes, carving wooden chairs, stools, benches and tables. These little Spanish towns must be among the last Western European strongholds of the craftsmen whose ancestors made up the medieval guilds. Here mass-produced factory goods are a rarity; the community to a great extent supplies its own wants by skilled local labour.

Along the comparatively wide streets near the Plaza Mayor women were busily sweeping the areas of road opposite their houses. The Spaniards are a very clean people and in the most isolated village the streets are thus tended. No litter is ever strewn about. I hate to think of the impression a Spaniard would get on strolling through some of our Irish towns.

### 'Irlanda!'

My presence in Maella was still causing covert speculation, though the majority of the citizens feigned to ignore me. At length one young woman paused in her sweeping as I passed, and boldly enquired, '*Francia?*' Immediately all her neighbours stood still, expectantly turning towards me. I shook my head and said '*Irlanda*' which produced a noticeable increase in the friendliness of the atmosphere – not because '*Irlanda*' conveys a great deal to the Spanish peasant, but because *Francia* is the most unpopular country in Spain. The information was quickly spread: '*Irlanda! Bicicleta! Sola!*' being shouted from group to group down various streets and the ice having been broken, I was greeted warmly by everyone as I proceeded on my way to the Fonda.

I was quite startled to observe a huge lorry parked in the centre of the Plaza Mayor. Only then did I realise that I had hitherto seen no trace of motor vehicles in Maella and their absence had seemed so natural in the little town that I would never have consciously remarked it but for the antique contraption which now caught my eye.

Upstairs in the *comedor* [dining room] I found the *patrona* placing my breakfast on the table. It consisted of the usual glass of sweetened warm goat's milk and three rounds of dry toast. The *patrona* explained regretfully that butter was never used hereabouts.

When I had paid my bill – total, five shillings – and secured my kit for the next lap, the *patrona* appeared to bid me goodbye and present me with a dozen delicious peaches, which she insisted on my carrying, though I found it very difficult to fit them into the knapsack. Then we shook hands and I received many motherly warnings of the dangers to be avoided en route. Five minutes later I had left Maella behind and was on the right road to Caspe. But I did not regret having gone astray, for my hours in Maella were unforgettable.

**Irish Times, September 28 1968**

**Review of *The Hills of Adonis* by Colin Thubron & *The Mountain Arabs* by John Sykes**

Recently in Turkey, an expatriate Englishman, long out of touch with home, asked me if any successor to Freya Stark had yet appeared on the literary horizon. I replied readily that I was aware of no such rising star – but that was before I had read Colin Thubron's *The Hills of Adonis*. The publishers' claim was that Mr Thubron's first book, *Mirror to Damascus*, established the author as 'the most interesting and readable young writer to combine travel and scholarship in his work'. A bold claim, yet one felt no inclination to dispute it.

In the spring of 1967, Colin Thubron walked 500 miles through the Helaneic mountains in quest of the Semite love goddess, Astarte – Aphrodite to the Greeks – and of her lover Adonis. He explains, 'to drive through such a land would be to receive no sense of it, for Lebanon is half the size of Wales and is best seen as centuries of people knew it, on foot or on a donkey. For this reason I trusted in the hospitality of "the people of the mountains", by walking down through the country; and besides, a goddess must be approached carefully and with humility.'

Nowadays almost every track is beaten and travel writers tend to be competent guides rather than inspired interpreters. But Colin Thubron is inspired and to journey with him through Lebanon is an unforgettable experience. Exultantly he responds to this old, old land – saturated with myth, solemn with history and effortlessly, by the flick of a phrase, he recalls the splendour of Lebanese landscapes, the nobility of Lebanese ruins, the significance of Lebanese customs. Delicately, he traces the magic past subtly flowing into and transforming the mundane present. Awful dangers attend a twentieth-century quest for ancient gods. But Mr Thubron's integrity preserves him from these dangers and no taint of the fanciful or the artificial ever spoils his pages. Probably it is not a coincidence that this twenty-nine-year-old author is a direct descendant of John Dryden. His prose contains more true poetry than half-a-dozen contemporary slim volumes, and his formidable erudition appears draped with such an easy grace that it never becomes aggressive or tedious. If there is a place in this beautiful book I failed to find it.

John Sykes also spent the spring of 1967 in Lebanon and *The Mountain Arabs* is a disconcerting but necessary complement to *The Hills of Adonis*. The original purpose of the Sykes' visit was to study the confrontation between Christian and Muslim traditions and beliefs. Soon the immanent Six Days War had deflected his interest to local politics, and an accidental close involvement with one of the most powerful Maronite clans gave him the opportunity to observe modern Beirut society from the inside.

As the author of seven novels John Sykes chose indirectly to present his observations and deductions by doing character studies of those influential individuals whom he came to know best and by indicating the dramatic complexities of their relations with each other, with their political approaches and with himself. Used by a less gifted writer this could be a dangerous technique, prompting the reader to suspect exaggerations for the sake of 'the story'. But there is no temptation to doubt the accuracy of Mr Sykes's brilliant analysis of this unstable, ambitious, calculating yet friendly city, where Phoenician ghosts are only now being laid with some difficulty – by the exorcism of the necrologists.

**Irish Times, October 15 1969**

**Why there's no going back for some travel writers**

Some weeks ago I received a letter from Ethiopia telling me that what I have written about that country has wounded and puzzled my Ethiopian friends. Anxiously, I examined my conscience – but could think of nothing that might reasonably have offended anyone. It seems that travel writers are doomed never to please their host countries. However strenuously one tries to avoid giving offence – by omitting amusing incidents that could hurt individuals, by ignoring domestic politics, by emphasising national virtues, by making every sort of allowance for national vices – inevitably there is an angry reaction from official or semi-official quarters. Then one's book is banned – an academic point, in such countries as Nepal and Ethiopia – one has no hope of getting a permit to return and the people who had been thought of affectionately as friends, proclaim that this scoundrel of a writer is their enemy.

Because travel is an essentially personal thing – an encounter between an individual and an unfamiliar land – travel books cannot be more than one foreigner's vision of a strange, stimulating and sometimes misunderstood country. Complete objectivity is impossible when the foreigner's personality is the sieve through which all impressions pass. If only for this reason, non-Europeans are bound to resent European comments. They have their own vision of their own land, which rarely coincides with the traveller's vision, and they are not interested, but outraged, when given an opportunity to see themselves as others see them. Obviously, the two visions are equally important, which is why the best travel books are so often written not by true travellers, but by sympathetic foreigners who have settled in a country, learnt its language and been able to see the natives' vision clearly enough for it to complement their own.

### Progress v. Tradition

It is sad that most underdeveloped peoples are now torn between pride in their countries' traditions and shame because of its technically backward state. Some conflicts are healthy and inspiring, but this one is stultifying all round. Inevitably, technical advances have to uproot ancient traditions; yet the power of the rulers who yearn for modernisation is often based on these traditions, so they must manoeuvre themselves and their people into a dishonest position where everyone tries to run with the traditional hare and the technical hound. The common results are that the social structure suffers from the impact of new ideas, the bearers of new ideas suffer from the suspicion of the very authorities who have invited them and the ordinary people suffer from muddled values.

This situation might be eased if non-Europeans could bring themselves to accept the fact that the foreigner's vision of their country has its own validity, and is related to the fate that awaits their civilisation when it has been partly remodelled on ours. They would then be better equipped to distinguish, in their cultural readjustment, between the baby and the bathwater; and they would also find it easier to understand why their particular modes of thought and behaviour are so often incompatible with the constructive use of 'Aid Program' funds and personnel.

### Misunderstood

One of my Ethiopian friends is quoted as having said that she cannot understand my motive for writing such a book on Ethiopia. This remark made me reflect – for the first time, oddly enough – on the subject of travel writers' motives in general. There is, of course, one obvious and sordid motive. In travel books, the subject matter predominates to such an extent that their creation requires less literary skill than almost any other form of writing. Publishers and the reading public will meekly accept, from a travel writer, the sort of mangled English and rickety construction that would forever confine non-travel typescripts to the bottom drawer; so if those with ambitions to write but limited talent happen to enjoy travelling, they are frequently luring into becoming travel writers.

A less sordid motive is the desire to communicate why one has come to love countries and people which, even now, are less known and less understood by the average European. This brings us back to the struggle for objectivity.

Every author very quickly finds out through the grisly medium of his fan-mail, that the pen, however feeble, is indeed mightier than the sword. Therefore, remembering the trustful library borrower who takes every printed word as gospel truth, travel writers sweat blood to be objective. The less a country is known the heavier is their responsibility, as they try to prevent affection from blinding them to the national warts – with the unhappy repercussions that have already been mentioned.

Yet another motive is the alleviation of the traveller's nostalgia after he has come home. At the deepest level a journey never ends, for one retains, as part of oneself, many valuable qualities gathered from civilisations that are in some respect superior to our own. Yet a certain nostalgia is felt for countries that are unlikely to be revisited, or that would be dismally changed if one were to return. And the writing of a book helps here, partly because, while working on it, the writer is reliving his journey during most of his waking hours – and partly because it forms, in some curious way, a new link quite separate from the links formed on the journey itself.

I feel that this last motive is the chief one behind Walter Gill's book, in which he describes his successful search, in 1931, for a then unknown tribe of Aborigines in the Petermann Ranges. The journey into their territory was made on camels, through almost unexplored country, and the Aborigines were pure primitives. The author had the good fortune to experience the real Australia before it was adulterated by development, and his descriptions of sights, sounds and smells are always vivid and often beautiful. His style takes a little getting used to, for it has the jaggedness commonly associated with the speech of tough, witty Australians; and this jaggedness is accentuated by the fact that most of the commas in his books have invisible tails – which is irritating to a degree, but not Mr Gill's fault.

It is obvious that when the author first met his spear-carrying Aborigines he was in some danger, but because he respected them they at once accepted him.

Comparing his book with the writings of many professional anthropologists one realises that his relaxed, unscientific approach gives him a tremendous advantage. Instead of tensely 'Observing Aborigines' he simply enjoyed his stay among fellow humans as different from himself as anyone of the same species could be – and so the Aborigines took him to their hearts and allowed him to witness scenes that would make any anthropologist writhe with envy. The recent history of Australia would have been much happier had there been more white Australians like Walter Gill.

*Irish Times,* **July 16 1975**

## Backward Social Mobility – Dervla Murphy Accounts for a One-Woman Battle against Inflation

Inflation takes us all differently. Some people go on strike yet again and get an extra £100 a week. (Or is it £10? But no matter at this stage …) Others blackmail their bank managers, or take an evening job, or pretend to live in Jersey, or make piteous, simpering noises within earshot of their publisher and/or editor.

This last ploy, however, is singularly ineffective. It merely draws forth details about other people's overheads. Also one is told that if there are any more tiresome squeaky noises about not having had a rise for nine years, no publisher or editor will ever again have anything to do with the mediocre drivel that drips from one's pen at irregular intervals. Discouraging …

One goes home to brood and slowly the awful truth dawns. As a writer, one's output is of no value to the nation, to the EEC, to the Third World, to God Almighty or to anybody but oneself. And it is of value to oneself only if it can be flogged, for however paltry a fee.

Obviously the thing is to economise, cut back, tighten the belt, count the pennies, recycle the tea-leaves and so on. But if, over the past five years, one has been becoming increasingly frugal (a nicer word than close-fisted), the means whereby further economies may be achieved are not immediately apparent.

In 1972 I gave up cigarettes (that was for health reasons, but it also saved money) and brandy was banished from my drinks cupboard. In 1973 whiskey was banished; in 1974, sherry and plonk; and recently, in this year of gracelessness, I have made the supreme sacrifice. My Guinness! – a tear springs to the eye as I write those dark and frothy syllables.

Now guests are offered a choice of tea or coffee. They try to conceal their horror, grip the arm of their chair and look at me with wild surmise, fancying I must have entered a phase of religious mania and taken the pledge. (It can happen to women in the mid-forties.) By 1976 coffee may have been banished, and by 1977 tea. Then perhaps we'll be down to rainwater from a barrel, very good for the kidneys, because in two years' time who knows what the water-rates may be?

This summer many people claim to be gaining pounds sterling and losing pounds *avoir-dupois* by taking the children for a walk on Sunday afternoons instead of motoring to the sea; but I cannot cut back on transport, never having risen out of the pedal-cycle class. Neither can I cut back on entertainments; I have no television set, I gave up buying new records years ago and in rural Ireland one's chief entertainments are in any case provided free by the generosity of nature.

Nor does my telephone account offer much scope. I am a passive subscriber; my friends can ring me if they are so disposed but except in emergencies I let sleeping receivers lie. Postage is intractable too. I rarely write social letters, for lack of time, and if one neglects business letters, all sorts of incomprehensible financial disasters occur and one ends up having to make four telephone calls to London in the middle of the morning. There is, of course, a third sort of letter which gives one pause. I received a good example the other day from an organisation called 'Genesis' with a London address – though my antennae suggested American provenance. The letter-writer is 'bringing together a major new-age community' and would very much like to meet me. So – do I spend 5p on a postcard, or do I forget Genesis? But how does one bring together a major new-age community? And what is it, anyway, when it has been brought together? And which is 'major'– the new-age or the community? Obviously Genesis can't be forgotten. Led astray by vulgar curiosity I squander 5p gloomily, reminding myself that really it is a shilling…

Yet correspondence is one of the few areas in which I can claim to have made significant savings over the past decade. Long before there was so much fuss about a paper shortage I deplored our shameful wastage. Recalling a few wholesome wartime devices, which we would have done well to retain when peace came, I began to reply to people on the backs of their own letters. This, however, had an unfortunate effect on some nervous systems so I took to writing to A on the back of B's letters, and vice versa. All went well until A wrote something about B which had been better not read by B. Then life became slightly more complicated because I made a rule always to censor my writing paper, which takes time. Nevertheless, this campaign is well worthwhile.

Just a few weeks ago, while tidying out a remote cupboard, I came on a huge brown paper parcel labelled 'Jumble'. It contained an assortment of garments in far better condition than anything I have worn for the past several years, and I gazed at these in awe, trying to remember what it felt like to be affluent enough to give *away* unflawed shirts, sweaters and slacks. It must, I reckoned, have been in 1967 that I made up that parcel and forgot to take it to the jumble sale. What a blessed lapse of memory! They will keep me going until 1984, at least. And any day now they may come back into fashion.

Actually, clothes bills have never over-strained my resources. During adolescence I studied Thoreau closely and marked his excellent advice to 'beware of all enterprises that require new clothes.' Even catering for a fast-growing child is no threat to the economy, because of London's Oxfam shops, where almost-new garments – for both children and adults – need cost no more than 20p or 30p.

Now we come to the nitty-gritty: one's daily bread. I don't know about city shops, but here in the backwoods we have a splendid institution called 'dog-bread'. This is perfectly good brown bread sold at half price, because it is more than twenty-four hours old; apparently the populace with wanton disregard for its collective digestion, must have *hot* bread. Dog-bread, they tell me, is given to greyhounds, mixed with beaten eggs, honey and other body-building delicacies. I have it with margarine.

Then there is 'dog-meat'. Because of our national improvidence, meat-laden bones which would be regarded elsewhere as the basis of a good square meal, are simply thrown out here. Or given away to the like of me, ostensibly for my dog. Our butcher must realise that these gifts are now my main source of protein, but having known me since the good old sirloin days, he tactfully plays the 'dog-meat' game.

Brown bananas also provide cut-price nourishment; seemingly the fact that yellow bananas are flatulent and almost devoid of food value is not widely accepted. Bacon-ends, too, can be acquired for as little as 10p or 15p a pound, depending on how many streaks of lean they contain. Fortunately, I relish any form of fat and can happily consume half a pound of bacon-end at a sitting. My more gullible friends swear I'll soon drop dead of some new disease invented in America. Unfortunately, however, all these economies are to a great extent counteracted by the fact that neither my dog nor my cat will have anything to do with stale bread, free bones or the cheaper brands of dog-meal or tinned meat. While I sit drinking recycled tea, and gnawing hard hunks of bread which have scraped a mere acquaintance with margarine, they gorge on the choicest chicken and liver, in rich gravy, at 18p a tin.

It has recently been pointed out to me that I can *grow* food. Potatoes, cabbage, carrots, lettuce, onions – that sort of thing. I took the suggestion on the chin and said brightly, 'Yes, of course! Why not?', while horror welled up in the depths of my soul. Growing food is synonymous with gardening, and gardening is (next to housework) my least favourite activity.

'It would give you exercise in the fresh air,' continued my non-friend. True enough, but if I have been writing flat out for eight or nine hours I consider myself entitled to an *enjoyable* form of exercise. I want, then, to walk or cycle or swim, not to rouse my latent lumbago by wrestling with acres of weeds. (Well, actually, my estate comprises one-sixteenth of an acre.) So I hastily sat down and calculated that, given the cost of seeds, fertilisers, insecticides, gardening implements and anti-lumbago lotion, vegetable growing for two people would be no economy, but an unforgivable extravagance. It's marvellous what can be done with figures.

However, one important economy that involves enjoyable fresh air 'n' exercise is firewood-collecting. If one collects just a little every day, during the summer, a really impressive pile has accumulated by the beginning of the winter. But here we are on delicate ground. Firewood-collecting is a very public economy and like bare feet, it carries, throughout rural Ireland, shameful connotations of a degraded degree of poverty.

Therefore, certain ultra-respectable neighbours recoil when they see me sweating home with a large branch in tow. *What* would her parents think – God rest them! – they mutter into their beards. (Within this sub-species both sexes tend to have beards.) Occasionally, indeed, I am openly reproved by those who have known me since I was born; but they cannot dispute that my parents would have condoned any honest activity that helped to avoid debts. Incidentally, I am almost the only firewood-gatherer left in my area; soon the species will be as extinct as food-gatherers.

Thirty years ago the only cleaning aids used in our house were Lux, Vim, washing soda and carbolic soap. But now, on the relevant shelves of any supermarket, one sees a sinister proliferation of strange substances in packets, tins, bottles, tubes, phials, jars, cartons, boxes, plastic phalluses and weird containers with nozzles at suggestive angles. All these substances are expensive, most are utterly superfluous and some are known to be downright deleterious. If the next generation is born with green nails or purple hair it may be our fault for having cleaned the windows with Shinier, or the lavatory with Sweeter or the oven with Swifter, while our children were growing up. Only within the last few months have I de-brainwashed myself and seen that here is the most obvious of all cutback areas – and one, moreover, in which cutbacks will benefit not only myself but our wretchedly ill-used planet. Mind you, I rarely tested the efficiency of all these new cleaning aids. Their main purpose was to give nosy visitors the impression that I had at one time cleaned the house and might be expected to repeat the performance at some unspecified future date.

Recently, one such guest complimented me on a stew, sounding rather puzzled, for I had been frank about its basis of free dog-meat. As I do not care to make a mystique out of cooking I at once explained that the subtle flavour came from a seasoning of horse medicine. '*Horse medicine?*' croaked my friend, going green beneath her suntan lotion. I then had to explain further. In Baltistan, a few months ago, my daughter's horse was bitten on the flank by a mongoose and developed an abscess, for which the locally prescribed treatment was an exotic mixture of herbs and spices. This medicine cost Rs. 70 per half seer (i.e. £3.50 per pound) but Hallam (the horse) was unimpressed and firmly refused every dosed feed. So, of course, I brought the residue home and found another use for it. At the end of this perfectly reasonable explanation my friend was silent for a moment. Then she said, 'You know, I think you *enjoy* inflation. You're naturally mean and it gives you an excuse to make a virtue out of parsimony.'

She could be right, too.

*Irish Times,* **September 4 1999**

**My Writing Day: What's wrong with a rut?**

'She's gone into purdah,' they say, meaning: gate locked, post unopened, telephone off the hook, social life in abeyance. Some excluded friends see this as neurotic behaviour. I would find writing much easier, they assert, if I relaxed at intervals and had a night – or at least an evening – on the tiles. They won't concede that I'm good at recognising my limitations. I'm a one-thing-at-a-time person. I'm by temperament inclined to get rather involved in other people's lives. If combined with a normal social life, my work would suffer from the distractions – other people's plans and problems, joys and stresses.

Also while working on a travel book I need to remain, mentally, in the country being written about, to avoid brooding over Ireland's problems. It may seem that in purdah I lead a lonely life, my only companions for months on end dogs or cats or both. But this is not so. While reliving a journey, one retains the companionship of certain individuals met en route. These are more than 'raw material' – the memory of their friendship and hospitality keeps me linked to faraway others.

There are seasonal variations in my writing day. I rise at 5 a.m., then, during summer, enjoy a swim in the Blackwater river, followed by my main meal of the day, a substantial breakfast of homemade muesli (known as Ma's Mess) and homemade bread with Knockanore or Bay Lough cheese and a few pint mugs of strong tea. In winter, breakfast happens first, while I listen to the World Service news, and exercise happens later when I cycle 20 miles or so, weather permitting.

Most of the day is devoted to the current book – not necessarily writing: at some stages much background reading or checking of facts is involved. The first longhand draft is severely pruned, then becomes the second roughly typed draft. The third draft is polished for the publisher with the aid of a scissors and sellotape to avoid more re-typing. For years numerous friends have been applying heavy pressure regarding a word processor. This machine, I'm assured, would save me countless hours, days – even weeks – of tedious labour. It would not produce a typescript but something called a floppy disc – or is it 'disk'? Anyway, however it's spelt, I can do without it. Those well-meaning friends deplore my being fixed in a rut from which the rest of the writing world has long since escaped. But I like my rut. I'm comfortable in it – and what's the hurry? People nowadays forget that when God made time he made plenty of it.

Moreover, I am so allergic to technology that an ugly machine dominating the workplace would certainly dry up my meagre flow of inspiration. And the likelihood of my pressing the right buttons in the right sequence is remote. Nor do I want to see my mortal prose on a TV-type screen; I only want to see it on paper, where it's supposed to be.

NB: I go to bed at 9.30 p.m.


*Irish Times*, **August 8 2011**

**Swept away on my own River of Life**

I have had an intimate relationship with the Blackwater since my father taught me to swim in 1934 – an important rite of passage, though I can't remember it. Here in west Waterford, the river has come a long way from its source near the Cork/Kerry border and is quite close to its Youghal Bay estuary. It flows between steep wooded ridges – sombre in winter, lacy green in spring, heavily green in summer and in autumn a glowing conflagration. To the north, in the near distance, rise the gentle blue curves of the Knockmealdown mountains.

East and west of Lismore one may walk all day, seeing nobody, through a dog's paradise of woodlands and riverside meadows where the terrain cannot have changed much since the second century.

Then, Ptolemy took time off from star-gazing and composed a map of the known world – including the Blackwater, already an important trading route. For lack of Romans, land transport inhibited Irish commerce until comparatively recently.

Gradually, over the decades, nature has wrought numerous changes in this tranquil corner of the Barony of Coshmore and Coshbride. Aged trees have surrendered to gales, or to the slow erosion of their supporting hedgerows, and now lie or lean at odd angles, wearing frills of fungi and housing an abundance of insects. An 18th-century salmon weir has been dismantled by floods. Banks of sand and gravel come and go, creating temporary current-free inlets suitable for teaching small children to swim. Every winter brings certain modifications, usually subtle, but dramatic when great chunks of pasture land are torn away. Other river-bed transformations can seem almost magical, as when a deep dark glossy stretch is replaced within a very few years, by a sparkling amber torrent, shallow enough for its stones to be visible.

In the 1950s and 1960s a dying willow was my diving board, but it now lies level with the bank, forming a highway for mink – beautiful creatures, though widely and rightly resented. Since their arrival, the swans that habitually nested on the islet near the collapsed weir, just upstream from Lismore Castle, have moved house. Responsible swans don't lay eggs within reach of mink. So I can no longer watch the tiny cygnets (little bigger than ducklings) rapidly becoming fawn-grey adolescents. Swan life, being such a joy to watch, encourages anthropomorphism. They seem the ideal family, parents mutually loving and faithful and sharing childcare, adolescents happy to hang out with parents until something hormonal tells them it's time to seek a mate.

Otter families are much rarer and even more endearing. In midsummer I like to swim at sunrise, and one year two adults and a juvenile often appeared nearby. If I was already in the water, they ignored me and played: all three having fun, chasing each other, doing gymnastics on a half-submerged fallen branch. Then one would move off to fish for breakfast while the others continued to frolic. It seemed I was no threat while swimming very slowly and quietly. But if they arrived first, and saw me walking towards them, they immediately vanished.

One memorable morning I met an otter on the path, sitting on his haunches, sucking a swan's egg. On an even more memorable morning, my dogs interrupted an otter's breakfast by the water's edge – an aberrant otter, no doubt: allegedly, they never catch salmon. That five-pounder became several suppers; I had carried it home furtively, wrapped in colt's-foot leaves, hoping not to be reported to the Duke of Devonshire's bailiff.

Along this valley, on an average day, one sees what I think of as 'the quintet': moorhen, duck, cormorant, heron, swan. The cormorants conspicuously colonise a dead elm for several years, then move on, then return. The herons stay put, always building their sprawling, noisome nests in the highest branches of towering sycamores or chestnuts. They are responsible for littering the banks with large horse-mussel shells, once used by the locals as spoon substitutes – a poignant reminder of bygone days when many in this area lived in extreme poverty, while up and down this valley stately homes were being embellished and spacious demesnes expanded.

On lucky days a winged jewel flashes past: kingfishers nest where tangled tree roots protrude from the bank above a semi-stagnant inlet. Occasionally the jewel perches on an alder branch and if I go still, treading water, I may see his lightning dive for something identifiable. On other lucky days flocks of wild geese follow the river, their powerful wing music stirring a mysterious emotion, a mix of reverence and diffuse nostalgia.

Less common, nowadays, are the iridescent curlew flocks, their plaintive cries not matching their joyous, precisely choreographed swirlings across a wide sky. In recent years a few newcomers have appeared among the cattle: slim, Persil-white egrets, suggesting climate change.

One May afternoon in 1941 I saw something unforgettable. My parents and I were approaching the Blackwater estuary, on our way to Whiting Bay, when suddenly a man waving a red flag leaped out of a ditch. He had probably been dozing; in those days motor traffic merely trickled and our Ford Ten was the only car on the road. Then, before my very eyes, Youghal bridge seemed to disintegrate. Quickly it came apart and a three-mast schooner with an auxiliary engine sailed past us on its way to Cappoquin – or maybe it was going to turn up the Bride with a cargo for Tallow. Twenty years later I was to see from my bicycle saddle one of the last merchant schooners taking advantage of the tide between Camphire and Dromana.

The sight of that splendid vessel sailing upstream, past waving fishermen grouped below Ballintray House, put my father into pedagogic gear. I associated the Blackwater with beauty, silence and solitude, but now I learned about it as a crowded thoroughfare of considerable commercial and military importance. For some two thousand years boat- and ship-building were a crucial part of riverside life; in the nineteenth century fifty-ton barges were still being built in such unlikely (to us) places as Ballyduff and Affane. The variety of cargoes carried up and down the Blackwater and Bride indicate how multi-skilled were these communities. Boat-builders, sail-makers, wool-combers and spinners and weavers, stone masons, fishermen, wood-cutters, sand-spreaders, iron smelters, lime burners, leather tanners, basket makers, flour millers, bacon curers, cider brewers, rope makers – each person valued for his or her particular contribution to the local economy. Such people must have enjoyed a high level of self-respect. Now too many of their descendants are reduced to using technologies that minimise physical labour but can't do much for the individual's *amour-propre*. ...

That summer [aged twelve] I was judged sufficiently mature, mentally and physically, to swim alone in a river I already knew so well. Thereafter my two favourite activities supplemented each other. Cycling allowed me to find various secluded swimming spots between Mocollop, some eight miles west of Lismore, and Villierstown, about the same distance to the east. Downstream from the Kitchen Hole one had to beware of the tide; elsewhere, one had to check for dense underwater weeds.

As a teenager, I once swam in the Bride, the Blackwater's main tributary, without first studying its tidal whims. I forget what prompted that lapse into mental immaturity but I shall never forget my fear when I realised that I could neither swim back to my starting point nor reach the bank. Along that stretch there was no visible bank, only treacherous, muddy reed-beds.

Not until the tide had carried me down to Camphire bridge was I able to scramble ashore, very cold and very shaken. Luckily haymakers had been near my starting point; otherwise I would have been naked. I set out to hitch-hike back to my belongings and soon a bemused elderly farmer, driving a cart-load of spires to Sapperton, bravely picked me up and hastily wrapped me in sacking. ... I wasn't the first reckless swimmer to have come ashore at Camphire bridge.

... Towards the end of the 1950s motor traffic began to replace draught animals to my great distress. Cyclists dislike sharing roads with other machines. Rapidly the pace of life changed, as did attitudes to farming, which around then became the 'agricultural industry' – an ominous semantic shift. (Similarly, publishing became the 'book industry', to the great detriment of non-bestselling authors.) ...

West Waterford disappoints some of my foreign guests. They protest, 'It's too like Sussex or Dorset, too unlike Kerry or Donegal.' I see their point yet to me west Waterford, south Tipperary and east Cork are incomparably satisfying. Everything is congenial: every curve of the hills and valleys, every bend of the rivers and streams, every distinctive seasonal scent of fields and woods. This territory is my natural habitat, where I'm at ease in all weathers. It doesn't do to forget that we too are animals, albeit with certain unique capabilities increasingly lethal to our fellow animals.

# Publisher's Afterword

'Whatever the theologians might say about Heaven being in a state of union with God, I knew it consisted of an infinite library; and eternity … was simply what enabled one to read uninterruptedly for ever.'

Dervla remembering her childhood self
in *Wheels within Wheels*

By the time she died, Dervla Murphy was under no illusions about that infinite library, but she had made impressive use of her 90 years on earth to read, and think, as much as anyone. 'So, Barnaby,' I remember her saying, as I stumbled into the kitchen bleary-eyed from the night before, when we'd matched each other beer for wine a few years ago. 'I've been listening to the World Service. What do you make of the latest horrors in the West Bank?' It was only 7 a.m., and Dervla was already engaged with one of the world's most intractable problems. Even when we went over to visit her in April 2022, six weeks before she died, the Curragh Mutiny of 1914 and the one-state solution in the Middle East were on the agenda.

I didn't realise how frail she had become. A couple of weeks before there had been a robust description of her *Lunch with the FT*, where she helped the journalist submit the lowest expense form ever. They had dined at Dervla's home on her incomparable lentil stew and a selection of cheese and bread, washed down by cider and beer, something that we had enjoyed on many an occasion. My wife, Rose, had intuited that we needed to visit, and sure enough when we arrived I saw that, though her mind was as sharp as ever, she was in constant, debilitating pain.

As well as keeping abreast of events, she had been worrying away at an issue closer to home. Dervla had been thinking back over her life and wondering about her father's emotional distance. She had come to the conclusion that the answer lay in the Curragh barracks, where he had been detained for ten days as an eighteen-year-old Republican. She was convinced that this, almost certainly brutal, experience at the hands of the British army was traumatic enough to affect his entire life. Her deep empathy for his experience was written all over her face.

Early in our professional relationship, Dervla told me she could read anything except a contract and would sign anything I put before her. It worked well for her, as I was so delighted by her trust that I always made our best offer right from the start. Her vagueness about money ended there, and though frugal about her own comforts, this was a matter of anti-consumerist principle not need. Money was reserved, like a cautious treasury minister, for the education of her granddaughters and for health, which were the two absolutes. Her house was spartan, and when she came to stay with us she insisted on sleeping on the sofa in her own sleeping bag, folding up the clean sheets we had provided for the use of our next, more profligate guest.

Dervla's books are also full of trust, trust that she would find somewhere to eat and sleep that night, trust in the kindness of strangers. Her method was one of random engagement. She rarely called on government ministers or followed up introductions, for she found that the story could be found more easily while you were waiting to catch a bus. She would install herself somewhere, like Balata refugee camp in the West Bank, and trust that people would open up to her, that the story would come to her. And I think people knew she was trustworthy, that in telling their story she would do so with utter respect for its complexity.

She was a one-off in the world of travel writing. She despised hotels and restaurants and every artifice of the worldwide travel industry, which separated tourists from reality and pocketed the difference. She was immune to the subtle corruption of an upgraded flight or to accepting the presidential suite furnished with complementary bowls of fruit. When she went to the Dubai literary festival, she was the only guest ever to insist on staying in a local hotel downtown rather than in a glass and steel skyscraper. In a like manner, she never accepted an advance from a publisher, travelled off her own bat to wherever drew her, and if and when a book came out of it, she would send it to her publisher. Instead of complaining about distractions, she put a padlock around her front gate for as long as was needed to produce a first draft, and after breakfast was over unplugged the telephone.

When we settled down in her home this last time and opened the first of many bottles, Dervla's immediate family were, as always, our first and foremost conversation: her only daughter Rachel and her three beloved granddaughters, but this time we were also treated to a loving sketch of her son-in-law, Andrew Hunt.

The other family that Dervla cherished were her first publishers, the Murrays. A chance meeting on two bicycles in Delhi, between her and Penelope Chetwode, led to an introduction to Jock Murray, who not only published Dervla's first book, *Full Tilt*, and made a great success of it, but the many that came after it. He and his wife, Diana, became the bedrock of Dervla's literary life, having her to stay for months in their home in Hampstead. Jock became godfather to Dervla's daughter, while Diana was the much-cherished editorial midwife to many of Dervla's travel books.

Dervla said that the only men whose advice she valued were Jock Murray and Colin Thubron, whose early talent she first spotted as a book reviewer for the *Irish Times*. In other ways the works of Isabella Bird, Mary Kingsley and Mary Wortley Montagu were her role models: how the real purpose of a journey was the search for chance friendships on the road. Dervla always travelled light but carried with her a profound sympathy for the oppressed, and a hostility for nationalist generals and their secretive allies within international corporations. To balance this, her ear was always primed to meet genuine patriots, aspiring towards self-sufficiency not just in sustainable resources but in governance. Although she would never agree with my suggestion that Tibet and the Republic of Ireland were her two role models – nations that at a terrible cost had tried to remain true to their own cultures and maintain an independence from greedy, neighbouring empires – I stand my ground.

It is not often that you get to talk with a beer-drinking prophet, so when I am asked if Eland will ever make a serious profit, I answer that we have already banked our greatest dividend – to talk the world with Dervla Murphy.

Barnaby Rogerson
London 2022

# ELAND

61 Exmouth Market, London EC1R 4QL
Email: info@travelbooks.co.uk

Eland was started forty years ago to revive great travel books that had fallen out of print. Although the list soon diversified into biography and fiction, all the books are chosen for their interest in spirit of place. One of our readers explained that for him reading an Eland is like listening to an experienced anthropologist at the bar – she's let her hair down and is telling all the stories that were just too good to go into the textbook.

Eland books are for travellers, and for readers who are content to travel in their own minds. They open out our understanding of other cultures, interpret the unknown and reveal different environments, as well as celebrating the humour and occasional horrors of travel. We take immense trouble to select only the most readable books and therefore many readers collect the entire, hundred-and-sixty-volume series.

You will find a very brief description of some of our books on the following pages. Extracts from each and every one of them can be read on our website, at www.travelbooks.co.uk. If you would like a free copy of our catalogue, email us or send a postcard.

# ELAND

**The Weather in Africa**
MARTHA GELLHORN
*Three novellas set amongst the*
*white settlers of East Africa*

**The Last Leopard**
DAVID GILMOUR
*The biography of Giuseppe di Lampedusa,*
*author of* The Leopard

**Walled Gardens**
ANNABEL GOFF
*A portrait of the Anglo-Irish: sad,*
*absurd and funny*

**Africa Dances**
GEOFFREY GORER
*The magic of indigenous culture*
*and the banality of colonisation*

**Cinema Eden**
JUAN GOYTISOLO
*Essays from the Muslim*
*Mediterranean*

**Goodbye Buenos Aires**
ANDREW GRAHAM-YOOLL
*A portrait of an errant father,*
*and of the British in Argentina*

**A State of Fear**
ANDREW GRAHAM-YOOLL
*A journalist witnesses Argentina's*
*nightmare in the 1970s*

**A Pattern of Islands**
ARTHUR GRIMBLE
*Rip-roaring adventures and a passionate*
*appreciation of life in the Southern Seas*

**Warriors**
GERALD HANLEY
*Life and death among the Somalis*

**Morocco That Was**
WALTER HARRIS
*All the cruelty, fascination and*
*humour of a pre-modern kingdom:*
*Morocco in the 19th and early 20th*
*century*

**Far Away and Long Ago**
W H HUDSON
*A childhood in Argentina, and a hymn to*
*nature*

**Palestine Papers 1917–22**
ED. DOREEN INGRAMS
*History caught in the making*

**Holding On**
MERVYN JONES
*The story of a London dockland street,*
*and the families who lived there*

**Mother Land**
DMETRI KAKMI
*A minutely observed Greek childhood on*
*a Turkish island in the 1960s*

**Red Moon & High Summer**
HERBERT KAUFMANN
*A coming-of-age novel following a*
*young singer in his Tuareg homeland*

**Three Came Home**
AGNES KEITH
*A mother's ordeal in a Japanese*
*prison camp*

**Peking Story**
DAVID KIDD
*The ruin of an ancient Mandarin*
*family under the new communist order*

**Scum of the Earth**
ARTHUR KOESTLER
*Koestler's escape from a collapsing France*
*in World War II*

**The Hill of Kronos**
PETER LEVI
*A poet's radiant portrait of Greece*

**A Dragon Apparent**
NORMAN LEWIS
*Cambodia, Laos and Vietnam*
*on the eve of war*

**Golden Earth**
NORMAN LEWIS
*Travels in Burma*